E·COMMERCE
Business on the Internet

Constance H. McLaren
Indiana State University

Bruce J. McLaren
Indiana State University

JOIN US ON THE INTERNET
WWW: http://www.thomson.com   A service of I T P®

South-Western Educational Publishing
an International Thomson Publishing company I T P®

Cincinnati • Albany, NY • Belmont, CA • Bonn • Boston • Detroit • Johannesburg • London • Madrid
Melbourne • Mexico City • New York • Paris • Singapore • Tokyo • Toronto • Washington

Team Leader: Karen Schmohe
Managing Editor: Carol Volz
Editor: Mark Cheatham
Art Coordinator: Mike Broussard
Technical Editor: Cinci Stowell
Production House: Electro-Publishing
Marketing Manager: Larry Qualls
Internal Design: Ann Small
Cover Design: Lou Ann Thesing

ISBN: 0-538-68918-8

2 3 4 5 6 7 8 9 10 BM 05 04 03 02 01 00 99

Printed in the United States of America

I⟨T⟩P®
International Thomson Publishing

South-Western Educational Publishing is a division of International Thomson Publishing, Inc. The ITP® registered trademark is used under license.

Explore the Web

With these exciting new products from South-Western!

- **E-Commerce: Business on the Internet** (McLaren and McLaren)
  20+ hours of instruction. The Internet is the place of choice to conduct business, and e-commerce is now an essential course of study for anyone trying to understand today's business climate.

Student book, soft cover	0-538-68918-8
Electronic Instructor Package	0-538-68919-6

Other Complimentary South-Western Titles

- **Understanding & Using the Internet** (Bruce McLaren)
  20+ hours of instruction. Provides a comprehensive overview of the Internet from a history of its development to the importance it plays in business today.

Student book, soft cover	0-538-72132-4
Electronic Instructor CD ROM	0-538-72133-2

- **Web Page Design** (Stubbs, Barksdale, Crispen)
  15+ hours of instruction. Essential preparation for using any brand of Web page design software, such as Microsoft FrontPage. Provides a common-sense approach to design fundamentals.

Student book, soft cover	0-538-68997-8
Electronic Instructor Package	0-538-68998-6

- **Microsoft FrontPage 2000** (Ciampa)
  20+ hours of instruction. FrontPage 2000 allows you to quickly create Web pages without programming. Use this text to get certified as a proficient user.

Student book, soft cover	0-538-69092-5
Electronic Instructor Package	0-538-69093-3

- **Microsoft Internet Explorer 5.0** (Gehris)
  15+ hours of instruction. Learn the nuts and bolts of the most widely used Internet browser through this excellent introductory text.

Student book, soft cover	0-538-69123-9
Electronic Instructor Package	0-538-69134-4

The Electronic Instructor CD ROM contains tests, Lesson Plans, and solutions, and much more.

Join Us On the Internet
www.swep.com

South-Western
Educational Publishing

Using This Book

Activities

Activities are written to support each chapter objective. These activities cover the E-Commerce topics that are most relevant to today's classroom and workplace. Each activity begins with a brief explanation of key concepts.

Step-by-Step Instructions provide hands-on reinforcement and simplify the process of working through each activity.

Sidebar Features

Special Features occur throughout the text to present important concepts in a brief, easy to read format.

NET FACT

Net Fact presents important technical information.

Net Careers provides information about types of Web-related career opportunities.

Net Ethics

Net Ethics provides a forum for discussion of important ethical and legal concerns in relation to the Internet.

Net Business examines the types of organizations that conduct business on the Internet and their successes and failures.

ACTIVITY 4.2

Objective:
In this lesson, you will find up-to-date information about stock and bond prices, track a portfolio of investments, and use online brokerage services.

NET FACT

What is a Discount Broker?

Discount brokers are agents who buy and sell stocks for you, but don't provide all of the market analysis and customer service that a full-service broker provides. Now, at least 75 online discount brokers are operating, and some are offering very deep discounts to lure customers to buy and sell with them. Researchers predict that by 2002, 14 million investors will trade stocks online, which will be about 5 percent of all traders. Why do people trade online? For the same reasons they bank online: it is fast, it is cheap, and it is easy. You can order your trade at any time of the day, not just when the broker's office is open.

All About Online Investing

Many financial sites on the Internet enable you to create a group of investments to watch. You don't have to own the stocks to keep track of their movements, and you can learn about companies' financial performance this way. In fact, you should thoroughly study a stock's history, along with the company's financial statements, before you consider purchasing some shares.

In Chapter 2, you saw how to find a company's information on its Web site. In this activity, you'll learn how to follow the financial markets on the Web. You'll learn how to create a collection of stocks and other investments, called a **portfolio**, to watch. And you'll also investigate ways to buy and sell stocks online.

1. Many Internet sites allow you to follow a stock. Even opening screens of some browsers, such as Netscape Netcenter, offer users the opportunity to request a current stock price. In this activity, you will be visiting several sites for stock information. Find the URL for each of the following companies, and check the services they offer.

Brokerage	URL	Free Quotes?	Free Portfolio Watch?	Trading?
American Express Financial Services				
E*TRADE				
Smart Money Interactive				
Discover Brokerage Direct				

2. All stocks have **a ticker symbol**, which is a company abbreviation made up of several letters. Ticker symbols are used for easy reference in stock quotes. For example, the ticker symbol for the Mauna Loa Macadamia Partners, a Hawaiian grower of macadamia nuts, is NUT. Go to the American Express Financial Direct site. Use the Symbols link to find the New York Stock Exchange ticker symbol for the following companies in the North American markets. By clicking the linked symbol, you will be able to see stock price information, such as that shown for Disney in Figure 4.5. For each company in the table below, record the symbol, today's high, the 52-week high, and the 52-week low.

End-Of-Chapter

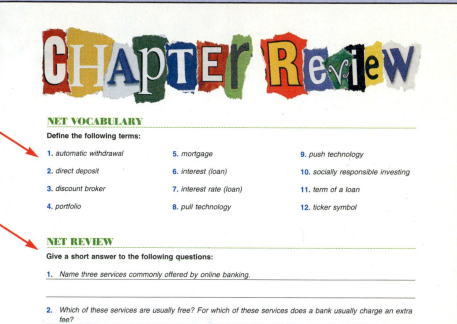

Net Vocabulary reinforces key concepts presented in the text in the form of a vocabulary exercise.

NET VOCABULARY

Define the following terms:

1. automatic withdrawal
2. direct deposit
3. discount broker
4. portfolio

5. mortgage
6. interest (loan)
7. interest rate (loan)
8. pull technology

9. push technology
10. socially responsible investing
11. term of a loan
12. ticker symbol

Net Review short answer questions test the retention of important chapter information. This serves as an excellent review for the chapter test.

NET REVIEW

Give a short answer to the following questions:

1. Name three services commonly offered by online banking.

2. Which of these services are usually free? For which of these services does a bank usually charge an extra fee?

Net Project puts the user's new tools and skills to work by applying them to an ongoing Web-based business project.

ONLINE BANKING IN YOUR NEIGHBORHOOD

Find the URL for your bank or for a bank in your community and visit the site. Why do you think the bank has an Internet presence? Does it offer online services? Make a list of them. What does a current customer have to do in order to access these services? If the bank doesn't have online services, then why do you suppose it has a Web site?

NET PROJECT TEAMWORK How "Online" Is Your Local Bank?

With your team, select a bank in your area to investigate. Different teams should select different banks. Make an appointment with someone at the bank who is familiar with the bank's online services. Each team should create a list of questions about online banking to ask the bank employee. Be sure to include questions about kinds of services offered, costs, and future online plans. Then meet with the bank employee, and present the results to the class.

Net Project Teamwork is a team option for the Net Project designed to emphasize the importance of working in teams to accomplish common goals.

WRITING ABOUT TECHNOLOGY Where Did the Paper Go?

Jeremy Clark is pleased with himself. He has one semester left in college, has a part-time job that pays reasonably well, and has just bought a new car. After watching a TV show, he's become convinced that it is not too early to start an investment program. He doesn't know too much about the stock market, but he'd like to buy a few shares of a good stock. Jeremy's downfall, though, is that he is not very good at keeping track of things. He pays his tuition monthly, but sometimes he forgets to send the check on time. His part-time job pays him every two weeks, and he is too embarrassed to tell the payroll department that he lost one of his January paychecks. Besides, he keeps hoping it will turn up somewhere in his room! Do you know anyone like Jeremy?

Write a letter to Jeremy, explaining how he might use his computer to help make his life easier and more organized. In about 100 words, give him suggestions on how he could use the Internet to help manage his personal finances.

Writing About Technology emphasizes the importance of developing writing and critical thinking skills within the emerging, complex world of Web computing. Each of these end-of-chapter assignments provides an opportunity for building a personal portfolio.

PREFACE

Businesses and organizations of all kinds have learned that it makes good business sense to use the Internet to reach their audience. Almost every magazine ad or TV commercial makes sure that you know the address of the company's Web site. Other organizations, like universities and nonprofit groups, realize as well that they can give you much more information if you visit them online than they could ever afford by other means.

Why do businesses find it essential to have an online presence that will attract customers? How can customers make the most of what is available online? These are the two key questions that we answer in this book. Here you'll learn all about the sites developed for businesses of many different kinds. You'll see how to find them and learn what they have to offer. You'll also see how they are developed and learn what separates an adequate site from a great one.

Technical advances and the ever-increasing number of customers with Internet access are among the reasons for the massive development in online business. E-commerce has spurred the development of the technology that enables a company to post a product catalog, a buyer to select items to order, and payment information to be transferred securely and privately. E-commerce allows investors to find out how their portfolios have performed and to make stock trades in the privacy of their own homes. E-commerce makes it easy to use your computer to schedule a flight and buy a plane ticket, to apply for a job, or to read a company's annual report.

Some experts predict that Internet spending will reach at least $1 trillion by the year 2003. Although consumer shopping might get the most publicity, transactions between businesses are expected to account for 80-90 percent of this activity. No matter whose projections you read, it is clear that electronic commerce is an important part of our economy and our society.

By studying the activities and examples in this book, you'll learn to use E-commerce effectively. You'll have the confidence to enter this arena, knowing what you can find and how to use what you find. Using *E-Commerce: Business on the Internet* as your guide, you'll find that you can gather corporate information, make a purchase online, develop an effective company Web site, or find global trading partners. The more you look, the more you'll find.

E-Commerce: Business on the Internet is divided into sections and chapters. You will learn a concept and then apply it through hands-on activities and site visits. The book will take you through each step in a logical, easy-to-follow manner.

In *Section 1: An Introduction to Electronic Commerce*, we'll introduce you to the impact of the Internet on our economy. We won't smother you with statistics, but you'll see enough trends to get the idea of the amazing success and growth potential of E-commerce. You'll also take a look at some typical business uses of the Net. Remember, it is not all about selling.

In *Section 2: Personal and Business Services Online*, you'll see the effect of nonsales E-commerce. A whole industry has sprung up to support online job searches. You'll see how one-stop career sites can help you discover what you want to do, how to prepare for it, and how to find the job you want. In another chapter, you'll learn how to manage your personal and business finances without ever going to the bank, the broker, or the insurance office. You'll also learn how to make travel plans, find a phone number, and get up-to-the minute weather bulletins.

In *Section 3: Buying Online*, you'll learn everything you need to know to be a savvy purchaser. You'll see examples of the goods and services you can shop for electronically—things like a paperback book, clothing for you to wear or to sell in your store, a shipment of light fixtures, or even a car. You'll see how to participate in an online auction or subscribe to an electronic magazine. Before you're finished, you'll know why it is important to deal with a reputable and secure online merchant and how to know that you are.

In *Section 4: Doing Business on the Web*, you'll take a look at E-commerce from the company's perspective. You'll learn how companies use the Internet for marketing, including e-mail targeted advertising, generating customer lists, and ways to deliver customer service over the Web. You will learn how banner ads can be linked to certain keywords in search engines. You will see how multinational corporations use the Web to reach customers in many countries. You'll also see how to use the Internet to research customs and economies of other countries before visiting those countries.

In *Section 5: Developing an Electronic Commerce Web Site,* you'll learn about E-commerce Web sites, including Web servers and HTML files. You'll visit some award-winning Web sites to view good designs. You will use Microsoft FrontPage to build your own small personal Web site and even build a small E-commerce site as a chapter project. You will learn about the details of processing credit card information securely and discover other ways to pay for goods and services purchased on the Internet.

Throughout the book you will find references to E-commerce Web sites with plenty of actual screen captures. Although you don't need to be connected to the Internet to learn about electronic commerce, you'll experience more by surfing the Web while you read this book. For those who have not had much experience with e-mail and Web browsers, the *Appendix* contains brief tutorials on popular tools.

HOME PAGE SUPPORT

At the Computer Education opening screen, click Products and Resources at left. Choose the Internet category. Scroll down the list until you locate the Web page for this book. Under the Resources heading, click on "Student Activities." Or access the Student Activities page directly through bookmarking this url: **e-commerce.swep.com**.

The Web page contains current hotlinks to most Web sites for the text activities. If, for some reason, a Web page cited in the book goes down permanently, visit our Web page to find a replacement site, since we'll update these links. If you bookmark our Web page, you can use it to go directly to the links for your assigned activities.

CONTENTS

SECTION 1 – AN INTRODUCTION TO ELECTRONIC COMMERCE 1

CHAPTER 1
The Internet in Our Economy 2

Activity 1.1   The Partnership Between the Internet and Business 6
Activity 1.2   Finding Company Information on the Web 9
Activity 1.3   E-Commerce Success Stories 12
Activity 1.4   Who Is Keeping Track? 14
NET PROJECT: Doing Business With The Government 17
NET PROJECT TEAMWORK: Shopping Online 17
WRITING ABOUT TECHNOLOGY: URLs Among Us 17

CHAPTER 2
Types of Internet Businesses 18

Activity 2.1   Retailing on the Internet 20
Activity 2.2   Electronic Catalogs 23
Activity 2.3   Organizations and Associations on the Net 26
Activity 2.4   What Can a Small Business Do on the Internet? 30
Activity 2.5   Corporations on the Net 33
NET PROJECT: Advice For Small Businesses 36
NET PROJECT TEAMWORK: Nonprofits on the Web 37
WRITING ABOUT TECHNOLOGY: Grow Your Small Business on the Web 37

SECTION 2 – PERSONAL AND BUSINESS SERVICES ONLINE 39

CHAPTER 3
Searching for a Career 40

Activity 3.1   Career Planning 42
Activity 3.2   Your Resume 45
Activity 3.3   The Job Search 48
Activity 3.4   Relocating 51
Activity 3.5   Back to School 53
NET PROJECT: Moving to Houston 56
NET PROJECT TEAMWORK: Career Potential in Houston 56
WRITING ABOUT TECHNOLOGY: The Low-Tech Job Search 56

CHAPTER 4
Personal Finance on the Internet 57

Activity 4.1 Banking Online...59
Activity 4.2 All About Online Investing 62
Activity 4.3 Financing Your Home 66
Activity 4.4 Searching for Insurance Online 69
Activity 4.5 Internet Tax Tips 71
NET PROJECT: Online Banking In Your Neighborhood.............................74
NET PROJECT TEAMWORK: How "Online" Is Your Local Bank? 74
WRITING ABOUT TECHNOLOGY: Where Did the Paper Go?......................74

CHAPTER 5
Internet Information Services 75

Activity 5.1 Travel Planning 77
Activity 5.2 Online News and Weather 84
Activity 5.3 Internet Information Providers 88
Activity 5.4 Internet Links to Government Information.............................90
NET PROJECT: Business Trip To Denver..94
NET PROJECT TEAMWORK: A Whirlwind Tour of Baseball Parks.................94
WRITING ABOUT TECHNOLOGY: Planning for Weather Emergencies 94

SECTION 3 – BUYING ONLINE 95

CHAPTER 6
Retail and Business Purchases 96

Activity 6.1 Shop 'til You Drop 99
Activity 6.2 Find the Good Life on the Internet 102
Activity 6.3 Would You Buy a Car from This Site?.................................106
Activity 6.4 When a Business Is the Buyer..109
Activity 6.5 Sold to the Highest Bidder! 113
NET PROJECT: Comparison Shopping 118
NET PROJECT TEAMWORK: Small Business Assistance..............................118
WRITING ABOUT TECHNOLOGY: It's a New World of Shopping 118

CHAPTER 7
Making Online Purchases...119

Activity 7.1 Bring the Music Home...123
Activity 7.2 Flowers for All Occasions 125
Activity 7.3 Downloading an Online Image..128
Activity 7.4 Online Subscriptions...131
NET PROJECT: Equipping The Pizza Restaurant 135
NET PROJECT TEAMWORK: The Good Sports! Store 135
WRITING ABOUT TECHNOLOGY: Customer Information 136

CHAPTER 8
Consumer Issues 137

Activity 8.1   Safeguarding Security and Privacy 139
Activity 8.2   Speaking Up 142
Activity 8.3   Wise Consumerism 148
NET PROJECT: The Baby Shower 154
NET PROJECT TEAMWORK: How Much a Minute? 154
WRITING ABOUT TECHNOLOGY: Savvy Shopping 154

SECTION 4 – DOING BUSINESS ON THE WEB 155

CHAPTER 9
Internet Marketing 156

Activity 9.1   Phase I: Pre-Sale 158
Activity 9.2   Phase II: Taking the Order 161
Activity 9.3   Phase III: Delivering the Products 164
Activity 9.4   Phase IV: Post-Sale 167
NET PROJECT: The Four Phases of Marketing Online 171
NET PROJECT TEAMWORK: Comparing E-Commerce Web Sites......171
WRITING ABOUT TECHNOLOGY: Invasion of Privacy? 171

CHAPTER 10
Digital Advertising 172

Activity 10.1 E-mail Advertising 174
Activity 10.2 Banner Advertising 179
Activity 10.3 Promoting Your Site..186
NET PROJECT: Concert Tickets 192
NET PROJECT TEAMWORK: Preparing Web Ads 192
WRITING ABOUT TECHNOLOGY: Creative Minds 192

CHAPTER 11
Global E-Commerce..193

Activity 11.1 Lowering Geographic Barriers 195
Activity 11.2 Asynchronous Business Activities............................199
Activity 11.3 Online International Business Information................204
Activity 11.4 Intranets, Extranets, and the Internet 208
NET PROJECT: World Ventures Limited 212
NET PROJECT TEAMWORK: Analyze Different Countries..............212
WRITING ABOUT TECHNOLOGY: Supporting Global Sales............212

SECTION 5 – DEVELOPING AN ELECTRONIC COMMERCE WEB SITE 213

CHAPTER 12
Creating a Web Site 214

Activity 12.1 Components of a Web Site 216
Activity 12.2 Methods for Developing a Web Site 226
Activity 12.3 Registering and Promoting Your Web Site 233
NET PROJECT: Create Your Own Personal Online Store 237
NET PROJECT TEAMWORK: Add Images to Your Online Store 237
WRITING ABOUT TECHNOLOGY: Managing Your Site 237

CHAPTER 13
Developing a Web Site with Microsoft® FrontPage 238

Activity 13.1 Good Web Design 240
Activity 13.2 Creating a Personal Web with FrontPage 98 244
Activity 13.3 Customizing Your FrontPage Web 248
NET PROJECT: Create a Small Business Home Page 255
NET PROJECT TEAMWORK: Perfect Your Site 255
WRITING ABOUT TECHNOLOGY: FrontPage: What's Your Verdict? 255

APPENDIX A
Browser Basics 257

The Hypertext Concept 257
Web Browsers 258
Using a Browser to Explore the Web 259

APPENDIX B
E-Mail Basics 267

How E-Mail Works 267
Using E-Mail 269
Using E-Mail Features 273

APPENDIX C
Web Security 277

Providing Privacy for E-Commerce Visitors 277
Paying for Merchandise Online 282

GLOSSARY 285

INDEX 289

Software and Hardware Requirements

Concepts in this book are illustrated using screen captures from Netscape Navigator 4. You should have a compatible Web browser (including Netscape Navigator 3.0 or higher or Internet Explorer 3.0 or higher).

Computer systems that support these browsers include PCs running Microsoft Windows and Macintosh systems. You should have an Internet connection with a modem or a direct connection to work the activities, exercises, and projects from this book. You need to have Microsoft FrontPage (98 or later) installed on your computer to work the exercises and projects in Chapter 13.

Home Page

Access the home page for this textbook at *e-commerce.swep.com*.

An Introduction to Electronic Commerce

"Electronic commerce" is a tremendously popular phrase these days. *Time* magazine and *Business Week* devote cover articles to the idea, newspaper and TV news stories weigh in on the future of traditional retailing, and everyone from The Gap to your grocery store wants to make sure you know their Internet address.

What do people mean by "electronic commerce"? How big is it, really? Will your company be left behind if it doesn't do business that way? Will you be left behind if you don't do business that way? And just what way are we talking about?

In this section, you'll learn what electronic commerce is to people in a variety of industries. You'll learn how the Internet affects our economy, both nationally and globally. You'll see, by the numbers, where it's been and where experts expect it to go. And by looking at the kinds of business that companies and organizations do on the Internet, you'll begin to see what part "E-commerce" will play in your future.

Chapter 1   The Internet in Our Economy 1
Chapter 2   Types of Internet Businesses 18

The Internet in Our Economy

Chapter Objectives:

In this chapter, you will learn how the Internet affects our economy. After reading Chapter 1, you will be able to

1. use the Internet to find information about electronic commerce.

2. use the Internet to find information about companies and products.

3. discuss companies that have achieved success with E-commerce.

4. find information about the past, present, and future developments of E-commerce.

Net Terms

E-commerce (electronic commerce)

business-to-business sales

NET TIP
Home Page

Access the E-Commerce: Business on the Internet *home page through the following URL:* e-commerce.swep.com. *Remember that a Web address may change at any time. An address given in this book as an example may no longer be valid. If so, either access the home page* (e-commerce.swep.com) *for the current link or do a search to find a similar site.*

E-Commerce–It's More Than Buying and Selling

Have you ever stopped to think that not so very long ago, the letters "www" didn't mean anything to most people? That comedians didn't use funny Web addresses as punch lines? And that a lady named "Dorothy Com," who uses the nickname "Dot," didn't make the national headlines?

From Limited Beginnings

The Internet, as we know it, really isn't very old. The forerunner of the Internet, Arpanet, was created in the 1960s for military and scientific use. Its main purpose was to maintain communications in case a nuclear war or natural disaster knocked out critical pieces of our communica-tions systems. At that time, only researchers and other specialized users could access the network. Later, several technological breakthroughs made the Internet accessible to businesses, educational institutions, and the average household.

As you might expect, the Internet provides a source of historical information about itself. Several sites offer timelines that can help you put the developments into perspective. Figures 1.1 and 1.2 show portions of a historic timeline created to accompany the PBS series, "Life on the Internet." To use the PBS timeline, click and drag the slide bar along the bottom of the window to a year of your choice. The window will tell you what happened in that year. As you will see, the Internet was not open to commercial use before 1991.

Businesses Establish a Presence

To get a feel for how widespread business use of the Internet has become, take your own informal survey. When you are driving down an interstate, check out the next semi you pass. It probably displays the URL of the trucking company. Look on the title page or cover of your textbooks, and you'll probably find the Web address of the publisher. Go to your pantry or refrigerator, and see how many companies include their Web address on their product label. The August 17, 1998, issue of *Time* magazine contained at least 20 URLs in ads. Only three companies did not display their Internet address in their ads. And *Time* puts *www.time.com* right on the front cover.

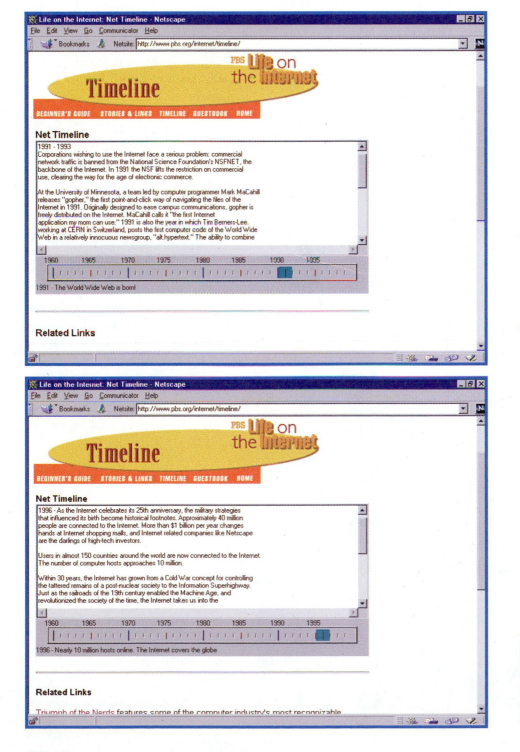

Figure 1.1
PBS Internet timeline, 1991-1993

Figure 1.2
PBS Internet timeline, 1996. Only five years after the Internet opens for commercial business, Internet shopping malls accounted for over $1 billion of activity.

So why do all of these businesses want the world to know where to find them on the Internet? Some use the Internet for sales to consumers, and some use the Internet for sales to other businesses. All use their Internet presence to provide information about their company and products. You can't order a new car from the Ford or Chrysler or Toyota or Honda Web sites, but you can read about models and options and configure the car you want to buy from your local dealer. If you visit General Mills' Web site, shown in Figure 1.3, you can't order a box of Cheerios, but you can learn that Cheerios were invented in 1941 and were originally called "Cheeri Oats." You can also find out about career opportunities at General Mills and read the latest news about the company. For most companies, the goal of a Web site is to interest potential customers, employees, and investors in their company.

Business-to-Business

For all the hype about the Internet replacing shopping malls, forecasters predict that the overwhelming majority of sales—as much as 89 percent of the projected dollar volume for 2001—will be business-to-business. **Business-to-business sales** are sales made by one business to another, rather than directly to a consumer. If you need to buy a replacement hinge for a kitchen cabinet, it may be easier for you to make a trip to your local hardware store than to order it over the Net. But if your company manufactures cabinets and you are searching for a supplier of hinges, examining online catalogs from hardware manufacturers can let you see at a glance which manufacturer has what you need.

The Internet also makes it easy for people who buy merchandise for their clothing stores to see new product lines in the fashion industry. The Liz Claiborne company has created a virtual product showroom that lets its business customers examine clothing details without having to travel to the physical showroom. The company hopes to eventually use the Internet to provide stores with business support and advertising materials.

Nonsales Benefits

A Web presence can have other benefits for companies besides sales. A company can enhance its image by providing corporate history, free advice for users of its products, and its financial information online.

It can post job openings and showcase new products. It can make its name familiar to customers in far-flung locations who would never hear of the company otherwise. And it can do all of this while gathering information on the number, and in some cases the individual characteristics, of the people who access its site.

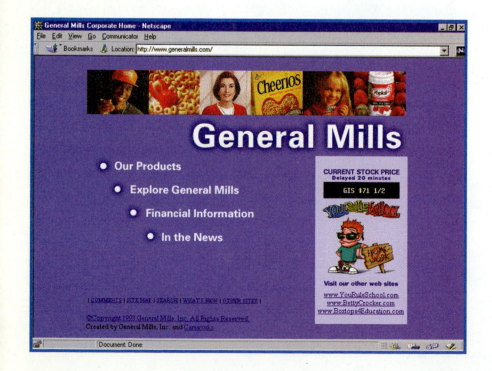

Figure 1.3
General Mills' home page illustrates the kinds of information a large corporation might want to make available over the Internet

E-Commerce

Although the features described above include all sorts of activities, they can be put into two categories. A company with a Web presence can use the Internet (1) to sell goods or services and (2) to distribute information. Some authorities use the term "electronic commerce" or "E-commerce" to mean buying and selling goods and services over the Internet. In this book, we'll use a broader definition: **E-commerce (electronic commerce)** is any electronic exchange of information to conduct business. ■

Net Fun

You may not be able to order a box of Cheerios from General Mills' Web site, but there are such things as online grocery stores. Some gourmet and specialty food shops have online catalogs. Electronic shopping services, such as Peapod, will even redeem your paper coupons. The number of supermarkets that encourage their shoppers to order electronically is growing. For information, search for "online grocery," and see if a grocery near you offers this service.

Net Business: Doctors on the Internet

Doctors may not be the first people you think of when you consider professions that would find the Internet useful as they go about their work. But several new companies think that doctors can, should, and will use the Internet to connect to hospitals, insurance companies, suppliers, and other doctors. WebMD even offers to give a free computer to doctors who subscribe to their service. Member doctors will be able to obtain test results and records online, verify insurance, have voice mail, e-mail, and fax service, and get news and information.

Doctors can't subscribe online to WebMD—a sales force will market the service. But WebMD does provide free online health information to the public. Consumers can find links to other sites and search WebMD's physician list for a new doctor. What possibilities can you see for ways such a site can serve consumers?

In addition to selling subscriptions, WebMD will sell advertising space on its pages. If you were a medical products or pharmaceutical company, wouldn't you want to advertise before a group of high-tech physicians?

You can visit the public side of WebMD by visiting the company's site. You can also learn more about combining medicine and the Internet by reading the October 4, 1998, issue of The Internet Standard.

Net Ethics   The Online Journal of Ethics

The Institute for Business and Professional Ethics at DePaul University conducts research into ethical business practices. Although the Institute's area of concern goes far beyond E-commerce, the Institute has chosen the Internet as a vehicle for publishing the latest research in business ethics. You can read current and past issues of the *Online Journal* by visiting the Web site at *www.depaul.edu/ethics*.

ACTIVITY

1.1

Objective:

In this lesson, you will learn how to use the Internet to find information about electronic commerce.

The Partnership Between the Internet and Business

One of the easiest ways to understand the close alliance between the Internet and business is to search the Internet itself. Popular search engines, like Yahoo and Excite, show categories for business and related subjects. Some provide immediate links to business topics, such as stock price quotes or company names, on their opening screens. In this activity, you will visit several search engines to see what you can learn about E-commerce.

1 Go to the Yahoo home page. Which categories could you investigate to learn about E-commerce?

_____

What link do you see under "Inside Yahoo" that relates to E-commerce? What other links on this page might provide useful information about E-commerce?

_____

Click the Business and Economy category, and then click the link to Electronic Commerce. Follow a link of your choice. What did you choose, why did you choose it, and what did you learn?

_____

_____

_____

_____

2 Go to the Infoseek home page. As you've learned, E-commerce includes just about any activity related to business. What link would you follow

to learn about a company? _____

to find a stock price? _____

to look at job openings? _____

to find office furniture? _____

to learn current mortgage loan rates? _____

to order a birthday present? _____

Figure 1.4 shows some of the Infoseek links to business sites. Tour the Infoseek business section to see today's business news and other useful links.

NET FACT

The Top Ten List

Relevant Knowledge reported these sites as the top ten "Web Properties" for March, 1998: Yahoo/Four11, Netscape, Excite/Webcrawler, Microsoft, AOL.com, Lycos/Tripod, Geocities, MSN/Hotmail, Infoseek, and CNET. Are you surprised at the number of search engines in this list?

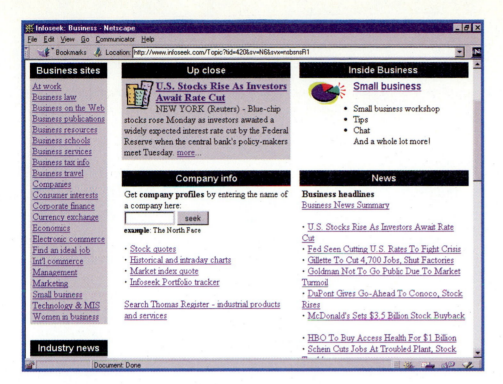

Figure 1.4
Infoseek's Business link

③ Go to the Excite home page, a portion of which is shown in Figure 1.5. Excite encourages you to personalize the home page. By registering a user name and password, and providing answers to some questions about yourself, you can use Excite's chat and mail services. You can also specify what information you want Excite to supply to you every time you log on by creating a personalized home page. Every section of the page that begins with the word "My" can be customized to your

NET TIP

Online Job Listings

In June, 1998, The Industry Standard reported that online job listings had increased by 30 percent in one week. Was this due to summer job seekers? Not entirely. One career site stated, "We are seeing a broader diversity of companies recruiting on the board." You will learn more about online job searching in Chapter 3.

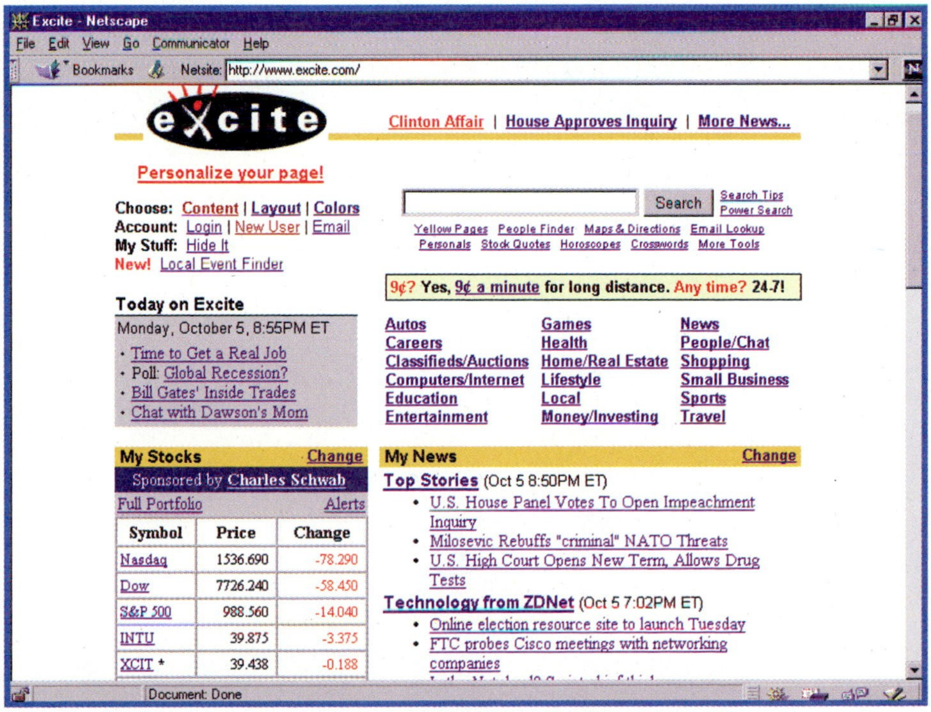

Figure 1.5
The Excite home page

choices. The selections shown in Figure 1.5 are the defaults for Excite. If you are working in a public computer lab, you may not be able to register. Registering with Excite is not required for this activity.

Click the "Personalize your page" link. Read the registration form. Name three benefits that Excite receives when its visitors register.

1. _____

2. _____

3. _____

There are several features of the home page that would be useful for a business owner. If you were starting a business to manufacture toys, you might want to keep track of your competition. Name three companies you would list in the My Stocks section.

1. _____

2. _____

3. _____

If you were preparing to go to a toy maker's convention, what Excite links might you follow, and why would they be useful?

1. _____

2. _____

3. _____

THINKING ABOUT TECHNOLOGY

How do you use the Internet? How do your friends use it? Is the Internet a way to communicate with people, a tool for doing schoolwork, a source of fun, a business tool, or all of these?

Finding Company Information on the Web

ACTIVITY 1.2

Objective:
In this lesson, you will learn how to use the Internet to find information about companies and products.

As you have seen, companies use the Web to sell products and services and to make information available. E-commerce can help them control costs by not having to print and mail catalogs and brochures. They can advertise and communicate on the Web, reaching a worldwide audience that they might never be able to reach otherwise. They can make themselves available to customers 24 hours a day, 7 days a week.

Why would you want to find a specific company on the Internet? There are many reasons. You might want to:

- learn more about the products and services a company offers.
- make a purchase.
- download information, such as a parts manual.
- apply for a job with the company.
- read the company's financial reports before you buy its stock.
- write an e-mail letter to the company's customer service representatives.

In some instances, you might have a product or service in mind, but not know the name of a company that sells it. You might need to buy a new copier for your business, and want to investigate copier models from a number of manufacturers and retailers. Or you might want to see which banks offer online banking arrangements.

In this activity, you will learn how to search for the Web presence of specific companies. You'll also learn how to locate companies by their products.

1 There are many ways that you could search for information about a company. If you want to get to the company's Web site, you could take a chance and guess at the URL you think it would have. You could also do a general search with a search engine for the company's name. Go to Yahoo, Excite, and Infoseek, and do a general search on the phrase "Pizza Hut." How many hits appear?

Search Engine	Number of Hits
Yahoo	
Excite	
Infoseek	

The list of matches picks up all kinds of references to Pizza Hut, as you can see by the titles that appear. The variety makes it a bit difficult to see exactly which one will lead you to the company. Luckily, each of these search engines makes it easier for you to go to a company site directly.

NET FACT

Growing Online

Some businesses really thrive on the Internet:
Music stores:
1996: $21.5 million in online sales
1997: $52 million in online sales
Software stores:
By 2001, Forrester predicts online sales of $3.7 billion.
Online auctions:
eBay, an online auction house, has 325,000 auctions every day, 600,000 registered users, and 8 million page views per day.

NET TIP

You Can Always Comparison-Shop

An AOL survey showed Web users were cautious about purchasing insurance online. Among potential insurance customers, 50 percent wanted personal attention, 34 percent were worried about security, and 8 percent found it too complicated. But even if you have these concerns, the Internet can be a valuable shopping tool for you. You can always comparison-shop online and then contact an insurance company directly.

2. Open Infoseek, and click the Company Profiles link. Type "Pizza Hut" in the first open box, as you see in Figure 1.6, and click Search. The first link in the list will open a brief profile of Pizza Hut, provided by Infoseek. What does this profile tell you about Pizza Hut?

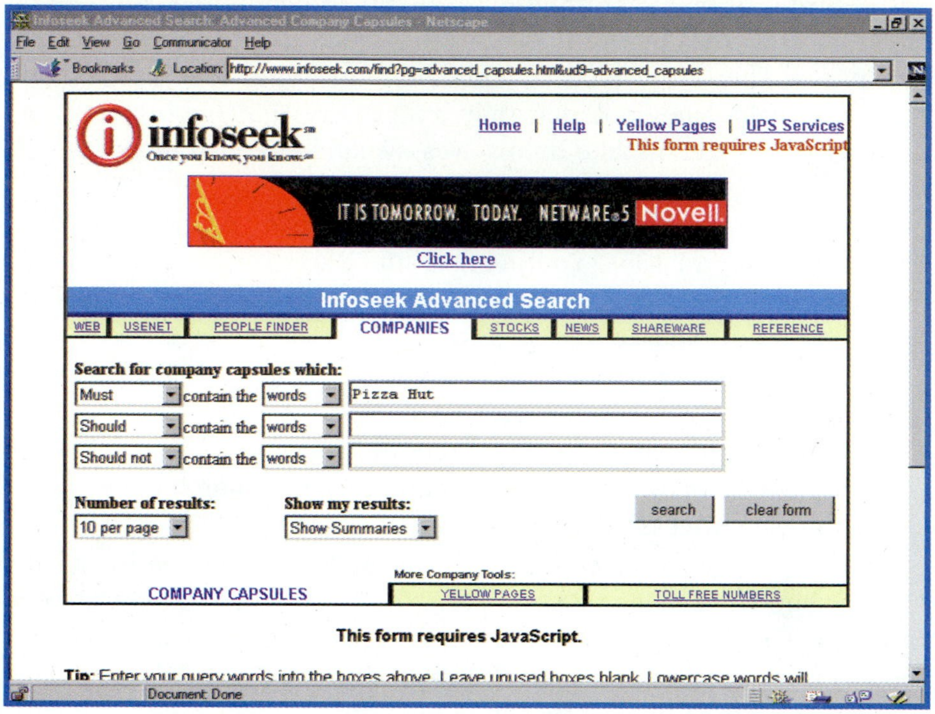

Figure 1.6
Infoseek search for company information

In what state is the company headquarters? ______________________

What is the company URL? ______________________

What company used to own Pizza Hut? ______________________

What company owns it now? ______________________

Click the link to go to the Pizza Hut company site. Take a look around. Maybe you'll get hungry!

3. Open Yahoo. To find company information in this search engine, you will need to click Companies under the Business and Economy category. What do you see?

____

____

4. Now search just this category for the phrase "Pizza Hut." Is it simple to tell which of these matches will lead you to the Pizza Hut corporate site? How do you think searching for company information with Yahoo compares to searching with Infoseek?

____

____

____

5 How would you search for information about specific products? Although you can narrow your search with most search engines by using successively more specific categories, you will eventually need to type in the product and do a search. Using the search engine of your choice, search for information about digital cameras by going through representative categories. You need to find Web sites of three manufacturers. What hierarchy of categories did you follow to find the companies?

Search engine _____

First category _____

Second category _____

Third category _____

Additional categories _____

Company 1 URL _____

Company 2 URL _____

Company 3 URL _____

THINKING ABOUT TECHNOLOGY

Would you like to see other "Find a product" links from your search engine? This would save some searching time. If you were determining the links, how would you decide what products deserved to have their own links?

NET FACT

Online Consumer Activity
The number of U.S. households making online purchases more than doubled from the second half of 1996 to the second half of 1997—from 3.2 million to over 7 million. One researcher expects the value of E-commerce transactions to be $2.16 billion in the year 2000.

ACTIVITY

1.3

Objective:

In this lesson, you will learn about companies that have achieved success with E-commerce.

E-Commerce Success Stories

There have been some marvelous successes in E-commerce. Established companies have found new customers and a new way of doing business by going online. Other companies have been created just to take advantage of this new technology. They may not have a physical presence anywhere. Still other companies have sprung up to provide a product or service for this new technology. Without the technology, there would be no company.

In 1993 and 1994, the Internet world was full of promise, and many companies jumped aboard. In 1995, things slowed a bit, and some companies found that they had moved too quickly, or that the early promise of E-commerce did not live up to their unrealistic expectations. Some small companies withdrew, and some large companies got burned. But many companies, particularly those with a niche, with a product or service attractive to Internet users, and with a clever plan, found great success.

① Number one on almost everyone's list of successful electronic commerce sites is Amazon.com. This bookseller has done everything right. In 1996, sales were $15.8 million. In 1987, sales grew to a fantastic $131.7 million. Customers can search for books by title, by author, and by subject. They can browse and read book reviews. Purchasing is easy and secure. Shipping is not cheap, but books are discounted. Figure 1.7 shows the results when you search for books by a popular mystery author.

NET FACT

What Sells Best Online?

Here are the top categories for purchasing online, based on a University of Michigan survey:

1. software
2. books
3. computer hardware
4. music
5. home electronics

Figure 1.7
Book search results from Amazon.com

Go to Amazon.com. Search for books by your favorite author. (Need an idea? Try Stephen King or John Grisham, or even Bruce McLaren.) Is it easy to perform this search? What do you like or dislike about it?

_____

For one of the books you found, do a bit of comparison shopping. With shipping, what would the book's price be from Amazon.com?

_____

What is the book's price at your local bookstore? Don't forget to include sales tax and your cost of going to the store.

_____

Which way would you order the book? Would it make a difference if you needed it by the end of this week?

_____

2 *New Media* magazine profiled five E-Commerce success stories in 1996. Go to the New Media site, and search for October 28, 1996. Read the "Selling Online" feature presentation to learn about the successes of these companies (yes, Amazon.com is included). From their stories, develop five principles that you think contribute to E-commerce success.

1. _____

2. _____

3. _____

4. _____

5. _____

3 One of the hottest services on the Internet is travel. In 1997, online travel sales accounted for $654 million in sales. By 1999, this number is expected to grow to $2.8 billion in total sales, making it the number one E-commerce category. Visit your search engine's travel category. What kinds of things can you do? What links appear? Would you feel confident making your own travel plans this way?

Net Fun

Tenagra Corporation, a public relations and Web design firm, presents awards to E-commerce sites it finds particularly effective. You can see the list of winners and visit their sites to judge for yourself. Go to www.tenagra.com, and click the link to Internet Marketing Excellence Awards.

THINKING ABOUT TECHNOLOGY

Dell Computer leads the way with online PC sales. It seems appropriate to sell computers over the Internet. Can you think of other products that would be particularly well-suited to sell this way? One successful product that might surprise you is gourmet food. Why do you suppose there is an online market for this kind of product?

Objective:

In this lesson, you will learn
how to find information about
the past, present, and future
developments of
E-commerce.

Who Is Keeping Track?

One industry that has flourished in the past few years is the industry dedicated to keeping track of the Internet and all of its associated activities. Old and new research companies have found a market for reports about the Internet. Consultants, economists, market researchers, and statisticians provide information to the public and sell research reports to subscribers.

Why is it important to know the numbers? The most obvious reason is to spot trends and understand how your company fits into the grand scheme of things. Research companies can supply anything from demographic information (age, gender, and other personal information) of Internet users to forecasts for market segments of the Internet economy. In this activity, you will visit some of these companies. Throughout the book you will see references to the information they can provide.

1 Figure 1.8 shows the home page for *The Industry Standard*, an electronic magazine about the Internet economy. One of its features is a link to Metrics, shown in Figure 1.9. This section reveals a variety of facts and figures about E-commerce. Other companies concentrate on E-commerce research. Begin by visiting four of them. Find the URL for these companies.

Company	URL
eStats	
CyberAtlas	
Forrester Research	
Relevant Knowledge	

NET TIP

More Than Just a Guess?

In a speech in 1997, the president of Cisco Systems, a computer hardware company, forecast phenomenal growth in electronic commerce. He used the figure $1.5 trillion as his estimate for revenues by the year 2000. How did he come up with this number? Forecasters frequently combine forecasts for pieces of a market to develop a forecast for the entire market. He anticipated that his company would have revenues of $15 to 20 billion by the year 2000, and estimated from there. It remains to be seen how accurate his forecast will be.

2 Visit each of these companies. Each offers some information to the visiting public. Look at their information, and record at least one statistic that is interesting to you from each site.

1. eStats _____

2. CyberAtlas_____

3. Forrester Research_____

4. Relevant Knowledge_____

3 What kinds of information do these sites sell, and what does it cost?

_____

NET TIP
Different Ways to Count

Are you wondering how the research companies count Internet users? If you'd like to find out, read the sampling information from eStats, CyberAtlas, and Relevant Knowledge. Do they follow different procedures? Would you expect their statistical results to be very different?

Figure 1.8
Home page for *The Industry Standard*

Figure 1.9
Link to Metrics, the facts and figures provided by *The Industry Standard*

Selling to Internet Clients

The research companies you've learned about in this chapter employ market researchers and other statisticians, and Web designers and other software specialists. They also need a sales force. Account executives sell research to new clients and work with clients to understand their information needs and how to meet them. With experience, this position can lead to other marketing positions. Being a computer genius is not a requirement for this kind of a job, but excellent communication skills are required.

THINKING ABOUT TECHNOLOGY

The Nielsen Company, the same company that measures the number of viewers TV shows attract, also measures the number of visitors Internet sites attract. Why might a business want to know how many Internet users visit its site? What similarities do you see between the reasons for measuring site visitors and the reasons for measuring TV viewers?

NET VOCABULARY

Define the following terms:

1. business-to-business sales

2. E-commerce
   (electronic commerce)

NET REVIEW

Give a short answer to the following questions.

1. What is E-commerce?

_____

_____

2. Name three reasons that businesses would want to use the Internet. Describe a company or a product for each reason.

_____

_____

_____

_____

3. What kinds of products sell well to consumers over the Internet? Why do you suppose these products work so well?

_____

_____

4. How could a business use the Internet to interact with another business?

_____

_____

_____

5. What kinds of information do companies that research Internet usage provide? Why is this information valuable to businesses that use the Internet?

_____

_____

_____

_____

Net Project

DOING BUSINESS WITH THE GOVERNMENT

The Department of Defense of the U.S. government has established an online Electronic Commerce Resource Center. This Web site was created to assist businesses that are, or want to become, suppliers and contractors for the department. Visit this site to learn about the support available for businesses. List at least five courses available through the ECRC Training Program. How would a small supplier benefit from doing business over the Internet? How would E-commerce help the Defense Department?

NET PROJECT TEAMWORK Shopping Online

Choose a consumer product that is interesting to the members of your group. Each member of the group should go shopping online for that product. Compare what you found. What range of prices did you find? Would you be able to buy that product online? What consumer information did you find about the product? Did the product come in a variety of brands or models? As a group, decide whether you would buy online, and if so, from which seller.

WRITING ABOUT TECHNOLOGY URLs Among Us

For one 24-hour period, write down every URL you see or hear. Exclude those that you find when you are surfing the Net, but include the ones you see in ads or on products when you are not at the computer. Group them according to the purpose you think they serve. Using about 100 words, describe the types of references you saw and heard.

Types of Internet Businesses

Chapter Objectives:

After completing the activities in this chapter, you will be able to

1 describe how the unique capabilities of the Internet benefit both retailers and their customers.

2 discuss the advantages for businesses of providing an electronic catalog.

3 explain how associations and professional organizations can use the Internet to help accomplish their goals.

4 discuss the benefits of an Internet presence for a small business.

5 explain how large corporations use the Internet to accomplish multiple goals.

Net Terms

retailing

consumer

entrepreneurship

market share

> ### NET TIP
> **Home Page**
>
> *Access the* E-Commerce: Business on the Internet *home page through the following URL:* e-commerce.swep.com. *Remember that a Web address may change at any time. An address given in this book as an example may no longer be valid. If so, either access the home page* (e-commerce.swep.com) *for the current link or do a search to find a similar site.*

A Net for All Reasons

As you learned in Chapter 1, many different kinds of businesses have a home on the Internet. Some use the Internet for **retailing**—selling goods and services to the **consumer**, the ultimate owner or user of the product. With or without a physical store, they can reach new consumers, take orders, and complete transactions electronically. Some companies use the Internet to sell things to other businesses rather than to consumers. Some businesses feature their product information online, but require a phone contact or a personal call in order to make the sale.

Not all electronic commerce involves a sales transaction. Businesses and organizations have discovered the value of the Internet for showcasing their operations and placing their information in front of a target audience. Web sites are also useful for an organization whose main purposes are information and public relations. It can put its best foot forward, share its story, and be available whenever anyone wants to look. By providing online access to corporate information, businesses can avoid mass mailings, improve communications with their customers and investors, and reach new audiences.

In this chapter, you'll look at several businesses that use the Internet for E-commerce. In later chapters, you'll learn more specifically how to go shopping for goods and services, and how to set up your own E-commerce site.

Journalists Find a Home on the Web

Graphic designers and Java programmers aren't the only people in demand for developing Web sites. Talented reporters and writers are needed to make certain that what the site says is said well. The Web is also home to a large number of columns and interviews. Print reporters have found their skills to be useful online as well. To understand the career paths of some Web writers, read about the hosts of Netscape's community forums at http://form.netscape.com/directory/community/html/host.htm. *Almost all of the hosts have a background in writing. Be sure to read about host Marc Frochtzweig, who hosts the "Rumor Mill" forum. Why does this host have to use a pseudonym?*

Net Ethics   Who Owns the Copyright?

In several references in this chapter, you'll see the ™ symbol for a company's registered trademark. This mark clearly indicates that no one else may use this name. Copyrighted material is a bit different. The *http://www.m-w.com* dictionary defines *copyright* as "the exclusive legal right to reproduce, publish, and sell the matter and form." Because the definition is copyrighted, this book has to show it in quotation marks and attribute its source. It is so simple to copy and paste text or graphic images from a Web document that companies must protect themselves legally by placing copyright, or terms of use, statements with their material. This doesn't prevent a user from lifting something from a site, but it does establish legal protection for the owner of the site. The only real protection is the sense of ethical responsibility shown by those who visit the site. Hundreds of Web pages are devoted to Internet copyright issues. These also address fair use policies and issues of intellectual property rights. For a sample, see the information from the Stanford University Libraries at *http://fairuse.stanford.edu.*

Net Fun

Netscape hosts forums at its small business source site. These online discussion groups let users exchange information at the "Consultant's Watercooler," "Keeping the Books," "Productivity Tools," and "Women in Business." To gain access to these forums, you need to complete an online registration form, but there is no cost. You can visit one of these forums to eavesdrop and see the answers to questions about small business. A piece of advice—you may be tempted to jump into the conversation immediately, but to avoid embarrassment, listen for a few days first. You may find that just listening is your best strategy.

ACTIVITY 2.1

Objective:
In this lesson, you will visit two online retailers to see how the unique capabilities of the Internet benefit both retailers and their customers.

At the CDnow site, when you are looking for music by a particular artist, click to see what the Album Advisor™ recommends. Check out the soundclips. You may discover some interesting new sounds.

Retailing on the Internet

The Internet offers many advantages for retailers and consumers, but physical examination of the product is usually not one of them. Although clothing retailers like The Gap have successful online stores, companies that sell items that don't have to be touched, tried on, or physically compared have been particularly successful when selling their products online.

You saw in Chapter 1 how Amazon.com has changed the way many people buy books. Amazon.com also sells music by marketing CDs. But two other online giants are leading the way in music sales. They will not only sell you a CD, but also make recommendations and give you information about the artist. In this activity, you'll visit two online music stores to discover some of the advantages of shopping for and selling consumer products on the Internet.

1. The first site you will visit is CDnow. Go there, and scroll to examine the entire page. As you look through the page, compare what you see to what you experience when you visit a music store in person. Use what you see to answer these questions.

    Whose music reviews can you read online?

    _____

    What do you click to find out this week's top sellers?

    _____

    Does CDnow allow you to ship outside the United States?

    _____

    What do you do to order a gift certificate?

    _____

    Can you search by artist? by title? How else can you search for music?

    _____

    What is My CDnow?

    _____

2. Searching is one of the Web's best features. If you look through a bin at a music store, you will see only the titles they have in stock. At the CDnow site, you can see what titles exist and follow links related to the artist. In the CDnow FastFind, key in the name of your favorite artist. (If you need a suggestion, look for titles by the Dave Matthews Band.) Click Find It to get to the artist's discography page. As you see in Figure 2.1, this page gives you the prices and other information for each album title. Choose an album by your artist to answer these questions.

What is the album's price for CD?_____ for tape?_____ for vinyl?_____

The discography page has links for related artists, to store your favorites, to make recommendations, and for reviews. How is CDnow's online store different from your music store?

_____

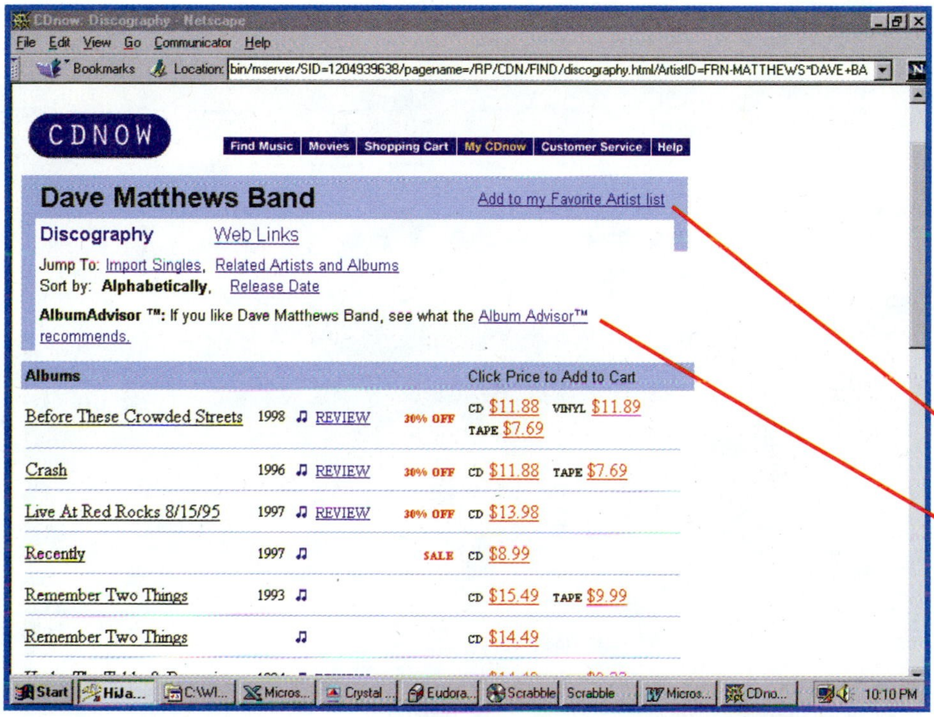

CDnow will keep track of your favorites.

CDnow can make suggestions for similar sounds.

Figure 2.1
CDnow Discography

3 Now look at another online music store. Go to the Music Boulevard site and answer these questions.

Whose music reviews can you read online?

_____

What does Store Pulse show you?

_____

Does Music Boulevard let you ship outside the United States?

_____

How many CDs do you have to buy before you qualify for a free one?_____

What do you do to order a gift certificate?_____

Can you search by artist? by title? How else can you search for music? _____

_____

Figure 2.2
Music Boulevard artist search results

④ Figure 2.2 shows the results of an artist search. Use the Search button to trace the same artist you used in step 2.

How do the prices compare to what you found from CDnow? (Don't forget the shipping.) _____

_____

What happens when you click the album title? _____

What happens when you click the music notes? _____

⑤ Both sites offer customers the opportunity to read reviews and hear sound samples. Can you do these things as easily in a music store? How do these features help online retailers make sales? How do these features help consumers make choices?

_____

_____

_____

THINKING ABOUT TECHNOLOGY

Do you think that one company checks the prices that the other one charges? If you started a music store in a mall, would you consider the online stores to be your competition? What would you have to offer to compete with the online stores?

Electronic Catalogs

ACTIVITY

2.2

Objective:
In this lesson, you will learn the advantages for businesses of providing an electronic catalog.

Businesses that use electronic commerce to sell goods, and even services, need to let the customer see what goods and services they offer. Sometimes just a list of specifications is sufficient. If you are in the business of selling parts in the automotive industry, you may have thousands of items in stock. Providing a picture of each of these is probably not necessary, but your ordering and inventory systems will have to make use of some sort of database that can distinguish one part from another.

Online catalogs with pictures and descriptions are necessary for some products. Like their printed counterparts, online catalogs with pictures still need to provide a clear description of the merchandise, including item number, size, color, and price. Whether customers can use online ordering, must order by phone, or must work personally with a sales agent, the online catalog can reach new markets with speed and convenience. Figure 2-3 shows a page from the Florida Level and Transit catalog, a company specializing in equipment for land surveying. Even though customers must telephone their order, they can price equipment online.

One product that is frequently featured in online catalogs but does not lend itself to online sales is real estate. In this activity, you will visit several real estate companies to learn why they feature some of their properties electronically.

Figure 2.3
Catalog page from Florida Level and Transit

1. Use your search engine to locate real estate companies with an Internet presence. You should find links for nationwide franchises, such as Coldwell Banker and Century 21, and for individual firms. Begin by visiting the Century 21 home page, shown in Figure 2.4.

Figure 2.4
Century 21 real estate home page

This home page offers customers much more than properties for sale. How does the company benefit from offering customers all of these links? _____

_____

2. Click the house to conduct a property search. Follow a link and view a listed property. If none of the agencies in your location displays properties electronically, search another location. Which of the following are provided for the property?

Feature of Electronic Listing	Provided?
Photograph	
Price	
Information (bedrooms, baths, square feet, etc.)	
Address	
Agent's name	
E-mail to agent	

Which of these features appear in printed real estate ads in your community? _____

_____

Why can an agency provide more information online than in the newspaper? _____

_____

3 Check the real estate section of your local newspaper or the telephone book to see if other real estate firms in your community publicize an Internet presence. Choose one that is not part of a national firm, and visit its site. Compare the amount and types of information it provides with the information you found at the national site above. How is the catalog different? (If you cannot find a local company that has a site, visit Williams and Associates, shown in Figure 2.5.)

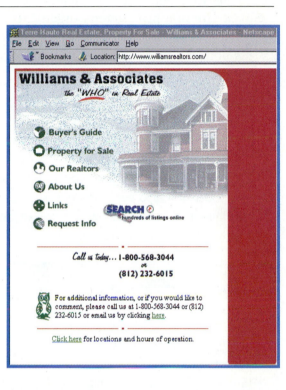

Figure 2.5
Williams and Associates real estate home page

THINKING ABOUT TECHNOLOGY

What other products are well suited for an online catalog? Why would these products work well for online catalog sales? Name three that are well suited to online ordering and three that are not. Why are some products better candidates for online catalog sales than others?

Net Fun

Traditional catalog retailers were among the first companies to use electronic catalogs. You can find specialty catalogs for everything from Gaelic music to golf carts. To see a list, go to "Companies" under Yahoo's Business and Economy category. Search for catalogs. If you like cartoon characters, visit the Acme Trading Company catalog, where you'll see merchandise featuring Scooby-Doo, Rocky and Bullwinkle, the Rugrats, and other cartoon characters.

Objective:

In this lesson, you will visit trade association sites to see how associations and professional organizations can use the Internet to help accomplish their goals.

Organizations and Associations on the Net

Trade and other professional organizations often create Internet sites to post information of interest to their members and to the public. As a business owner, you might search for a trade organization that deals with your merchandise. As a consumer, you might visit the Web site of a professional organization to find a member business near you, or to learn about new developments in the industry. In this activity, you will visit this kind of site to see how it helps businesses and consumers alike.

1. Some trade organizations are associated with a particular product. Farmers and growers frequently form an association around their crop. You can see in Figure 2.6 the home page of the Michigan Blueberry Growers Association site. There is also a site for the North American Blueberry Council. To see how an Internet presence can help the members and also serve the public, search for the associations for the products in the table below and answer the questions. There may be more than one site for a product.

Figure 2.6
Home page of the Michigan Blueberry Growers Association

Product	URL	Name of Association
onions		
eggs		
rice		
watermelon		
milk		

Name three things you found that are particularly useful to growers.
How does each one benefit growers?

1. _____

_____

2. _____

_____

3. _____

_____

Name three things you found that are useful to consumers. How does
each one benefit consumers?

1. _____

_____

2. _____

_____

3. _____

_____

2 Other trade associations are associated with particular industries.
These associations also act as information sources for members and
consumers alike. Many of them provide educational material and Web
links to their members' sites and to related sites. If you have a business, it would be valuable to be able to learn from others who face the
same issues you do. The Internet can make it easy to find and communicate with your peers. A portion of the Web site for the American
Sportfishing Association is shown in Figure 2.7. Not only can individuals
visit this site to learn more about fishing, but professionals involved in
the industry—such as fishing equipment retailers and manufacturers,
environmentalists, and camp owners—can also find each other in the
database, learn about legislation, and benefit from the association's
research.

NET TIP:

Search for Contacts with Yahoo

*To see a list of trade organizations, you can follow the links from Yahoo
through Business and Economy, Organizations, and Trade Associations.*

Outreach Menu drop-down choices

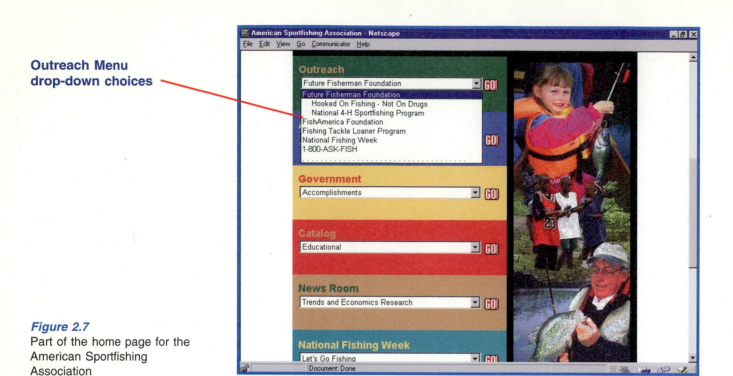

Figure 2.7
Part of the home page for the American Sportfishing Association

NET FACT

Entrepreneurship Programs

If you have studied French, you may recognize that both "entrepreneur" and "enterprise" come from French roots and are related to "undertake." Entrepreneurs get to undertake just about everything associated with a business. Although they may have employees and even partners, they usually have sole responsibility for the undertaking— the risks, rewards, decisions, and all. St. Louis University offers academic programs and support for entrepreneurship through the Jefferson Smurfit Center for Entrepreneurial Studies. They also sponsor the National Collegiate Entrepreneur of the Year contest. To learn more about their programs, visit their eWeb site at www.slu.edu.

Search for trade associations for these industries, and then use what you find to answer the following questions.

Occupation	URL	Name of Association
textiles		
lighting		
publishing		
soap		
toys		

The term **entrepreneur** usually refers to someone who starts and operates a new business. To be an entrepreneur, you don't have to invent a new product, but you do need to be responsible for a new venture. What information do you see at these sites that would be particularly useful to an entrepreneur in each of these industries?

_____

_____

_____

What links do you see at these sites that would be informative for someone looking for career advice in each of these industries?

_____

_____

_____

THINKING ABOUT TECHNOLOGY

Many professional organizations hold meetings and conventions. How could the Internet be used to hold a meeting of individuals engaged in the same sort of business?

If you like to fish, visit the American Sportfishing Association site and see the FishToid of the day. Figure 2.8 shows the fact for October 10. And yes, the cartoon fish swims.

FishToid for Saturday, October 10, 1998

Fish Fact 25:
Anglers spent more than $500 million on camping equipment in 1996.

Source: *1996 U.S. Economic Impact of Sport Fishing in the United States, American Sportfishing Association*

Figure 2.8
American Sportfishing Association FishToid

ACTIVITY
2.4

Objective:

In this lesson, you will see the benefits of an Internet presence for a small business.

What Can a Small Business Do on the Internet?

As you're beginning to notice, the Internet is a vast store of information for almost any subject you can imagine. In addition to sales, the small business owner can use the Net for two basic reasons—to gather information and to spread information.

Search engines have categories just for small business owners. By searching, they can find information about opportunities, legal issues, financing, government assistance, software, taxes, and just about any other issue they face. As you've seen in Activity 2.3, they can find contacts through associations and organizations.

Small business owners can also expand their own business by using the Internet. In advertising alone, they can save thousands of dollars and simultaneously reach thousands of customers by developing an Internet presence. In later chapters, you'll see precisely how this is done. For now, let's take a tour of a couple of small business sites.

1. Begin with a visit to the government's Small Business Administration Web site, shown in Figure 2.9. The SBA was founded in 1953 and provides a wealth of support for new and existing small businesses. Follow the link labeled "Starting" and answer the following questions.

   How is a "small" business" described? Give three features that distinguish a small business from a larger one.

   1. _____

   2. _____

   3. _____

   Read the answers to Frequently Asked Questions about starting a small business. How much money should a small business have on hand, after the initial startup costs have been paid? _____

   _____

   What is a Small Business Development Center (SBDC)? Hint: follow Offices and Services. _____

   _____

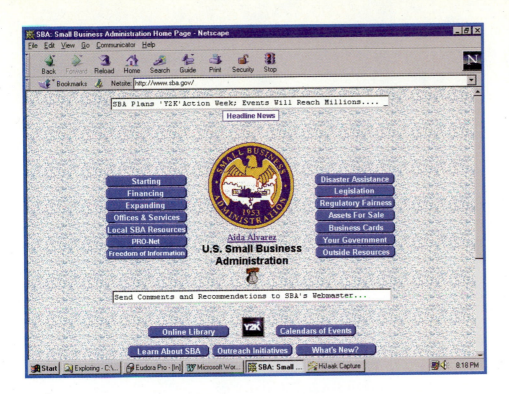

Figure 2.9
Small Business Administration
home page

2 Small businesses deal with everything from advertising to zippers, and many of them have discovered the benefits of an Internet presence. Visit a travel agency now to see how its Internet connection helps the agency do business. Visit the Web site of I.T. Travel and answer the following questions.

What do you click to ask the company, online, about your travel plans?

_____

How will the information be sent to you? _____

_____

What service do you reach when you do online booking? _____

_____

Online booking would be very convenient for someone who traveled regularly and knew which flights to choose. What might the company do to encourage other customers to use the online service? _____

_____

_____

3 Why would a restaurant want to have an Internet site? If a restaurant in your community advertises its Web address, go to the site. If not, use a search engine to find a restaurant with a Web site. If you use Yahoo, it is helpful to follow threads through regional travel to reach a chosen state, and then search for restaurants. Figure 2.10 shows the menu link from Shaffer's, a restaurant in Indianapolis.

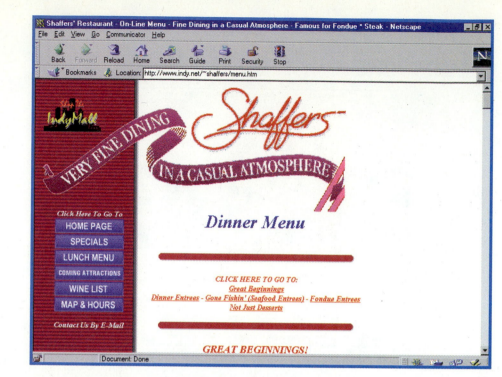

Figure 2.10
Shaffer's restaurant menu page

Which of the following pieces of information were you able to find on the restaurant's Web site?

• Hours of operation?	Yes _____	No _____
• Telephone number and address?	Yes _____	No _____
• Directions to the restaurant?	Yes _____	No _____
• Menu?	Yes _____	No _____
• Online reservations?	Yes _____	No _____
• Can you e-mail your order for take-out?	Yes _____	No _____

Does this restaurant's site make you more likely or less likely to eat at the restaurant? Why? _____

_____

_____

THINKING ABOUT TECHNOLOGY

It would be unusual for a computer-related business—a computer store, an Internet service provider, or a Web design firm—not have an Internet presence. What other businesses can you think of that would consider a Web site critically important? Can you think of any businesses whose customers would not be likely to look for them on the Internet? Why might these businesses want to have a site anyway?

Corporations on the Net

In Chapter 1, you took a look at the General Mills Web site. As you learned there, the site was not created to take orders and sell products to you, but rather to provide corporate information, to advertise, and for public relations. In this activity, you'll take a closer look at a site from a large corporation—Kodak. Here you will get a feel for the wide variety of ways that a corporation can use a Web site to accomplish its goals, even if it doesn't sell products online.

ACTIVITY 2.5

Objective:
In this lesson, you will see how large corporations use the Internet to accomplish multiple goals.

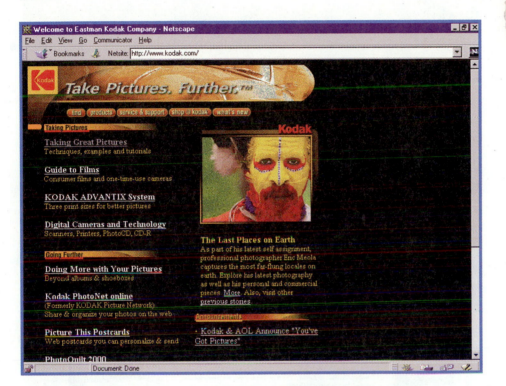

Figure 2.11
Kodak's "Take Pictures. Further™" Web site

1. Open the home page at *www.kodak.com*, shown in Figure 2-11.

   How can this Web site help you take better pictures?_____

   _____

   How can this site help Kodak sell more cameras, film, and processing?

   _____

   How can you use this site to find the Kodak company's annual report?

   _____

   Are student internship opportunities available at Kodak? How can you apply?

   _____

2. Click the link to Shop@Kodak. What is the price range for the digital camera packages you can buy online? _____

   _____

Business advisors and management textbooks are unanimous when it comes to stressing the importance of a comprehensive business plan. This document should spell out in measurable terms what a business intends to do and what it will cost. Lenders use the business plan to help determine whether or not they want to finance the business. One company that specializes in online business planning is BizPlanIt. This company creates customized business plans for customers, but it also offers a free online newsletter and online advice through Ask Mr. BizPlanIt. The Virtual BizPlan page, shown in Figure 2.13, has explanatory links to all the sections of a good business plan.

Figure 2.13
The Virtual BizPlan page from BizPlanIt

3 **Market share** is a particular company's portion of a product's total sales. For example, according to *MacWeek* (October, 27, 1997), Compaq Computer Corporation has 13.5 percent of the worldwide market for computers. This means that at this time, approximately 13.5 percent of all computers sold were Compaqs.

Increasing its market share is a corporate goal that Kodak, and every other company, considers to be important. List three things you found on the site that would make you feel more inclined to use Kodak products, and explain why.

THINKING ABOUT TECHNOLOGY

Ten years ago, if you had to write a biography about George Eastman, the founder of Kodak, you probably would have looked in an encyclopedia on a bookshelf, or searched for other printed material on his life. Now, you can visit the corporate site and read about Eastman and the history of the company. How do you suppose the information the company provides would compare to what you would find in an encyclopedia?

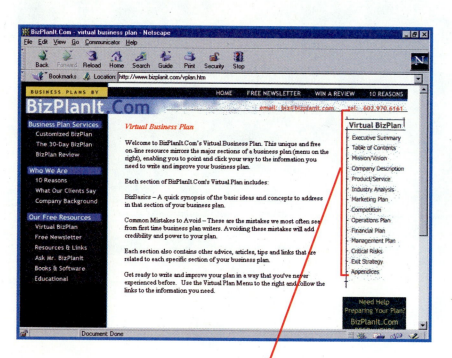

Components of a good business plan.

Net Fun

Use Kodak's Picture This link to send an e-mail postcard to a friend. To do this, choose a category and a picture, add a border and greeting, type your message, and address and send the card.

CHAPTER REVIEW

NET VOCABULARY

Define the following terms:

1. consumer

2. entrepreneurship

3. market share

4. retailing

NET REVIEW

Give a short answer to the following questions:

1. How can a business use the Internet to its advantage without making a sales transaction?

2. What kinds of information can a business put on its Web page to support sales? Use a music store as an example.

3. Why would a business that knows it will not be making online sales still want to have an online catalog? Use a business that sells antique cars as an example.

4. How can a business benefit by linking its Web page to a trade association Web page?

5. What is the Small Business Administration? What can a company learn from its Web page?

6. How can a very large company use a Web site to educate its customers?

ADVICE FOR SMALL BUSINESSES

In addition to the Small Business Administration's site, many other organizations and companies offer online advice to small businesses and new companies. Four of them are shown in the table below.

URL	Source	Title
http://www.cbia.com/mgmtsvc/tipsinde.htm	*Connecticut Business and Industry Association*	*Tips for Small Businesses*
http://www.quicken.com/small_business/	*Quicken.com*	*Small Business*
http://www.lowe.org/smallbiznet/	*Edward Lowe Foundation*	*smallbizNet*
http://smallbizhelp.net/	*Scott Direct*	*smallbizhelp*

The smallbizNet site offers some additional links to "Hailed Sites," sites that the organization judges to have the best business information on the Net. Figure 2.12 shows some of the smallbizNet's Hailed Sites.

Figure 2.12
smallbizNet links to Hailed Sites

Visit the four sites listed in the table. Compile a list of the three best suggestions from each site for a small business that wants to do E-commerce.

Connecticut Business and Industry Association Suggestions:

1. _____
2. _____
3. _____

Quicken Suggestions:

1. _____
   _____
2. _____
3. _____

Edward Lowe Foundation Suggestions:

1. _____
2. _____
3. _____

Scott Direct Suggestions:

1. _____
2. _____
3. _____

NET PROJECT TEAMWORK   Nonprofits on the Web

Some not-for-profit organizations have established a Web presence. With your team, choose as many charities as there are team members. Each person should search to see if that particular charity has a Web site. Gather information from the sites. What is their mission? How do they spend their contributions? What assistance do they provide for people who want to know more about the cause they represent? Do they have a way to take contributions online? Compile your results in a summary table, and present your report to your class. Include conclusions about how nonprofit organizations can benefit from a Web presence.

WRITING ABOUT TECHNOLOGY
Grow Your Small Business on the Web

Imagine that you have been asked to give a speech to the clients of a local Small Business Development Center. Your topic is "How the Internet Can Improve Your Business." In about 100 words, write a sentence outline of your speech.

Personal and Business Services Online

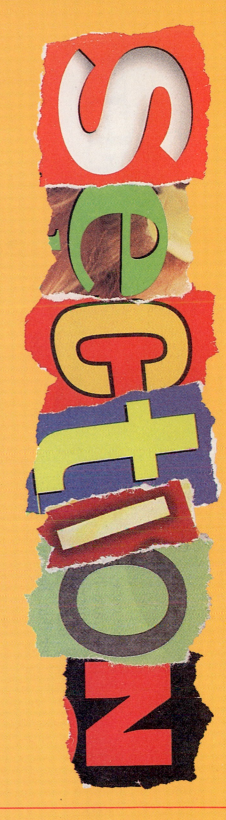

As you're seeing, E-commerce means more than buying and selling goods online. It describes business conducted electronically to take advantage of the speed, access, and data handling capabilities of the Internet.

Organizations that provide services can take advantage of these capabilities in the same way that organizations that sell goods do. Even though they may not have an object to sell, they still have customers (or clients) and need to reach them. With the Internet, they can bring their story to anyone with a connection.

Your work in this section will take you through some of the most common online services. In Chapter 3, you'll learn how to access information about careers and see how the Internet can help you decide what you want to do with your life. You'll be able to find information about a particular career and explore how to prepare for it. You'll learn how to find job listings in online job banks and at a company's Web site, and see how to prepare an electronic resume.

The Internet's immediate access to information makes it an excellent medium for distributing timely financial data. Businesses such as banking, investing, lending, and insurance have all found the Internet to be an effective way to attract and service their customers. And customers like it because it is never closed, easy to use, and economical. In Chapter 4, you'll see how personal finance works online.

You can use the Internet as your personal source for any information you want to know. Want to plan a trip—complete with airline schedules, fares, and reservations—and have a hotel room and rental car waiting when you arrive? You can do it online. Want to know what the weather and local headlines are in any corner of the world? Simple to do with the Internet. Need to find the phone number for an old friend, the address for a dentist in Tampa, or how to contact your elected representatives in Washington? In Chapter 5, you'll see how to make the Internet your information provider.

Chapter 3   Searching for a Career 40
Chapter 4   Personal Finance on the Internet 57
Chapter 5   Internet Information Services 75

CHAPTER 3

Searching for a Career

Chapter Objectives:

After completing the activities in this chapter, you will be able to use the Internet to

1 locate career-planning information.

2 prepare an electronic resume and post it.

3 search for job listings.

4 find relocation information.

5 match educational institutions with your needs.

Net Terms

resume

meta-sites

job

career

assessment tool

clearinghouse

acronym

Your Career Awaits... on the Internet

You probably already know that computers are necessary to do almost any job today, whether you are in the medical profession or manufacturing, law enforcement or sales. What you might not realize is that you can use the computer, and the Internet, to help determine what career might be best for you and to find your dream job. Sites available on the Web will teach you how to present information about your qualifications and experience in an attractive resume. A **resume** is a list of your personal information, educational background, and professional experience. Through the Internet, you can post your resume, view position announcements, make

contacts, and even calculate the cost of living and look for an apartment in your new location.

And there's more. If you are an employer wanting to hire capable employees, what better place to look for them than on the Internet? You have instant access to a huge number of resumes, and you can reach applicants all over the world. By listing open positions on your company's Web site or through a job bank, you get immediate and extensive exposure for your openings. With available software, you can automatically scan the resumes you receive to filter out the ones that aren't appropriate for the position.

NET TIP
Home Page

Access the E-Commerce: Business on the Internet *home page through the following URL:* e-commerce.swep.com. *Remember that a Web address may change at any time. An address given in this book as an example may no longer be valid. If so, either access the home page* (e-commerce.swep.com) *for the current link or do a search to find a similar site.*

The Internet has a huge amount of employment information. Individuals post resumes on their personal home pages, and company Web sites post openings. Government and academic placement centers list openings, and many commercial sites have links to thousands of jobs. There is also a large and growing amount of career-planning advice online. Career-related super- or **meta-sites** (the prefix "meta" means "going beyond or higher") can be gigantic. These sites offer not only their own information, but also indexes of related information.

In this chapter, you'll learn how job applicants can use the Internet to help with career planning and resume writing. You will also learn how applicants and prospective employers can find each other. ■

NET TIP

Search Engine Job Links

Some sites appear on everyone's list of the top Web employment sites. Most of these are multipurpose, allowing you to read career-planning advice, work on and post your resume, post and search for jobs, and learn about industry trends. You can find the National Business Employment Weekly, JobWeb, CareerMosaic, The Monster Board, America's Job Bank, and other super sites by following your search engine's business and employment links.

ACTIVITY

3.1

Objective:
In this lesson, you will learn how to locate career-planning information.

Career Planning

You may already have a clear idea of the career you'd like to pursue. But whether you do or not, you'll benefit from doing some career planning. Experts recommend that you always have both short- and long-term career goals, and that you examine them frequently. And circumstances, or your interests, might lead you in directions you have yet to consider.

Most people change jobs several times during their lifetimes. What some don't realize is that there are differences between jobs and careers. A **job** is simply a specific position you have with a specific employer. A **career**, on the other hand, is a profession, including the training you receive and the goals you set. A person with a career in pharmaceutical sales may have jobs with several different companies over the years. You need to devote time and energy to career planning, and the Internet can help you. In fact, a recent survey listed "Managing Your Career" as the third most popular activity on the Internet.

1 Most search engines have a category for jobs. Go to this category and look for links to career-planning sites. Eliminate sites that seem to be selling materials for career counseling or are for particular geographic areas, and go to five sites that seem to offer useful online guidance. One site you might want to check is shown in Figure 3.1. This site is a link from the *Washington Post* newspaper and features advice from the author of the book *What Color Is Your Parachute?* Write the addresses of your five sites below, along with helpful advice you found at each one.

Career-Planning URLs   **Helpful Information at Each Site**

1. _____

2. _____

3. _____

4. _____

5. _____

Figure 3.1
Career advice from author Dick Bolles

2 Some career-planning sites offer free online **assessment tools.** These are questionnaires that help you discover characteristics about yourself, such as your interests, aptitudes, or skills. Check to see if any of your sites lead you to an assessment tool. Figure 3.2 shows part of an online assessment tool from Bowling Green State University. Many times, university placement offices will provide a wealth of helpful information. And, you don't always have to be a student at that school to take advantage of the Web site.

Career Planning URLs   **Assessment Help Available**

1. _____   _____

2. _____   _____

3. _____   _____

4. _____   _____

5. _____   _____

The AltaVista search engine has a Careers category that offers one-stop shopping for anything dealing with careers. Take a tour of its links, and be sure to check out advice from the Career Coach.

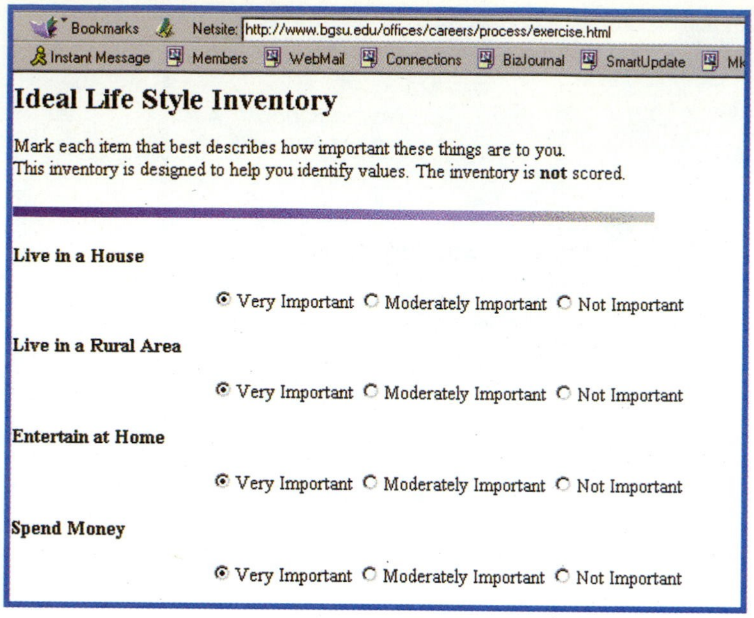

Figure 3.2
Bowling Green State University's online assessment tool

(3) Have you ever been interviewed for a job? Some applicants are very apprehensive when they sit down to talk with a prospective employer. Knowing what to expect, and practicing what you have to say, can help you make a better impression. Read through the interviewing advice at Career Consulting Corner and four other general sites. Record five hints that would be helpful to you.

Interview Information URL	Useful Hint
1.	
2.	
3.	
4.	
5.	

THINKING ABOUT TECHNOLOGY

After reading the career planning advice you've found, what do you think you need to do before you can begin searching for a job? What careers are you considering now? How can you use the Internet to gather information about your options?

Your Resume

ACTIVITY

3.2

Objective:
In this lesson, you will learn how to create and post a resume.

How do you present yourself to a prospective employer? When you answer a newspaper ad or visit a placement center, you submit a copy of your resume. Electronic job searches are no different. Your resume needs to present you in the best possible light, and it needs to reach the right people. The Internet can help you with both.

1 Search for advice on creating a good electronic resume. You may want to first limit your search to a Business or Jobs category. Write down the addresses of five sites you find that you think will help you. List five tips you discovered for writing an effective resume. Figure 3.3 shows links to resume writing on the Job Web site.

Resume Advice URLs	Resume-Writing Tips
1.	1.
2.	2.
3.	3.
4.	4.
5.	5.

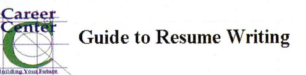

Figure 3.3
Links to resume-writing tips

> **NET TIP**
> **Check Out Your Competition!**
>
> *Many individual resumes are available for viewing and will show up when you search for resume links. You can see what you like, and what you don't, in a resume by looking at examples.*

2 One way that you can submit your resume is by pasting parts of it into a company's application form. Search for Ameritech's online job openings. Select a location, career interest, and business unit that interest you. Examine how you could submit resume information. Unless you are interested in proceeding, don't complete the submission. You can see the beginning of the form in Figure 3.4.

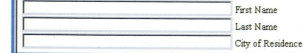

Figure 3.4
Ameritech's resume submission form

3 Applicants can also submit their resumes to online job **clearinghouses.** These are large databases that store information about jobs and job seekers, and match jobs with people. Go to the CareerMosaic site's resume-posting link, shown in Figure 3.5, and examine the form an applicant would complete. This service is free.

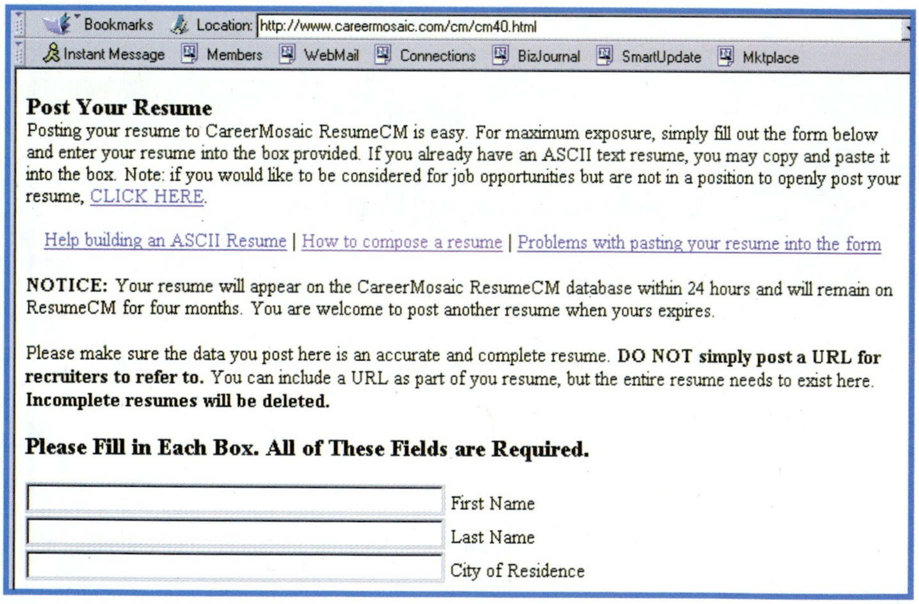

Figure 3.5
CareerMosaic resume submission form

4 Some commercial services will review and post your resume for a fee. Investigate three of these. What does the service cost? What do they guarantee for your investment? What might you do to decide which of these to use?

URLs for Resume Posting	Cost of Service	Service Provided
1.		
2.		
3.		

THINKING ABOUT TECHNOLOGY

How can a good resume help you find employment? How will you know that your resume is attracting attention?

NET FACT

Resume Scanning

Both electronic and paper copies of resumes are likely to be scanned if the company has to evaluate a large number of applicants. Artificial intelligence software searches for key words and phrases that match the employer's needs. Then it determines which candidates should be dropped and which should stay in the list of potential employees. Some authorities believe that applicants can improve their chances if they load their resumes with buzzwords that they think the software will look for. Others say it makes no difference. All seem to agree, however, that an applicant should use up-to-date terminology when describing experiences. Resumes should also avoid fancy fonts and formatting—these can confuse the scanning software.

Net Business *Rebecca Smith: Author, Consultant, and Web Designer*

If you are the author of books and articles about electronic resumes, it makes sense for you to use the Internet not only to describe your service but also to post your own resume. One very well-regarded site is that of Rebecca Smith at www.ersumes.com. This author, consultant, and Web designer offers reprints of her articles, tutorials for resume design, and links to other career-related sites. Her own resume is available for your examination. Why do you suppose this author and consultant has a Web site? Does she sell anything online?

ACTIVITY

3.3

Objective:

In this lesson, you'll see how both applicants and employers use the Internet for job searches.

The Job Search

Employers and applicants gain huge advantages by using the Internet. Employers can post job openings with no geographical limitations or response delays. Using search tools, employers can narrow applicant lists to just the most suitable for the position. As an applicant, you can use search tools to narrow the list of positions to just the most promising. If you find a job posting that interests you, you can use the Internet to learn more about the company and its location. If you decide to apply, you can get your resume to the employer immediately.

1 If you are looking for a job, you can look at one of the large clearing-houses, or you can go directly to a company's listings. Let's begin by looking at some of the general sites. Most of these ask you to specify a location and a job title or category. For this activity, select a location and job title or category that interest you. If you need an idea, search for positions in health care in the Midwest. In the space below, write the choices you want to investigate.

Position or job category _____

Location _____

Other key words _____

2 Go to America's Job Bank, The Monster Board, and CareerWeb. Record the URL of each service in the spaces below. Search for openings that fit your criteria, and list the three that interest you most from each service. Next to each opening, list the company offering it. As you can see, you can find out more about the job and the company, and in some cases submit your application through these services. Figures 3.6 and 3.7 show steps in a search from The Monster Board.

America's Job Bank	**URL:**
Position:	*Company:*
1.	1.
2.	2.
3.	3.

The Monster Board   **URL:**

Position: *Company:*

1.   1.

2.   2.

3.   3.

CareerWeb   **URL:**

Position: *Company:*

1.   1.

2.   2.

3.   3.

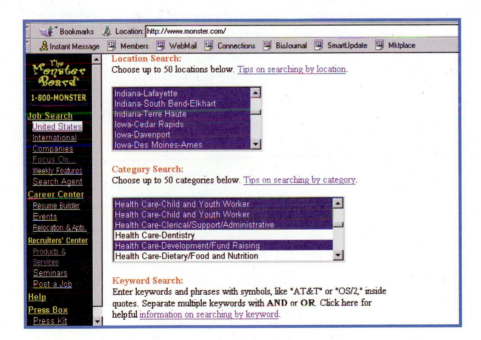

Figure 3.6
The Monster Board search form

Just for the fun of it, use one of the job-search sites to
see what jobs are posted in your neighborhood.

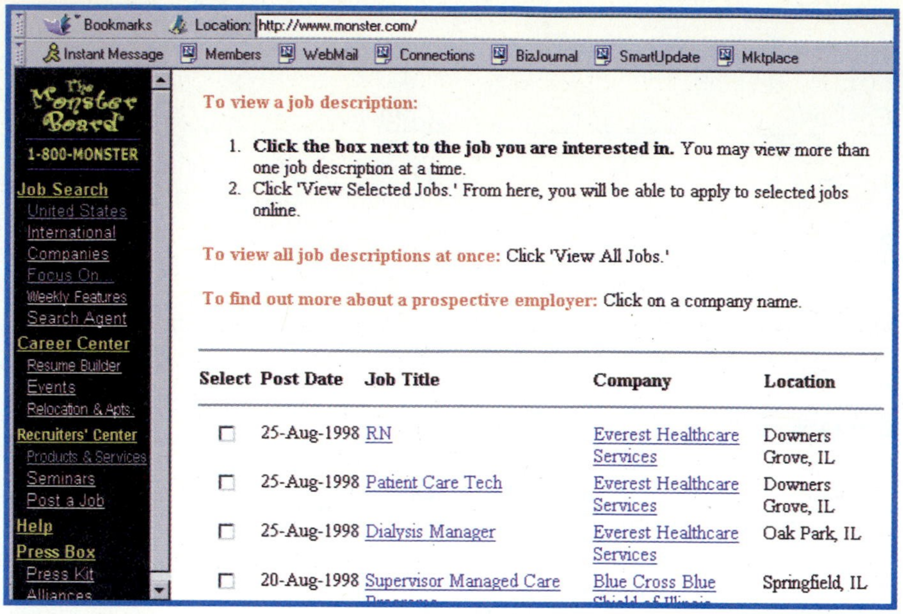

Figure 3.7
The Monster Board search results

The following is the content shown in Figure 3.7:

Bookmarks | Location: http://www.monster.com/

Instant Message | Members | WebMail | Connections | BizJournal | SmartUpdate | Mktplace

The Monster Board
1-800-MONSTER

Job Search
United States
International
Companies
Focus On
Weekly Features
Search Agent
Career Center
Resume Builder
Events
Relocation & Apts.
Recruiters' Center
Products & Services
Seminars
Post a Job
Help
Press Box
Press Kit
Alliances

To view a job description:

1. **Click the box next to the job you are interested in.** You may view more than one job description at a time.
2. Click 'View Selected Jobs.' From here, you will be able to apply to selected jobs online.

To view all job descriptions at once: Click 'View All Jobs.'

To find out more about a prospective employer: Click on a company name.

Select	Post Date	Job Title	Company	Location
☐	25-Aug-1998	RN	Everest Healthcare Services	Downers Grove, IL
☐	25-Aug-1998	Patient Care Tech	Everest Healthcare Services	Downers Grove, IL
☐	25-Aug-1998	Dialysis Manager	Everest Healthcare Services	Oak Park, IL
☐	20-Aug-1998	Supervisor Managed Care Program	Blue Cross Blue Shield of Illinois	Springfield, IL

③ What if you are an employer? How do employers post openings in these three banks? Go to America's Job Bank, The Monster Board, and CareerWeb and read the instructions for posting a job. Be sure to see the FAQs (Frequently Asked Questions) for America's Job Bank. What does it cost to post a job with each of these services?

Service: **Cost to Post an Opening:**

1. *America's Job Bank* _____

2. *The Monster Board* _____

3. *CareerWeb* _____

THINKING ABOUT TECHNOLOGY

If you were an entrepreneur with a small business, which of these job services would you want to use? Which contact methods would you want to publicize in your listing: your e-mail address, your phone number, your street address, or your URL? Why?

ACTIVITY
3.4

Objective:
At the end of this lesson, you will be able to find cost-of-living and quality-of-life information about your new location.

Congratulations! You've successfully used the Internet to post your resume, search for open positions, and get past the first interview. Now you're ready to talk about salary and your new community. How expensive is it to live there? What recreational activities does the area offer? What are the schools and health care like? The Internet can help you gather all of this information.

1 Using a location you've always liked, or one you found in Activity 3.3, decide on a city to use for this activity.

2 Search for a cost-of-living calculator at Virtual Relocation, Student Center, Pathfinder, or NewsEngin. Use one of these calculators to see what a salary of $50,000 in Chicago would equal in New York, Los Angeles, and your new location.

City	Amount Equal to $50,000 in Chicago
New York	
Los Angeles	
Your New Location:	

3 Search for your new location, and see what information you can find about schools and health care. How do the schools and health care services in the new location compare to the place you live now? How do the recreational activities in your current and new locations compare?

School, Health and Recreation	New Location	Current Location
School Information		
Health Care Information		
Recreation		

NET TIP
Go to the Source!

You can learn about a location's interesting features, and also limit the number of sites you need to wade through, if you go through your search engine's Travel category. Look for sites sponsored by state or local tourism agencies.

4 How would you find a place to live? You may find real estate links when you look up the new location, and most major real estate firms have Web sites. You also can search for nationwide apartment information, as shown in Figure 3.8. See what rental property is available in your new location, and determine what it would cost.

Type of Property	Cost per Month

Figure 3.8
Apartment hunting with Rent.net

THINKING ABOUT TECHNOLOGY

List the characteristics of your ideal place to live. Now prioritize your list. What characteristics of a new location are most important to you? Which characteristics would you be willing to give up to get others?

Yahoo, Excite, and AltaVista each let you draw a map based on an address. You can even get driving directions, which would be a big help if your job interview were in a strange city. Try out one of these by asking for a map and directions to a place you know well.

Back to School

ACTIVITY

3.5

Objective:
At the end of this lesson, you will be able to search for educational programs and educational institutions.

An important part of career planning is an understanding of the education and training required to enter and stay current in a field. What do you do if the career you want requires certification or continuing education? Most educational institutions have a Web presence. By searching for a particular school, you can find its home page. But you can also use the Internet to search for institutions that offer a particular program that interests you.

1 Assume you want to enter the medical field and become a nurse-practitioner. Look for information about requirements for this degree.

Requirements for Nurse-
Practitioners:_____

2 **Acronyms**, which are abbreviations made up of the first letters of words, can become confusing, particularly in the computing field. Search for the meanings of CNA, CNE, MCP, and MCSE. How can you achieve certifications for these computer careers?

Acronym	Meaning	How to Achieve?
CNA		
CNE		
MCP		
MCSE		

3 You may decide you need to investigate colleges and universities to see what programs they offer. Visit CollegeNET or the U.S. News college site and search for schools that offer a program of interest to you. Figure 3.9 shows how CollegeNET lets you search for schools that meet your criteria.

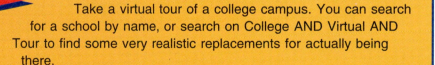

Take a virtual tour of a college campus. You can search for a school by name, or search on College AND Virtual AND Tour to find some very realistic replacements for actually being there.

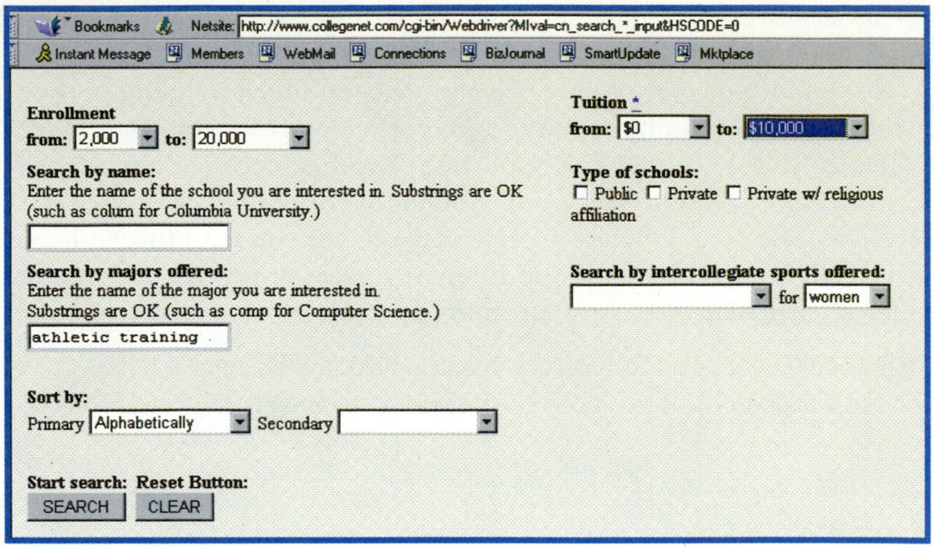

Figure 3.9
CollegeNet search

THINKING ABOUT TECHNOLOGY

What education or training do you need for your current career or one you are considering? Is certification required? If so, how can you get it?

Net Ethics — Acceptable Site-Use Considerations

When a job applicant or an employer looks for information in an online database, each would like to be assured that the listings are correct and accurate. However, postings tend to work on an honor system. If you are an employer, you trust that the information provided in a resume is factual. If you are a job seeker, you trust the position is as advertised. Undoubtedly, though, this kind of system can be abused. Participants are open to scrutiny by anyone who comes across their listing, and they should give careful thought to the amount of information they wish to publicize. For an interesting discussion of the legal and ethical concerns involved, read the Copyright notices and Acceptable Site-Use Rules of some of the big job-search companies you've found.

NET VOCABULARY

Define the following terms:

1. acronym
2. assessment tool
3. career
4. clearinghouse
5. job
6. meta-site
7. resume

NET REVIEW

Give a short answer to the following questions:

1. Why is career planning important?

2. Using the experience of someone you know, illustrate the difference between a job and a career.

3. Describe five types of information that you, as a prospective employer, would expect to see on a resume.

4. Your nervous friend has a job interview tomorrow. Give three pieces of useful advice for the interview.

5. What makes using the Internet to look for a job or an employee so effective?

6. What kinds of information can you find on the Internet about a new community?

7. How can the Internet help you with decisions about continuing education?

MOVING TO HOUSTON

Simone Landes has always been interested in moving to Houston. She likes the idea of living in Texas. Also, she has followed America's space program since she was very young, and Houston is the nerve center for space exploration. Although Simone grew up in Minnesota, she doesn't think that she'll have any trouble adapting to Houston's warmer weather.

What Simone doesn't have, though, is a job waiting for her in Houston. She is currently working as the assistant director of a corporate child care center, although her college degree is in creative writing. Simone would prefer to find a position that makes use of her education. However, she would be willing to consider other positions as long as

- she can work for an established company and receive health and retirement benefits,
- she can start at a salary of at least $30,000 annually, and
- she is, or can become, qualified for the position.

1. Visit one of the career-planning sites. Put yourself in Simone's situation. What careers might be possible for someone with an interest in creative writing? for someone with experience working with young children? for someone with interest, but little formal training, in physics and astronomy?

2. Draft a rough copy of Simone's resume, using the information you know about her. You will have to be creative with the missing pieces, but make them consistent with the facts you do have.

3. Use one of the large job-search sites to find at least five open positions in the Houston area that fit Simone's criteria. For each, record the position, company, salary, and application procedure.

4. Visit the Web site of at least one of the five companies. What can you learn about the company? What kinds of products or services does it offer? Does the Web site make the company appealing to you?

5. Visit NASA's Web site. Write a paragraph telling Simone about space-related tours she can take in Houston.

NET PROJECT TEAMWORK Career Potential in Houston

Share the careers you found for Simone with your teammates. Then, as a team, vote on one career to investigate further from among those everyone discovered. Use links to government data to investigate the potential for growth in that career. You may want to visit the Department of Commerce, the Department of Labor, and the Census Bureau. Divide up tasks among team members. After everyone has gathered their information, write a memo from your team to Simone, describing the projections for this career. Act as career counselors and conclude with your recommendations to her.

WRITING ABOUT TECHNOLOGY The Low-Tech Job Search

Interview a friend or family member who has had the same job for at least eight years. Ask how the person found out about the job and applied for it. On a separate piece of paper, use about 100 words to compare and contrast that job search with an Internet job search. Will you use the Internet to help find your next job? Why or why not?

Personal Finance on the Internet

Chapter Objectives:

After completing the activities in this chapter, you will be able to use the Internet to

1 discover which banks and other financial institutions offer online banking and learn how to access the services they offer.

2 find up-to-date information about stock and bond prices, track a portfolio of investments, and use online brokerage services.

3 search for mortgage outlets and see how a buyer can apply for a mortgage online.

4 investigate online sources of insurance information and learn to use the Internet to comparison-shop for insurance.

5 find tax preparation help from both the government and private agencies, and learn how to file your taxes electronically.

Net Terms

direct deposit

automatic withdrawals

portfolio

socially responsible investing

ticker symbol

discount broker

mortgage

interest (loan)

interest rate (loan)

term of a loan

push technology

pull technology

Managing Your Money Without Leaving Home

Although you might enjoy holding your actual paycheck in your hand, going to the bank to deposit it can be a nuisance. Considerations of time and security have led many people who receive regular checks, like employees and Social Security recipients, to sign up for **direct deposit** of their checks. With this system, your employer electronically deposits your paycheck to the account you have specified.

You might also instruct your bank to make **automatic withdrawals** to pay bills due at

regular intervals and for the same amount of money each time, such as a car payment. With this system, you authorize the bank to remove the amount you specify from your account and actually make the payment for you. You could also set up an automatic withdrawal to transfer money regularly to a savings account or other investment.

Electronic transfers save time, help you make your payments and deposits on time, and reduce your need to write checks. If it is this easy to do some of your banking electronically, why not consider doing the rest of it that way?

With the Internet, you can "write checks" and not have to address envelopes, buy stamps, or remember to put them in the mail. You can research the financial performance of your favorite companies and buy and sell stocks. Do you need a mortgage or want to buy insurance? Some banks and insurance companies allow their customers to apply online. You can get help with your taxes and even submit payments online. And this is just a small sample of the many ways you can manage your finances online.

Companies such as CNN (pictured in Figure 4.1), CNBC, CBS, and *Smart Money* magazine, among others, have established financial metasites. These sites give you financial news and tools to use for personal and corporate finance. They also provide wonderful learning opportunities to help you get started with financial planning. These sites can help you do just about anything you want with your money! ■

Figure 4.1
The home page for CNN Financial

NET TIP
Home Page

Access the E-Commerce: Business on the Internet *home page through the following URL:* e-commerce.swep.com. *Remember that a Web address may change at any time. An address given in this book as an example may no longer be valid. If so, either access the home page (e-commerce.swep.com) for the current link or do a search to find a similar site.*

Banking Online

How does online banking really work? Most banks offer two ways for you to pay your bills electronically. You may use a personal financial software package that links to the bank with a modem, or you may link to the bank through the Web.

When you pay your bills electronically, the bank immediately withdraws the money from your account. If your payee—say, the phone company—has established an electronic system with your bank, then the amount will go immediately into the phone company's account. But sometimes the payee has no electronic relationship with your bank. In this case, the bank holds the payment. Later, after collecting more customers' payments to that company, the bank sends the total owed to the company by check or wire transfer.

Why would this kind of system be attractive to a bank? There are several reasons, but they all have to do with the bank's profitability. First, by moving money electronically, a bank can keep deposits for the maximum amount of time to earn as much interest as possible. But probably more enticing to a bank are the cost savings. With less paper, less processing, and a reduced need for human employees, banks can achieve tremendous cost savings.

The Online Banking Association is a trade association of banks and other financial institutions. Although its main goal is to serve the banking community, its Web site offers useful information about online banking, including a glossary of online terminology. It also has links to award-winning bank Web sites. Let's take a look at one of these banks.

1. In 1997, the Online Banking Association recognized the Bank of America (BofA) for its excellence in home banking. Go to the Bank of America Web site, shown in Figure 4.3, and see what links appear on its home page. Go to the Home Banking area and take a test drive. Name three banking activities described in the test drive that you can do from this site.

Activity 1: _____

Activity 2: _____

Activity 3: _____

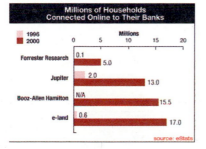

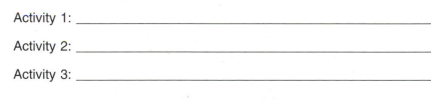

ACTIVITY 4.1

Objective:
In this lesson, you will discover which banks and other financial institutions offer online banking and learn how to access the services they offer.

NET FACT

Online Banking Today and Tomorrow

Statisticians at the eStats company estimate that under a million U.S. households were connected online to their banks in 1996. Forecasters predict that number will grow to somewhere between 5 and 17 million by the year 2000. By 1999, more than 1,000 American banks are expected to have Web-based banking services, and banks in other countries are progressing just as quickly. Figure 4.2 shows expected growth.

Figure 4.2
Forecasts for online banking

Figure 4.3
Bank of America home page

2 Click the Learn More button of the Home Banking area.

Customers who enroll in online banking can pay bills online. What does this service cost? _____

What software does the bank make available to help you track your finances? _____

How much does this cost? _____

3 Click the Business block on the home page. This section is specially tailored for entrepreneurs and small businesses. Follow the Your Home Office link, and read about setting up a home office. What kind of Internet capabilities does the bank recommend for your home office?

_____

4 Read about business banking online. The BofA recommends its home banking services for sole proprietors. What is the name of the bank's cash management service for other kinds of small businesses? Name five activities it offers.

BofA's Cash Management Service: _____

Activity 1:_____

Activity 2:_____

Activity 3:_____

Activity 4:_____

Activity 5:_____

5 Banks offer many other services online. Follow the links to find out how to apply for a car loan with BofA, as illustrated in Figure 4.4. Can you apply in your state? Go to the application form. Scroll down to see what the form requires, but don't fill it out.

What happens when you finish looking at the first page of the form and click Continue?

_____

Why do you think the bank finds it useful to separate the parts of the application?

_____

Figure 4.4
Information needed for a car loan application

THINKING ABOUT TECHNOLOGY

Some banks charge an extra fee to customers who use a human teller instead of an ATM. Do you think this fee will influence even more people to bank online? What local services would you miss if you began banking online? What would you like about banking online?

Net Fun

Banking Around the World

Want to know what banks are like in other countries? Go to *aaadir.com*. By listing a continent, then a region, and then a country, you'll find a directory of local banks. Information is listed for each one, including the availability of Internet banking. For example, five banks are listed for Finland, and two of them offer Internet banking.

ACTIVITY

4.2

Objective:

In this lesson, you will find up-to-date information about stock and bond prices, track a portfolio of investments, and use online brokerage services.

All About Online Investing

Many financial sites on the Internet enable you to create a group of investments to watch. You don't have to own the stocks to keep track of their movements, and you can learn about companies' financial performance this way. In fact, you should thoroughly study a stock's history, along with the company's financial statements, before you consider purchasing some shares.

In Chapter 2, you saw how to find a company's information on its Web site. In this activity, you'll learn how to follow the financial markets on the Web. You'll learn how to create a collection of stocks and other investments, called a **portfolio**, to watch. And you'll also investigate ways to buy and sell stocks online.

1. Many Internet sites allow you to follow a stock. Even opening screens of some browsers, such as Netscape Netcenter, offer users the opportunity to request a current stock price. In this activity, you will be visiting several sites for stock information. Find the URL for each of the following companies, and check the services they offer.

Brokerage	URL	Free Quotes?	Free Portfolio Watch?	Trading?
American Express Financial Services				
E*TRADE				
Smart Money Interactive				
Discover Brokerage Direct				

2. All stocks have **a ticker symbol**, which is a company abbreviation made up of several letters. Ticker symbols are used for easy reference in stock quotes. For example, the ticker symbol for the Mauna Loa Macadamia Partners, a Hawaiian grower of macadamia nuts, is NUT. Go to the American Express Financial Direct site. Use the Symbols link to find the New York Stock Exchange ticker symbol for the following companies in the North American markets. By clicking the linked symbol, you will be able to see stock price information, such as that shown for Disney in Figure 4.5. For each company in the table below, record the symbol, today's high, the 52-week high, and the 52-week low.

NET FACT

What is a Discount Broker?

Discount brokers are agents who buy and sell stocks for you, but don't provide all of the market analysis and customer service that a full-service broker provides. Now, at least 75 online discount brokers are operating, and some are offering very deep discounts to lure customers to buy and sell with them. Researchers predict that by 2002, 14 million investors will trade stocks online, which will be about 5 percent of all traders. Why do people trade online? For the same reasons they bank online: it is fast, it is cheap, and it is easy. You can order your trade at any time of the day, not just when the broker's office is open.

DISNEY CO WALT HLDG CO (DIS)
USA - New York

As of: Sep 17, 1998 @ 0:16 am ET

Last Trade: Sep 16,1998 @ 05:01 pm ET;
20 MIN. DELAY

Last	25 3/4	Change	+0 1/4
Currency	USD	% Change	+0.98%
Open	25 3/8	Tick	
Day Low	25 3/16	Day High	26
Previous	25 1/2	Volume	9,691,900
52 Week Low	23 7/8 09/14/98	52 Week High	42 51/64 05/04/98
EPS	0.95	P/E Ratio	27.11
Dividend Amount	Quarterly 0.0525	Ex-Dividend Date	07/22/98
Volatility	0	Current Yield	0.8
# Shares	2,047,246,000	Market Cap	52,716,584,500

NET TIP

Several Internet sites allow users to rate and comment on online brokerage firms. You can also find general guidance about online investing by searching your browser's investment category for reference and guides.

Figure 4.5
Stock price information for Disney

Company	Ticker Symbol	Today's Date	Today's High	52-Week High	52-Week Low
Disney					
Procter & Gamble					
Chrysler					
Maytag					
Merck					

3 Go to the E-TRADE home page and take the tour to learn about the site. Visit the Stocks and Options section of the tour and look at the sample detailed quote.

Compare the information E-TRADE supplies to what you saw from American Express. Which items are the same? What does E*TRADE show you that American Express doesn't?

_____

Click the link to the Stocks and Options section. Which corporate financial reports are available to members?

_____

4 Now you will create a portfolio to watch. Go to the Smart Money Interactive site, and click the Portfolio button. This service has no cost, but you will have to register a user name and password. You may make up whatever you wish. If someone else has already selected your choice, you will be asked to revise it.

NET TIP

Spend some time touring the E-STATION Learning Center to learn not only about using E-TRADE but also about investments and markets.

NET FACT

Push and Pull

When you search the Internet and retrieve information from a location, you are using **pull technology**. However, you can also have information sent to you. Using **push technology,** you can specify the kinds of information you want, and the system finds and downloads it automatically to your computer. For example, with Internet Explorer's channels, you can subscribe to have information sent to you on several different subject categories, such as stock market reports or news stories. Using push technology, Internet Explorer gathers the information for you.

5. After you have successfully registered, click the Create New Portfolio button. You are going to create a portfolio of the stocks from step 2 of this activity. Name your portfolio Activity 2, and type the ticker symbols, number of shares, and share price as shown in Figure 4.6. By doing this, you are assuming that you purchased 100 shares of each of these stocks for the price shown. Click Submit.

You will receive a report for your portfolio. This report compares today's prices with your purchase prices, and it shows whether your total portfolio value has increased or decreased. An example is shown in Figure 4.7. Did your portfolio show a gain or a loss? ___________

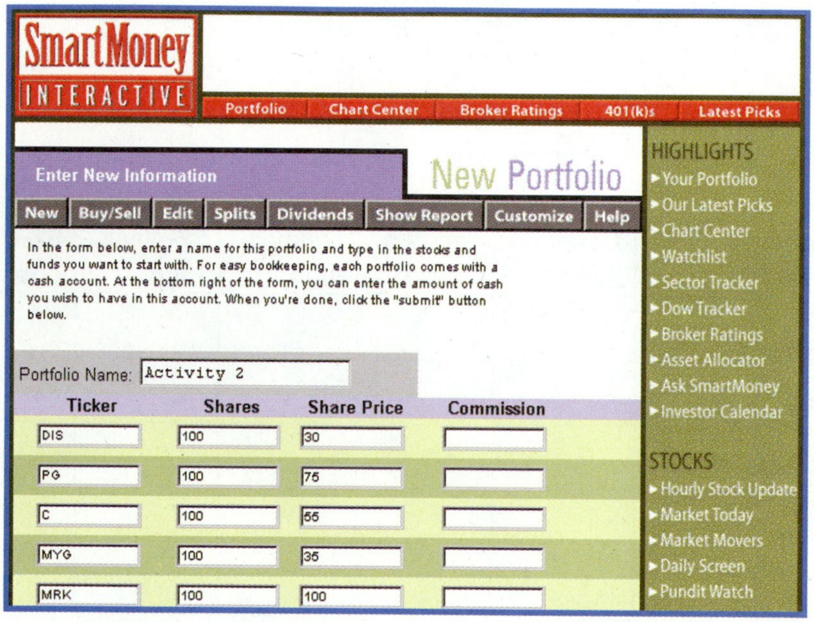

Figure 4.6
Setting up the Smart Money portfolio

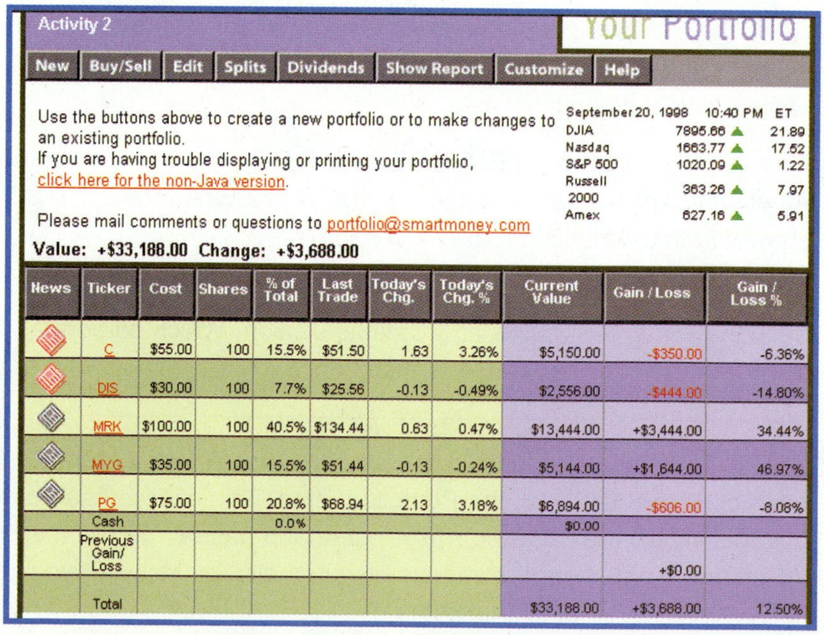

News	Ticker	Cost	Shares	% of Total	Last Trade	Today's Chg.	Today's Chg. %	Current Value	Gain / Loss	Gain / Loss %
	C	$55.00	100	15.5%	$51.50	1.63	3.26%	$5,150.00	-$350.00	-6.36%
	DIS	$30.00	100	7.7%	$25.56	-0.13	-0.49%	$2,556.00	-$444.00	-14.80%
	MRK	$100.00	100	40.5%	$134.44	0.63	0.47%	$13,444.00	+$3,444.00	34.44%
	MYG	$35.00	100	15.5%	$51.44	-0.13	-0.24%	$5,144.00	+$1,644.00	46.97%
	PG	$75.00	100	20.8%	$68.94	2.13	3.18%	$6,894.00	-$606.00	-8.08%
	Cash			0.0%				$0.00		
	Previous Gain/ Loss								+$0.00	
	Total							$33,188.00	+$3,688.00	12.50%

Figure 4.7
Portfolio results from Smart Money

6 How does online trading actually work? To see, go to Discover Brokerage Direct. You won't actually make a trade, but you will view the Trading Demo. Click the button to begin. As you view, answer these questions.

What ways can you invest through Discover Brokerage?

_____

_____

What does the Investor Center let you put on your own home page?

_____

_____

Click the Trading Center button. This site allows you to give the broker instructions about buying and selling. Why would you want to receive a real-time quote before buying or selling?

_____

_____

What is the minimum cost for a trade? Hint: Look at Services and Investments.

Minimum Cost: _____

THINKING ABOUT TECHNOLOGY

What are the relative advantages of a full-service broker and a discount broker? Would you rather be able to discuss your stock purchases with an advisor? What are some other ways you could gather information before making a trade?

Net Ethics   *Socially Responsible Investing (SRI)*

If you feel strongly that companies should consider the best interests of society and the environment in their operations, then you may want to use your investment dollars to promote such corporate behavior. Socially responsible investing is a policy of promoting environmentally and socially responsible operating practices by investing in corporations with good records in these areas.

Several Internet sites provide guidance and information about SRI. One of these is Goodmoney. Unlike some organizations that publicize companies *they* feel have poor social or environmental histories, the Goodmoney site presents positive, and in some cases negative, company information. This enables you to decide if a company's practices are in line with your values before you invest.

Being a socially responsible investor does not mean that you have to make financial sacrifices. Socially responsible companies can be just as profitable as any other. You can find out more information about SRI by following your browser's links to the S-R-Invest resource guide.

ACTIVITY 4.3

Objective:

In this lesson, you will search for mortgage outlets and see how a buyer can apply for a mortgage online.

Financing Your Home

When you get ready to buy a house or other property, you will most likely need a **mortgage**, a loan for a major part of the purchase price. Mortgages are usually for quite large amounts of money, typically about 80 percent of the purchase price of a home. Borrowers usually repay their mortgages over 20 or 30 years.

A mortgage, like most loans, requires the borrower to pay **interest**, which is a fee for the use of the money. This fee is usually figured as a percentage of the loan amount, called an **interest rate**. Over the 20- or 30-year life of a mortgage, a difference of just a half of a percentage point in the interest rate can mean thousands of extra dollars you must pay. The **term** of the mortgage—the number of years you have to repay—also dramatically affects the overall cost of the loan. So when you shop for a mortgage, it's worth the time to look around for a low rate and a term that suits your repayment abilities.

Banks, credit unions, savings and loans, and other financial institutions offer mortgages. Some of these institutions are encouraging their customers to make mortgage applications online. The Internet can also provide expert advice to help you understand mortgages and compare features. One site with links to a variety of information sources is The Mortgage Mart. Its home page links to the Resource Center shown in Figure 4.8.

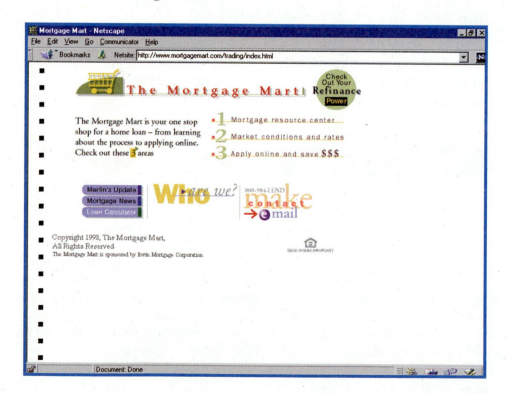

Figure 4.8
Resources available at The Mortgage Mart

1. Go to The Mortgage Mart Resource Center. Click the link to Mortgage Overview and then the Loan Application Process.

What is Form 1033?_____

Why does the lender prepare a final copy of the application?

_____

Give three of the questions you should ask yourself before you choose a loan.

1. _____

2. _____

3. _____

2. Go to the Mortgage Rates section. What are the current rates for 30-, 20-, and 15-year loans with no points?

30-Year Rate _____ 20-Year Rate _____ 15-Year Rate _____

3. Quicken.com, a multiservice financial site, has an extensive Home and Mortgage link, as shown in Figure 4.9.

Click "How much house can you afford?" in the Interactive Tools section. Submit a gross annual income of $43,000, monthly debt of $347 for your car loan, and $12,000 for cash available. Leave the term as 30-year fixed, and leave the rest of the optional areas blank. Click the

Figure 4.9
Quicken's Home and Mortgage site

Calculate button. How much house can you afford with the middle interest rate? What monthly payment would be required for this mortgage? How large would the down payment be?

Interest Rate: _____   House Price You Can Afford: _____

Monthly Payment: _____   Down Payment: _____

4 Click the "Find me a loan!" button, and look at the sample results. If you were applying for a loan for real, what information would you get in your loan summary?

_____

_____

_____

THINKING ABOUT TECHNOLOGY

Could automobile lenders use a Web site like this? What tradeoffs would you need to weigh when you consider a Web-based loan versus a loan from your local banker?

If you like to dream about living in your own "castle," visit one of the more upscale real estate sites. You can look at property in some of the world's most spectacular locations by going to the DuPont Registry. Of course, you can always bring yourself back to earth by calculating the monthly mortgage payment for one of these!

Searching for Insurance Online

Enabling customers to comparison-shop without actually having to contact assorted retailers is one of the features that has made Internet marketing so attractive to buyers. Experts state, and common sense agrees, that comparison shopping works best for products that the customer doesn't need to examine in person, like books and computers. Although insurance is not considered to be a retail product, it has the same potential for Internet marketing. Customers need to comparison-shop, but they don't need to see or touch the product to make their buying decision.

In 1997, Forrester Research reported that online insurance sales were over $40 million. The company projects online insurance sales of well over a billion dollars in 2001. Online life insurance sales are expected to lead the way as a percentage of total sales. Auto insurance sales should have the largest dollar amount. In this activity, you will investigate ways to learn about and buy insurance online.

1 Quicken's financial site that you visited in the last activity also includes insurance information. Go to the Quicken home page and click Insurance. Go to Insurance Basics and then to "Speaking Cool Insurance Terms." Write definitions in your own words for the following terms:

1. deductible _____

2. replacement value _____

3. term life _____

4. whole life _____

2 To learn about the kind of life insurance that might be right for you, return to the Insurance page and select the "60 Second Selector." Follow the directions and choose the quotes that sound the most like you. Request agents in your Zip code area, and record the names of three of them below. Do any of them have their own Web pages?

Agent 1: _____ URL: _____

Agent 2: _____ URL: _____

Agent 3: _____ URL: _____

3 Experts predict auto insurance online sales of over $800 million in 2001. To see how purchasing auto insurance online works, return to the Quicken Insurance page. Follow the Auto Insurance link in the Find Insurance box. Select Quotes, Purchasing, and Agents. Enter your Zip code, and click Auto Insurance.

Should you be able to receive an online quote in your state?

_____

Which insurance companies provide online quotes through this system?

_____

_____

Which insurance companies provide offline quotes?

_____

_____

Continue answering the questions in the form, using your personal information. This will take about ten minutes. If you need assistance with a question, press the Advice button. Default values are given for deductibles and coverage required by your state. Accept these unless you have reason to change them. Are any online quotes available for you?

_____

THINKING ABOUT TECHNOLOGY

What costs would an insurance provider have to consider when processing applications? List three pieces of customer information that the insurance company would want to verify before selling you a policy.

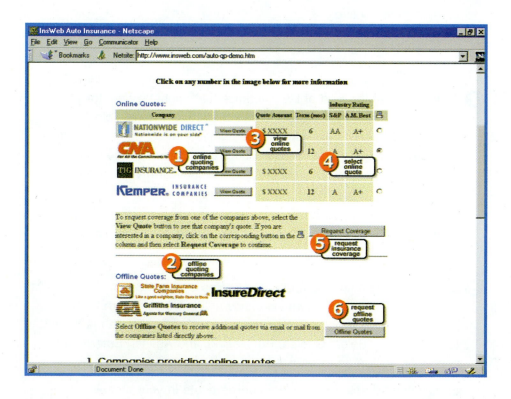

Figure 4-10
Sample auto insurance quote from InsWeb

Internet Tax Tips

If you earn a paycheck, paying taxes is probably one of your least-favorite activities. The Internet can make it just a bit simpler for you. The Internal Revenue Service Web site has links to forms, publications, instructions, and revenue departments in all 50 states. Let's take a tour.

1 The IRS home page is *www.irs.gov*. Go there, click the mailbox to enter, and click the link at the bottom of the page to electronic services. As Figure 4-11 shows, the IRS has instituted a number of online services for you. Scroll through the rest of the page to see what's available.

Welcome to Electronic Services. Sure, there may be times when you will need to send materials to the Internal Revenue Service via the US Postal Service. However, with advancements in technology, there are times you will want to take advantage of the latest methods of filing your return electronically, filing Federal and state returns simultaneously, downloading information and retrieving up-to-date information from the IRS. This year the Service is promoting the benefits of IRS *e-file* (electronic filing). You will now see "IRS *e-file*" in many places where electronic filing services are being offered.

2 Follow the link to "e-file Options for Individuals." Go to "Use a Personal Computer" under File from Home, and answer the following questions.

Who can use the program? _____

What equipment do you need? _____

How much does it cost? _____

e-file software providers:

1. _____

2. _____

3. _____

How do you submit your payment? _____

_____

_____

_____

_____

ACTIVITY
4.5

Objective:
In this lesson, you will find tax preparation help from both the government and private agencies, and learn how to file your taxes electronically.

Figure 4-11
The IRS introduction to electronic services

3 Return to Electronic Services and follow the link to "e-file Options for Businesses." Follow the link to "IRS *e-file* and Employees, Business and Organizations."

What advantages does this system offer to customers and employees?

_____

_____

THINKING ABOUT TECHNOLOGY

Taxpayer dissatisfaction with the IRS caused quite a stir in 1997 and 1998. In its quest to be more responsive to taxpayers, the IRS increased the number of online services it provides. Do you think this will help to improve taxpayer satisfaction? Did you know that even if you don't file electronically, you can still download copies of forms and publications? What do you think the IRS can do to encourage taxpayers to use these services?

NET VOCABULARY

Define the following terms:

1. automatic withdrawal

2. direct deposit

3. discount broker

4. portfolio

5. mortgage

6. interest (loan)

7. interest rate (loan)

8. pull technology

9. push technology

10. socially responsible investing

11. term of a loan

12. ticker symbol

NET REVIEW

Give a short answer to the following questions:

1. Name three services commonly offered by online banking.

2. Which of these services are usually free? For which of these services does a bank usually charge an extra fee?

3. What information can you find from an online portfolio watch? Do you have to own the stock to take advantage of this feature?

4. Explain why you should comparison-shop for a mortgage.

5. What kinds of insurance can you purchase over the Internet? Why would an insurance company that does not provide online quotes want to be included in an online insurance quote search?

6. Why would the IRS let taxpayers download forms?

ONLINE BANKING IN YOUR NEIGHBORHOOD

Find the URL for your bank or for a bank in your community and visit the site. Why do you think the bank has an Internet presence? Does it offer online services? Make a list of them. What does a current customer have to do in order to access these services? If the bank doesn't have online services, then why do you suppose it has a Web site?

NET PROJECT TEAMWORK How "Online" Is Your Local Bank?

With your team, select a bank in your area to investigate. Different teams should select different banks. Make an appointment with someone at the bank who is familiar with the bank's online services. Each team should create a list of questions about online banking to ask the bank employee. Be sure to include questions about kinds of services offered, costs, and future online plans. Then meet with the bank employee, and present the results to the class.

WRITING ABOUT TECHNOLOGY Where Did the Paper Go?

Jeremy Clark is pleased with himself. He has one semester left in college, has a part-time job that pays reasonably well, and has just bought a new car. After watching a TV show, he's become convinced that it is not too early to start an investment program. He doesn't know too much about the stock market, but he'd like to buy a few shares of a good stock. Jeremy's downfall, though, is that he is not very good at keeping track of things. He pays his tuition monthly, but sometimes he forgets to send the check on time. His part-time job pays him every two weeks, and he is too embarrassed to tell the payroll department that he lost one of his January paychecks. Besides, he keeps hoping it will turn up somewhere in his room! Do you know anyone like Jeremy?

Write a letter to Jeremy, explaining how he might use his computer to help make his life easier and more organized. In about 100 words, give him suggestions on how he could use the Internet to help manage his personal finances.

Internet Information Services

Chapter Objectives:

After completing the activities in this chapter, you will be able to use the Internet to

1 plan a trip and make lodging and transportation reservations.

2 find up-to-date news and weather information.

3 reach information providers for reference and location services.

4 search for government information useful to a business.

Net Terms

data port

database

powered by

> **NET TIP**
> **Home Page**
>
> *Access the* E-Commerce: Business on the Internet *home page through the following URL:*
> e-commerce.swep.com.
> *Remember that a Web address may change at any time. An address given in this book as an example may no longer be valid. If so, either access the home page*
> (e-commerce.swep.com) *for the current link or do a search to find a similar site.*

Information as an Internet Service

The Internet is a rich source of information that can support businesses in their daily operations. As you've seen, a large amount of E-commerce consists of one business selling a product to another business or to a consumer. Sometimes, this "product" is a service, and there is no direct charge. Companies, agencies, organizations, and individuals publish a huge amount of information on the Web, and wise business and consumer users have learned how to find the information they need.

Internet search engines can be particularly useful if you are trying to find information and you are not exactly sure what is out there or where to look for it. Spend some time looking at several search engines to see what they feature and how their links are organized. Figure 5.1 shows part of the opening screen from Yahoo. The links above the horizontal line show some of the services Yahoo provides. How might a small company use these links?

For an example, suppose you are the owner of a small company that manufactures tennis rackets. If you wish to approach retailers in a new location, you could use the Yellow Pages listing to search for sporting goods stores for sales contacts. The Maps and Travel Agent listings could help you arrange trips to tournament sites. And knowledge from News, Sports, and Weather could help you react quickly to changes on the tournament circuit. The other search categories are also useful. You could read about fitness in the Health section or find community recreation programs in the Regional section.

Figure 5.2 shows part of the opening screen from Netscape Net Search. In earlier chapters, you've looked at job searches and financial advice. What other services do you see here that might be useful if you were a tennis racket manufacturer? The links to Yellow Pages are here too, as are people searches. And by clicking the Add Your Site link, your tennis racket company could be listed at Netscape.

In this chapter, you'll explore several of the services the Internet offers. Although you'll concentrate on business uses of these services, many of them are valuable to consumers, too.

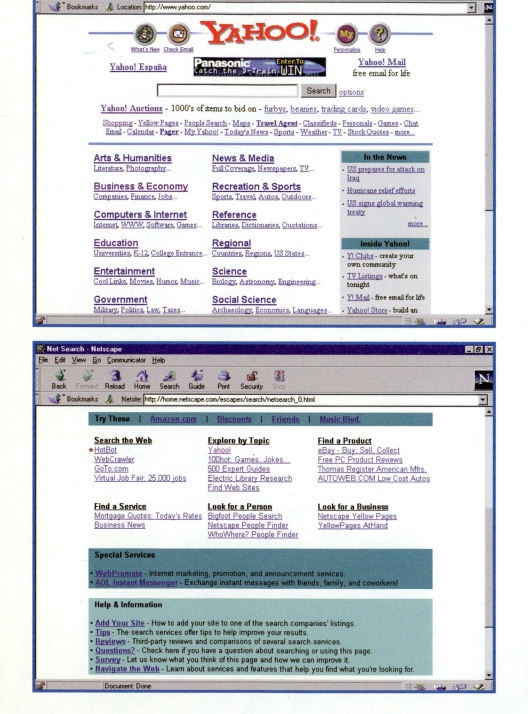

Figure 5.1
Yahoo home page services

Figure 5.2
Netscape Net Search home page services

Travel Planning

Objective:
In this lesson, you will learn how to plan a trip and make lodging and transportation reservations.

Professional travel agents have used computerized databases for years to keep track of flight schedules and airfares. A **database** is a large collection of information arranged in linked tables for easy search and retrieval. A travel agent's database contains flights, fares, passenger reservations, and schedules. Authorized users can easily search the system electronically for the information they want.

The huge amount of very detailed information used in the travel industry lends itself perfectly to electronic storage and retrieval. Although the Internet certainly hasn't replaced travel agents, consumers now have the ability to search for deals and make arrangements on their own. You can buy tickets online if you wish. You can also be looking at available flights while you talk with the travel agent on the phone. This can sometimes help you find a special deal. In this activity you'll look at several online travel services and plan a trip.

1. Go to the search engine of your choice and look for a travel category. Click to see what links appear. Figure 5.3 shows part of the screen that appears when you click Netscape's travel link. This is an all-purpose travel site whose developers have tried to anticipate any need you might have and provide a link for it.

   Figure 5.4 shows the result of clicking the Yahoo Travel link under Recreation & Sports. As you can see, the information is presented in a much different format. The presence of all of these categories may help you focus your search in a very specific way.

   How is your search engine's site different from these? _____

   _____

   _____

   _____

   _____

   Which kind of site would you rather use if you were planning business travel? _____

   _____

   _____

   _____

   Would your choice be different if you were planning a family vacation? Why or why not?_____

   _____

   _____

   _____

Figure 5.3
Netscape's Travel Channel

Figure 5.4
Yahoo's Travel link

② For this activity, you will use the Netscape Travel Channel. As you saw in Figure 5.3, this site comes from Travelocity, an Internet travel agency. Travelocity is powered by a system called Sabre. Here, the phrase **"powered by"** means that a mighty search engine or database provides the background resources for the site.

Begin by clicking Book a Flight. Then click Be Our Guest. As you can see in Figure 5.5, you'll complete dialog boxes to tell Travelocity where you want to go.

NET TIP
Travel Search Services

You can visit the Travelocity site directly if you wish. It requires you to register in order to access information, but registration is free. It is also possible to visit airline and hotel Web sites directly, but using one of the travel search services is much easier.

Book a Flight - Netscape

File   Edit   View   Go   Communicator   Help

Bookmarks   Location: http://dps1.travelocity.com/lognlogin.ctf?Service=NETCENTER&tr_module=AIRG

Netscape **Netcenter**   Net Search | WebMail | Personalize | Members | Download

You are here: Home >Travel >Reservations

Book a Flight   by Travelocity

Select the type of trip you want to take.

⦿ **Round Trip**   ○ One Way   Multiple Destinations

Select from these options to find the best fare for your needs.

⦿ **Lowest Price (formerly 3 Best):** My travel dates are not flexible but my travel times are. Show me the lowest fare for the date(s) I select.

○ **Specific Dates and Times (formerly Flights & Prices):** I need to travel on specific dates and times. Show me the fare for the flight(s) I select. (We will also find up to three lower-cost alternatives)

Enter the details of your trip.
You can use city names or airport codes

Leaving from: [   ]   Find the closest airport
Going to: [   ]
Leave: Nov ▾ 12 ▾ Calendar   ⦿ Departure time   7:00 AM ▾

Document: Done

Figure 5.5
Travelocity's Book a Flight screen

Plan a round trip using the Lowest Price search. You will be leaving from Columbus, Ohio, and traveling to Atlanta, Georgia. Leave a week from today and stay for five days. Use whatever times you wish. Plan for one adult traveler. Fly coach class without restrictions. Search all airlines. The search results will show you information about the flights that meet your requirements. Figure 5.6 shows the flights that appeared in November, 1998.

Quality Assurance Engineer

Who makes sure that a Web site does what it is designed to do? Who tests the systems and tools, and makes sure that the databases work properly? When companies develop online services, quality assurance engineers participate from the beginning of the design stage. They help create and execute test plans, work with software engineers, track problems, and work with outside vendors and customers. QAEs work in a team environment with other software professionals. They need to be trained in testing and programming, and they should have excellent written and oral communication skills.

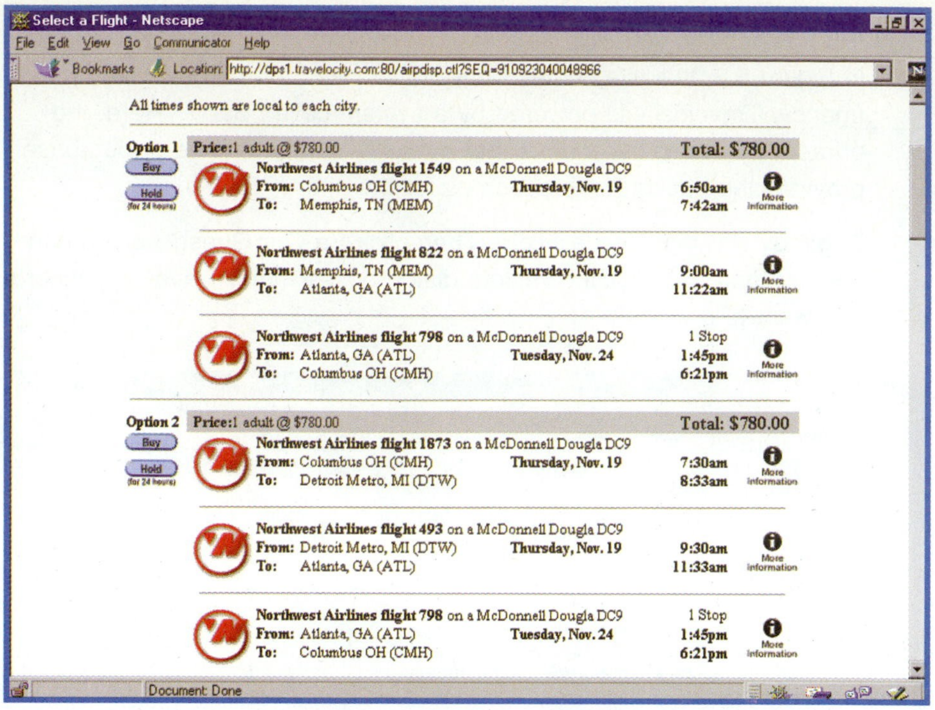

Figure 5.6
Results from Lowest Price air-fare search

Complete the table below with your three lowest fares. The first line of the table is completed as an example.

Airline	Flight	Depart at	Arrive at	Nonstop?	Plane	Cost
Northwest	*1549*	*6:50 a.m.*	*11:22 a.m.*	*no*	*McDonnell Douglas DC9*	*$780*

3 Return to the Netscape Travel Channel and click Reserve a Hotel. In the request form (shown in Figure 5.7), enter information for a single traveler in Atlanta for the dates you used above. Search for Hampton Inns in Atlanta, and use the defaults for the optional information. Click Submit. When the hotel list appears, select one of the Hampton Inns with available rooms, and click the information symbol or the hotel link.

How many rooms does your hotel have? _____

Is breakfast included?_____

Does it have a pool?_____

Do the rooms have refrigerators and microwaves? _____

How would you find out if your room has a **data port**, so you could connect to the Internet with your laptop through the hotel telephone? Many hotels wire their telephones into the wall to prevent theft, so don't plan to unplug the phone and plug in your computer. Also, some hotels have a digital phone system. A data port is a jack in the side of the telephone. By plugging into the jack, you are assured of an analog line, which is essential for making your connection.

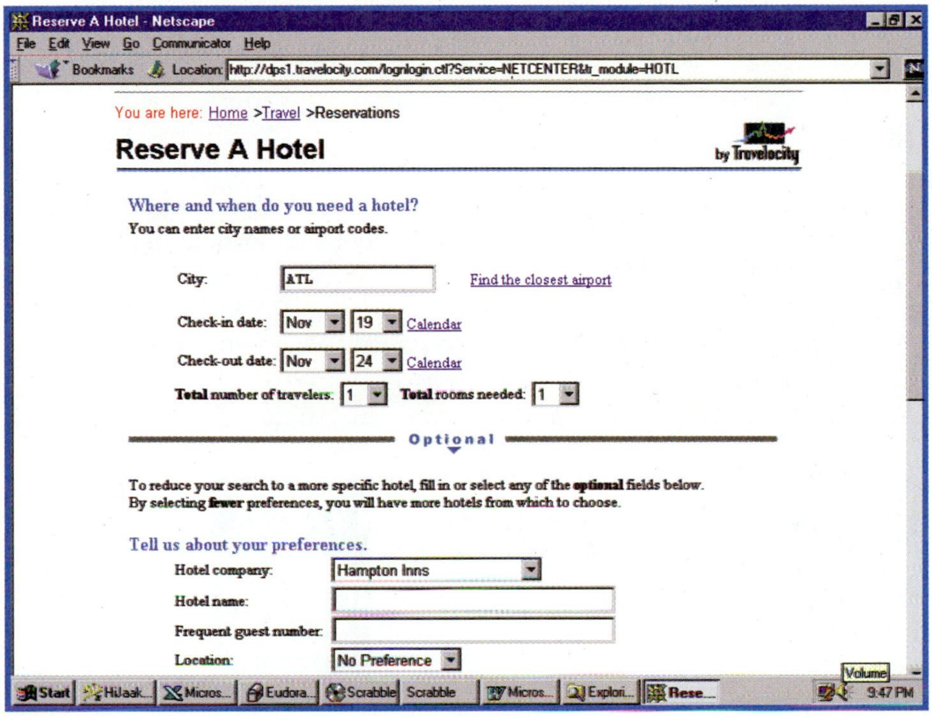

Figure 5.7
Travelocity's Reserve a Hotel form

4 What will you want to do in Atlanta when you are not working? Return to the Netscape Travel Channel, and this time click Local Guides. Select Atlanta under Select a City. Within Entertainment, click Events. Use the Event Search to choose a category that is interesting to you and an appropriate date. Then click Find Events. What three events would you enjoy? Write their information here.

1. _____

2. _____

3. _____

5 If you're not familiar with a new location, it is helpful to have a map to find your way around. There are many commercially available types of map software, and you can get free maps from many Internet sources. You'll tour several sources here.

After you land at the Atlanta airport, you need to visit your company's attorneys, whose office is in the downtown area. You can get directions from the rental car company when you get there, but why not print out your own map before you leave home?

Return to Netscape Travel Channel and click Driving Directions under Traveling Today. When you reach MapQuest, use the From Here to There section. You are looking for directions from Hartsfield International Airport to the attorneys' offices, which are near City Hall. Figure 5.9 shows the map you should find. Scroll down to follow the driving directions. How far is it from the airport to City Hall? _____

_____

Net Fun

If you want to indulge your sense of adventure, look at some of the featured bargains or discounts you'll see in travel sections. Figure 5.8 shows an ad for a trip to Rome. You can also plan a dream vacation by clicking a destination and reading about a new location.

Figure 5.8
Travel special from Netscape Travel

See Rome from $879- airfare included!
Enjoy a winter getaway to Rome, Italy! Includes airfare from select US departure cities, six night's hotel accommodations and continental breakfast daily. Book your trip now.

Net Business *Snap.com*

Does the Internet need another search engine? CNET, Inc. evidently thought so when it developed Snap.com. CNET: The Computer Network is involved in technology news and information on the Web, and also produces television programming. CNET has Web sites that deal with product reviews, technology news, computer hardware information, a computer products shopping service, and sites for games, searching, and software downloads.

CNET has partnered with the NBC television network to publish Snap.com, an Internet directory and search and navigation service. It describes its searches as being "professionally organized to give users the quickest route to what they're looking for on the Web."

Like the other search engines you've examined, Snap's home page offers local news and weather, breaking news headlines, maps and directories, and information services. Many of its categories resemble Yahoo's, but you can also find Aliens and UFOs under the Oddities category. Will Snap be a commercial success and find loyal users? Time will tell. You can check it out at www.snap.com.

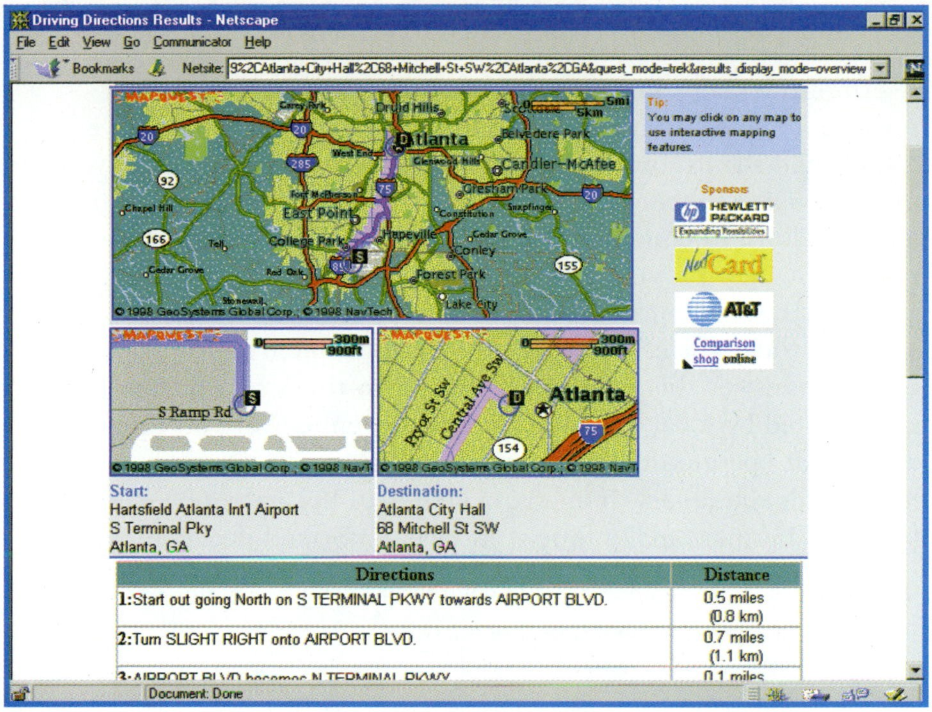

Figure 5.9
Map of driving directions from Hartsfield International Airport to downtown Atlanta.

6 Investigate the Maps section of several other search engines. Do these provide the same services you found above? Compare them.

Search engine	Search based on	Maps?	Driving Directions?
Excite			
Infoseek			
Yahoo!			
Altavista			

In Activity 5.3 you'll learn how to search for street addresses.

THINKING ABOUT TECHNOLOGY

How can the Internet make traveling easier? You've seen how to plan trips, find maps, and learn about local destinations. If you were writing a guidebook for travel to a vacation spot like Hawaii, would you worry that all the information available on the Internet would harm the sales of your book? Would you consider having a Web site for your book? How could you use that site to encourage people to buy the book?

Objective:
In this activity, you'll learn how to find up-to-date news and weather information.

Online News and Weather

All of the major television news networks have an Internet presence, and so do many local stations. Newspapers also have established significant Web sites. Through these media sites, you can find television schedules, follow breaking news, read feature articles, and find links to community information. As businesses, these media have seen how providing an Internet site for their users can increase the number of viewers or readers they have.

Why would businesses want to monitor a media site? It may be easier to answer this question if you try to think of a business that is not affected by local, regional, or world events. Can you think of many that operate in a vacuum? If not, then you know why a business needs the media. Immediate access to the news of the day can help any business make timely and well-informed decisions.

1 Which search engines provide links to breaking news stories? Check the home pages of each of these to see.

Search Engine	Links to breaking news?
Altavista	
Excite	
Infoseek	
Netscape Net Center	
Yahoo!	

2 Find the URL for each of these major television networks. Do they allow you to search for local news? Do they show breaking news headlines?

Network	URL	Link to local news?	Headlines?
ABC			
CBS			
CNN			
Fox			
NBC			

3 Weather reports are important to all kinds of businesses. If you use an agricultural commodity, you would certainly be affected by price increases following droughts, floods, or freezes. If your company sells snow removal equipment, you'd base your order quantities on the long-range weather forecast. If you are involved in transportation, you would certainly want to know weather and road conditions. You can find links to weather information through each of the search engines and networks above. However, there are other dedicated weather sites, and we'll visit several of these to see what they provide.

Figure 5.10 shows the results of searching Infoseek for the National Weather Service. You may find other weather links that are especially interesting to you. Some of them are designed for users with knowledge of meteorology, but others can be understood by any visitor. Begin by visiting the National Weather Service at *www.nws.noaa.gov*. Its home page is shown in Figure 5.11.

Figure 5.10
National Weather Service Sites

Humor Services

Some Internet services come to users by e-mail through a free subscription. You sign up for service by subscribing to a mailing list, and you can just as easily unsubscribe. You can get financial information this way, or join an interest group. There are also joke services. Using a joke in a business situation can break the ice, and humor services can be good sources of one-liners and funny stories. As you'd expect, there are some humor services that are G-rated, and many that are not. Remember, though, that not all jokes are funny to all people, and you should never tell a joke that is offensive to others. If you find that you don't appreciate the jokes a humor service sends you, then unsubscribe.

Figure 5.11
National Weather Service home page

4. Click the U.S. map to see current weather activity. Go back to the home page and click Public Forecasts. This connects you to the IWIN system. You will see a map of the United States with color coding for weather warnings. Figure 5.12 shows the map for November 14, 1998. Click your state. What kinds of information can you find? Name at least five.

1. _____

2. _____

3. _____

4. _____

5. _____

Figure 5.12
National Weather Service severe weather warnings

Go to Zone Forecast and read the weather forecast for your location. Are there any current warnings and advisories for your area? _____

_____

5 The National Hurricane Center provides a Web site at *www.nhc.noaa.gov*. During the hurricane season, this site receives a huge amount of traffic. In fact, the service has at times been overloaded when a hurricane is bearing down on the U.S. Use the links on the NHC home page to answer these questions.

What is the most expensive Atlantic hurricane in history? _____

_____

When did it occur, and what was the cost? _____

_____

How often are North Atlantic hurricane names reused? _____

_____

THINKING ABOUT TECHNOLOGY

At least one major U.S. insurance company keeps televisions (and likely the Internet) at its corporate headquarters tuned to breaking news and weather stories. What effects would this instantaneous knowledge have on the way an insurance company operates?

Net Fun

If you like adventure, you might want to travel with the hurricane hunters on a "Cyberflight Into the Eye," shown on the National Hurricane Center page. These pictures and descriptions follow the flight of the aircraft that fly into the midst of a hurricane to gather the data forecasters use.

Objective:
At the end of this lesson, you will be able to reach information providers for reference and location services.

Have you ever wondered what the difference is between a Webmaster and a Web guru? How about between Cold Fusion and Hotmail? NetLingo, the Internet Language Dictionary, defines these terms and hundreds more. You can learn to speak cyberspeak with the best of them by checking out *www.netlingo.com*.

Internet Information Providers

You are no doubt coming to the conclusion that you can find the answer to almost any question you might have by searching the Internet. You've seen how to find a location and directions to get there, and how to find out what is going on in the world. You can also use the Internet to find reference information. Publicly accessible databases, such as phone books, are also accessible online. And if you need to know something—whether it is how to spell a word, the population of Richmond, Virginia, or a quote on decision making—you can find it in a Web reference section.

1 Most public libraries have a collection of telephone books from major cities around the world. If you need to look for Jane Doe in Los Angeles, you can make a trip to your library and look for her in the LA phone book. If you want to find a dry cleaner in Milwaukee, you can check out the Milwaukee yellow pages. You can also do both of these searches on the Internet. Search engines offer data searches for phone numbers, street addresses, and e-mail addresses for individuals and businesses.

To find information about a person, look on a search engine's home page for a link to People Finder or People Search. For business information, look for Yellow Pages. All search engines support such searches. The results you find will vary slightly, depending on who powers the search. Some search engines even have a link to send a gift to the person you look up, and some help you get a map to the person's house.

Some companies also provide searches. One of these is Bigfoot.com, whose home page is shown in Figure 5.13. Go to this site and search for people in your state who have your last name. Do you recognize any of the listings? Are they correct for the people you know?

_____

_____

_____

Now use Bigfoot's yellow pages to search for printers in Seattle. How many do you find? _____

_____

2 You can find links to many kinds of reference materials by looking at the links from your search engine. For example, if you are using Infoseek, click Education, and scroll to find links to dictionaries, fact books, encyclopedias, grammar, bibliographies, thesauri, and quotes. Other search engines provide similar links. Using the search engine of your choice, locate an example of each of these reference tools. Record its URL, and tell how a landscape design company could use the information in its business. The first one in the table is done for you.

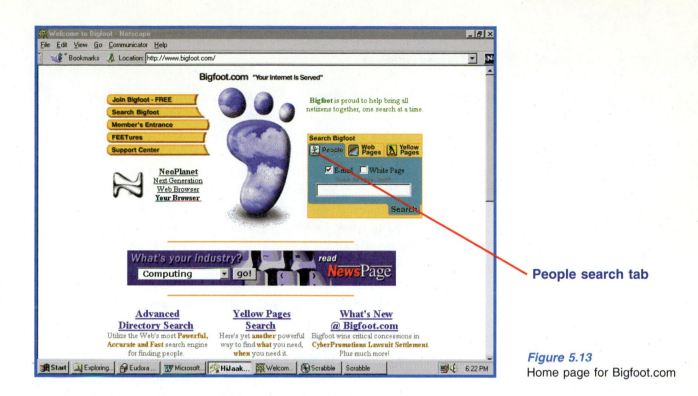

People search tab

Figure 5.13
Home page for Bigfoot.com

Reference Tool	URL	Example
Dictionary	http://www.m-w.com/home.htm	*Check the spelling of a word in an advertising brochure*
Fact book		
Encyclopedia		
Grammar		
Bibliography		
Thesaurus		
Quote		

NET TIP

More Information Sources

You can find Zip code lookup information from the post office at www.usps.gov, and search for toll-free phone numbers at www.tollfree.att.net.

THINKING ABOUT TECHNOLOGY

Businesses that advertise in the Yellow Pages do so in order to reach more customers. Residents who have listed telephone numbers agree to have their information available in their community telephone book. How do you feel about the fact that anyone with access to the Internet can find your listed information? How might other people feel? Should search services offer ways for individuals to block publication of their information?

ACTIVITY
5.4

Objective:
In this lesson, you will search for government information useful to a business.

Internet Links to Government Information

Federal, local, and state governments maintain massive amounts of information, and much of it is open to the public. By creating Internet access to the information, the government saves printing and storage costs, and users can retrieve exactly the information they need at any time. Information that is arranged logically and organized according to search patterns makes it relatively easy for users to locate the facts they need.

A good place to start looking for federal information is the Federal Web Locator at Villanova University. The Villanova Center for Information Law and Policy has organized this site according to the federal executive branch of government. It begins with links to the presidency and vice presidency. Following these, each of the federal departments has a section. You can visit the departments of Agriculture, Commerce, Defense, Education, Energy, Health and Human Services, Housing and Urban Development, Interior, Justice, Labor, State, Transportation, and the Treasury. Each section has link after link to the agencies under its jurisdiction. In this activity, you'll look at just a few of them.

1 Go to the Federal Web Locator, shown in Figure 5-14, and follow the link to the Commerce Department and then to the Bureau of the Census. Click Just for Fun. Click Map Stats. Select your state and then your county. Click the USA Counties General Profile from the most recent year.

What is the total population of your county? _____

Were there more births or deaths that year? _____

What is the unemployment percentage? _____

Net Fun

The National Park Service recruits volunteers to work in the parks. You could be an associate naturalist at the Grand Canyon or a harbor host at Biscayne. Almost 90,000 people volunteered in the parks in 1997. You can learn about volunteer opportunities online and read stories about some of the volunteers at *www.nps.gov/volunteer.*

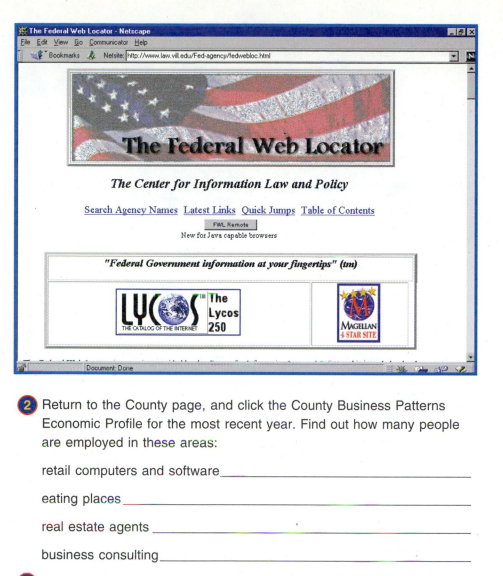

Figure 5.14
The Villanova Center for Information Law and Policy Federal Web Locator page.

② Return to the County page, and click the County Business Patterns Economic Profile for the most recent year. Find out how many people are employed in these areas:

retail computers and software_____

eating places_____

real estate agents_____

business consulting_____

③ Return to the Federal Web Locator and visit the Women's Bureau of the Department of Labor, shown in Figure 5.15. Click the Final Honor Roll Report. Examine the report's Figure 1 in the Knowing What Works section. What four company policies are most valuable to working women?

1. _____

2. _____

3. _____

4. _____

Net Ethics   **Online Ethics Training at the Department of the Interior**

The Department of the Interior requires employees to receive annual ethics training. This enables employees to behave according to written law and ethical standards. The department uses the Internet to make the training sessions available online. Visit the site at *www.doi.gov/ethics* to read about the requirements and download the training.

Figure 5.15
Department of Labor Women's Bureau home page

4 The laws passed by the U. S. Congress affect businesses. Senators and representatives are keenly interested in electronic commerce and the potential for taxation and regulation. If you are running a business, you will want to keep up with congressional hearings and know how to contact your elected representatives. One way you can find them is to go to *www.Congress.org*. Go there now, and type your Zip code in the Rep Finder box.

Who is your representative in the House? _____

_____

Who are your senators? _____

_____

Click the link to one of your elected representatives. Does this person have a Web page? _____

_____

Is there a link to send an e-mail
message to this person? _____

_____

THINKING ABOUT TECHNOLOGY

The Internet makes it possible for government offices and elected officials to offer detailed information to citizens. What benefits do you see when you compare this capability to earlier times? What responsibility remains with the government to be sure that all citizens, whether they are online or not, can receive the information they need?

CHAPTER REVIEW

NET VOCABULARY

Define the following terms:

1. data port   **2.** database   **3.** powered by

NET REVIEW

Give a short answer to the following questions:

1. Give examples of three organizations that use the Internet to provide information but who are not involved in sales transactions.

2. How could you use the Internet if you were running a bed-and-breakfast business?

3. How could you use the Internet to find your way to a job interview?

4. How could you use the Internet to find information about a winter storm warning in South Dakota if you live in Ohio?

5. How could you use the Internet to learn the correct pronunciation of a word?

6. How could you use the Internet to learn if a bill was scheduled for a vote in the House of Representatives?

NET PROJECT

BUSINESS TRIP TO DENVER

Plan a business trip from Pittsburgh to Denver, one week from today. Stay for four days. Find the three cheapest flights. Check for room availability in two moderately priced hotel chains, one near the airport and one downtown. Use an information service to find the address for a company called Decisioneering. Locate Mile High Stadium. Use the Department of the Treasury site to find information about the U. S. Mint in Denver. Find driving directions from the airport to each of these locations. To help decide what to pack, get a weather forecast for Denver.

NET PROJECT TEAMWORK A Whirlwind Tour of Baseball Parks

You and your teammates work for a company in Kansas City, Missouri, that makes souvenir baseball apparel. To launch a new product, you are planning to travel from Kansas City to attend games at five different major league parks in five days. The parks are located in San Diego, New York, Chicago, Atlanta, and St. Louis. Each park has a home game in the afternoon of each day.

There are many different orders in which you can visit the parks. Each person on the team should take one order and put together an itinerary of flights that will let you visit all five parks. Assume that you would need to arrive in each city no later than noon, and you wouldn't be able to leave until 6:00 p.m. Compare your flight schedules and the total cost. Which of these would you choose, or would you keep looking? What criteria are the most important in this scheduling?

WRITING ABOUT TECHNOLOGY Planning for Weather Emergencies

During severe weather, the Internet weather sites are sometimes jammed with traffic. Write about 100 words describing how the availability of constantly updated weather information has changed the ability of business owners to make plans. If you knew a blizzard was coming to your area, what decisions would you have to make about your hours of operation, protecting your building from damage, and cleaning up afterward? How would the up-to-the-moment information you'd find online help you plan?

Buying Online

The Internet can teach you to use your computer, help you find a job, download an e-mail program, or book a flight to Cancun. It can also let you buy, without visiting a store, just about anything you or your company would need. It doesn't matter if you are an individual buying a best-selling book or a company making a wholesale purchase. Buying online is quick, easy, and safe if you know what to do. The activities in this section will teach you how.

All kinds of products and services are offered for sale online. In Chapter 6, you will see how to shop online. You'll visit online malls and investigate small consumer products. You'll see how to use the Internet for large, expensive products like cars. Through the Internet, businesses can buy wholesale products to resell or component parts and raw materials for manufacturing. Online auctions provide another way for buyers and sellers to exchange goods, and you'll see in this chapter how they work.

In Chapter 7, you'll learn how to fill an online shopping cart, pay for your items, and take delivery. Music CDs and flowers are just a few of the items that are popular online purchases. But not everything bought online arrives in a mailbox. Here, you'll also see how to take delivery of items on your own computer.

Consumers have few qualms about using their credit cards at the gas station, a restaurant, or on the end of a toll-free phone number, but some are concerned about providing a credit card number when they buy online. In Chapter 8, you'll see how wise consumers can check a site's security before they make a purchase or provide personal information. You'll also see ways to discover what other consumers and agencies have found when they made an online purchase or worked with a site. The Internet helps you find links to consumer resources from the government, from companies and agencies, and from stores.

Chapter 6 Retail and Business Purchases 96
Chapter 7 Making Online Purchases. 119
Chapter 8 Consumer Issues 137

Retail and Business Purchases

Chapter Objectives:

After completing the activities in this chapter, you will be able to use the Internet to

1. find shopping services and online malls to help you locate a gift.
2. search for flowers, food, or tickets.
3. configure big-ticket purchases.
4. locate business suppliers.
5. participate in an online auction.

Net Terms

cookie

online mall

wholesale

auction service

zine

SOHO

The Internet–A Buyer's Dream

A television commercial for a major credit card company shows a harried mom chasing her three young children in the back yard. The announcer tells us that she shopped online for the Cozy Coupe™ and other things the children are using. Her comment—go shopping with these three? No way. I shop online!

One of the Internet's most attractive features is that it allows users to access information at any place and at any time. This can be as appealing to the investor who needs to track a stock portfolio on Saturday afternoon as it is to a family that wants to shop after the kids are in bed. In the early days of this country, the

"wish book" catalogs allowed people living in remote areas access to consumer goods. Today, anyone with an Internet connection can buy gourmet food from New York, tulips from Holland, tickets to a concert in San Francisco, or clothing from stores in far corners of the world. It doesn't matter where you live or when you shop, as long as you have an Internet connection and a way to pay for the item.

All of the major search engines have shopping sections. Yahoo's shopping link shows a number of major categories, as you can see in Figure 6.1. Clicking one of these leads to other links within the category. You can also search for the product. If you were shopping for an electronic organizer, you could either follow links or enter the phrase in the search box.

Infoseek also has many shopping topics within its shopping category. You'll see special sections for Lifestyle, Computers, Music, and Auctions. One of the shopping topics is Weddings. Clicking on Weddings brings up topics and Web site lists similar to what you see in Figure 6.2. Notice that this list of hits is different from one you would receive if you searched Infoseek using "weddings" as a keyword. Here, the search engine restricts the hits to *shopping* for weddings, saving you from wading through hundreds of wedding-related, but nonshopping sites.

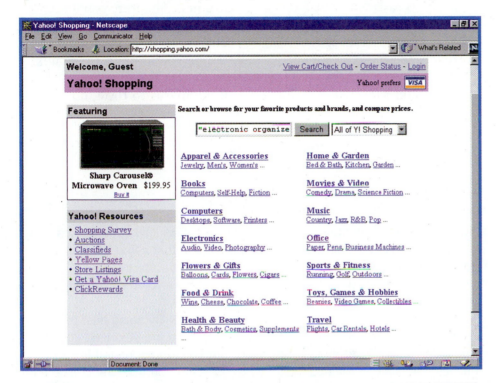

Figure 6.1
Yahoo! Shopping

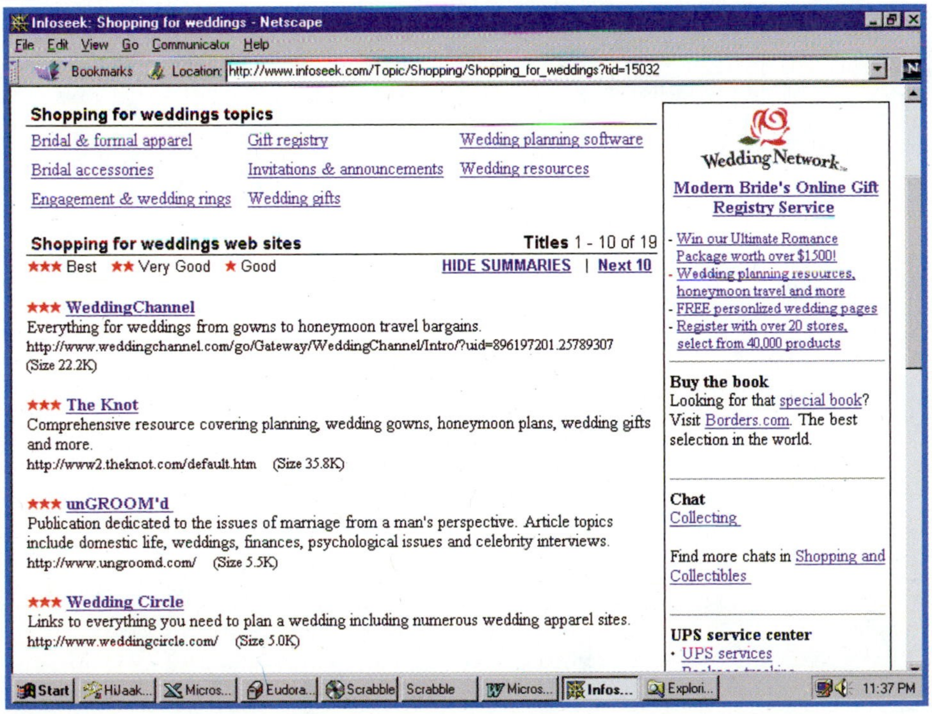

Figure 6.2
Infoseek's Shopping for weddings links

What portion of Internet traffic is online shopping activity? How does shopping online fare as compared to all retailing? What do experts predict will happen in the future? Are traditional stores going to be left in the dust as consumers stampede to online shopping? As you learned in Chapter 1, millions of Internet users have made an online purchase. Estimates have reached dizzying heights for the future of Internet malls and other online retailing centers. Yet, most Internet transactions are expected to continue to be business-to-business. *Comput-erworld* magazine reports at its "emmerce" Web site that total online retail purchasing in 1997 was $2 billion, one fifth of the total purchases over the Web that year. The percentage of U. S. retailers who offered online shopping programs grew from 11% in 1996 to 20% in 1997. If estimates come true and the total purchases over the Web reach about $220 billion in 2001, then business-to-consumer sales will be substantial. You can expect to be part of that market, so you need to know how to use online shopping tools wisely.

This chapter will give you a general overview of Internet buying. You'll look at the choices in shopping summaries and malls, and then you'll see how to search out specific items. You'll even have a chance to see how to shop for big-ticket items like cars. In the next chapter, you'll see how to actually make purchases. As you experience online shopping in these next two chapters, think about how it compares to the kind of shopping you've done all your life.

NET FACT

Cookies

When we talk about Internet cookies, we're not talking about an online bakery, although you can buy your favorite edibles electronically. A **cookie** is a file of information about you that some Web sites create and store on your hard drive when you visit the site. Then when you return to the site, it can pull up the information from the cookie file on your computer, so that you don't have to enter your identifying information again.

Some companies use cookies to keep track of your navigation through the site. By doing this, the company can determine your preferences and even personalize the site for you the next time you visit. For example, an online clothing catalog might note from your travels that you are interested in hiking boots. Then the next time you visit, the site can retrieve this information about you from the cookie and immediately show you its best deals on hiking boots and hiking-related products, like backpacks.

Some sites will ask your permission before storing a cookie on your computer. Also, you can set up your browser to refuse cookies, but doing so may keep the site from operating properly in your browser. You'll learn more about cookies in Chapter 9.

Shop 'til You Drop

Objective:
In this lesson, you will learn how to find shopping services and online malls to help you locate a gift.

The Web doesn't just have online stores. It has online malls and even shopping services that help you navigate through all the sites that want to sell you something. In this activity, you'll see how to find these sites and use them to help you find a present.

1 The easiest way to begin online shopping is to go to your search engine and look for its shopping category. Click the Shopping category in AltaVista, Netscape, and Yahoo to see how they are organized. Which search engine's category list seems to group links in the most logical way? Why do you think so? _____

_____

Do the opening pages in each search engine's Shopping category have links to specific stores? Do you think the store had to pay to be listed?

_____

Do these Shopping categories allow you to conduct a search, or do you have to follow links? Which seems more efficient to you? _____

_____

Which one of these search engines seems easiest to use? Why?_____

_____

2 Internet shopping services will search online stores for the price and availability of an item you specify. Some of these require you to become a member or to download software. One that doesn't, and is straightforward to use, is *shopguide.com*. Go there and search for basketball shoes. Figure 6.3 shows some of the results you might get. Notice the symbols beside each site. They can help you understand what a site holds. What benefits do you get from an online shopping service that you don't get from a direct online search?_____

_____

_____

NET TIP

Caution!

You will learn more about consumer issues and security later in this book. For now, keep in mind that they are both important. The phrase caveat emptor—let the buyer beware—applies to online shopping just as it does to any other purchase you make.

Figure 6.3
Shopguide.com search results

3 **Online malls** serve the same purpose that other shopping malls do: they give you access to a large number of stores in one convenient place. Hundreds of Web sites bill themselves as online malls, as you will see if you search for one. ShopNow and iMall are two of the largest. Visit these online malls and search for a portable CD player that you can plug into a car tape player. What steps did you have to follow at each one to get where you were going?

iMall _____

ShopNow _____

Which seemed easiest? Why? _____

What features of a physical mall would you like to have when you shop online? _____

Net Fun

You can go shopping at online malls around the world. To go to England, visit *www.Barclaysquare.co.uk*. For mall shopping from Iceland, go to *superhighway.is/megastore*. You might find some different sorts of merchandise than you have seen before.

4 How can online shopping give the service you would get in a physical store? Imagine that you want to give a present and have decided to buy perfume online. You certainly can't smell the fragrances online—how will you make a choice? Almost all shopping directories have a category for fragrances or beauty, where you are likely to find these products.

Visit *Fragrancecounter.com*, shown in Figure 6.4. What information can a shopper find at the Gift Advisor? Does this provide enough information to compensate for your being unable to see (and smell) the merchandise and talk with a sales clerk? _____

_____

Figure 6.4
Home page for Fragrance Counter

What information do you get when you click a specific fragrance? _____

_____

Under what circumstances would you buy this way? _____

_____

THINKING ABOUT TECHNOLOGY

How do you feel about having shopping services or search engines do the "browsing" for you? Are there instances in your life when you would appreciate being able to shop online? Are there times when you would prefer to wander through a store? What makes the difference to you?

ACTIVITY
6.2

Objective:
In this lesson, you'll see how to search for flowers, food, or tickets.

Find the Good Life on the Internet

Have you ever needed to buy flowers—in a hurry? You may have forgotten a family birthday, or wanted to send a congratulatory bouquet or express sympathy. If you need to send flowers to someone in another location, you probably don't know the name of a reliable florist there. And although you could visit a local florist to look through pictures of arrangements, choose one, and arrange for it to be delivered, you can do all of these things with much less difficulty online.

You can also shop for food online. You can find luxury gourmet items from shops and suppliers around the world, or you can order your everyday bread and milk from a grocery service.

If you've bought entertainment tickets recently, you know that most of these sales are done electronically through ticket services. You can jump into that role yourself by buying tickets online.

As you examine sites that provide flowers, food, or tickets, think about what they provide and how they provide it to the customer. Some of these Internet businesses are online branches of existing operations; others are solely online. Why did they choose to operate this way? And why do customers choose to buy this way?

1. Every search engine with a shopping category lists Flowers as one of the titles in the category. Figure 6.5 shows part of what appears at Infoseek.

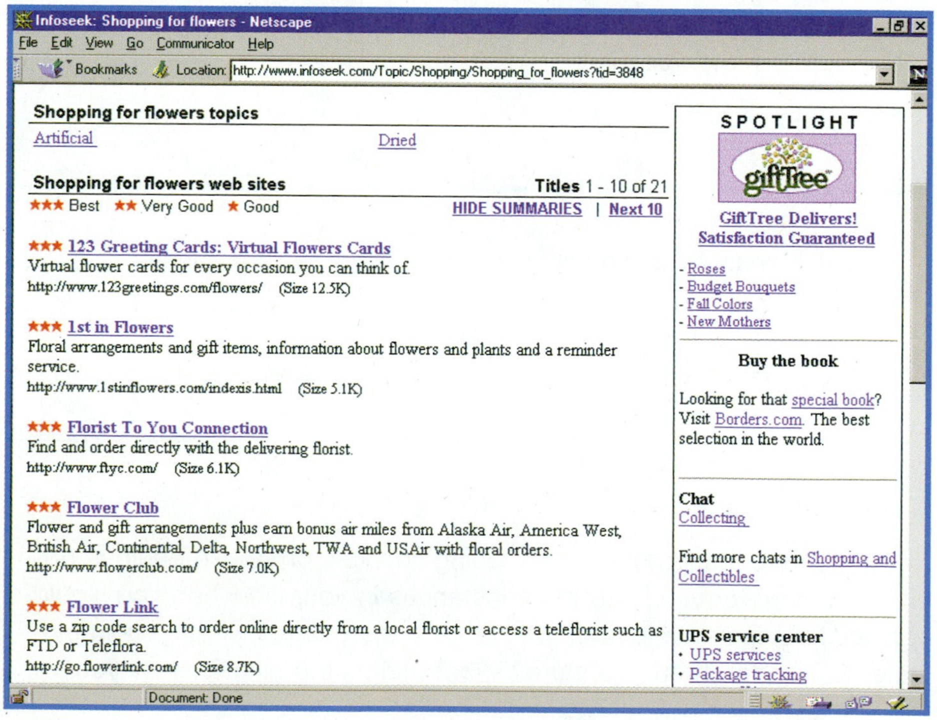

Figure 6.5
Infoseek's Flower links

Visit the Infoseek Flower category, or one from another search engine, and scroll through the list of links. Based on the descriptions shown, note four features of the floral companies that appeal to you as a consumer.

1. _____

2. _____

3. _____

4. _____

2 Go to the *1800flowers.com* Web site. Customers can contact this company by telephone, at retail locations in large cities, or interactively. Company forecasts use 10% as the portion of total revenue that will come from interactive sales in 1998. To see how the selection process works, search "Occasions" for a "Best for Business" plant that costs around $50. What does the site provide that would help you choose a plant?

_____

_____

Click My Flower Shop. Then click My Flower Shop Benefits. Read about the 1-800-FLOWERS Gift Reminder program. Would you like to receive a reminder e-mail, or would you find it intrusive? _____

_____

3 Food and groceries also appear in many search engines' shopping lists. Begin your examination of this kind of Internet shopping by looking at a specialty food shop, Balducci, from New York. Read the "About Us" section. Why does the Balducci family think you will like to shop online?

_____

_____

Click the link to Balducci's Catalogo Per La Cucina, shown in Figure 6.6. Then go to Pastas and Sauces. Read the descriptions of the pastas. Do these sound like the pastas you find in your local grocery store? Why can an online shop offer more variety? _____

_____

_____

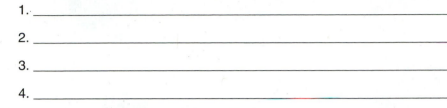

Plan, and price, a perfect celebration. Search for flowers, fill a gourmet picnic basket, and find tickets to an event of your choice. You can do all of this online. How much will it cost?

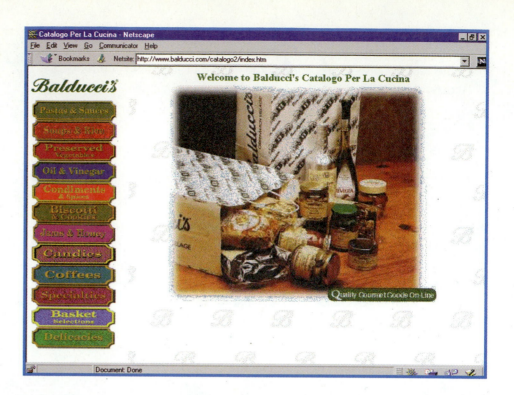

Figure 6.6
Balducci's Catalogo
Per La Cucina

4 Gourmet food sites might appeal to you for a special occasion, but probably aren't the best way to stock your pantry with everyday items. One online company that is trying to do just that is netgrocer. Like many superstores, netgrocer offers household items, pet supplies, baby goods, and health and beauty items in addition to food. Go to the netgrocer page and look at its categories. Read netgrocer's help topics to find the answers to these questions:

Does netgrocer have perishable items, such as milk and fresh fruit?___

_____

How do netgrocer's prices compare to your local grocer's? _____

_____

Where does netgrocer get its items? _____

_____

How long does it take for items to be delivered?_____

_____

What would netgrocer have to do to entice you to buy dog food online rather than from your neighborhood supermarket? _____

_____

5 Peapod bills itself as America's Internet Grocer. Visit the Peapod site and compare its services to those of netgrocer, using the first four questions above. You can find the answers by selecting Learn More.

Why would Peapod want you to begin with your Zip code? _____

6 Hundreds of Web sites sell tickets to concerts, sporting events, and theme parks. You can contact the event site directly for ticket information, or you can contact a ticket clearinghouse. Some sites specialize in hard-to-find tickets or resale of tickets. But for a good source, go to the Ticket-master site. Here, you can search for a particular artist or event, or even search just to see what is coming to a particular location. Figure 6.7 shows the results from searching for upcoming events in Indiana.

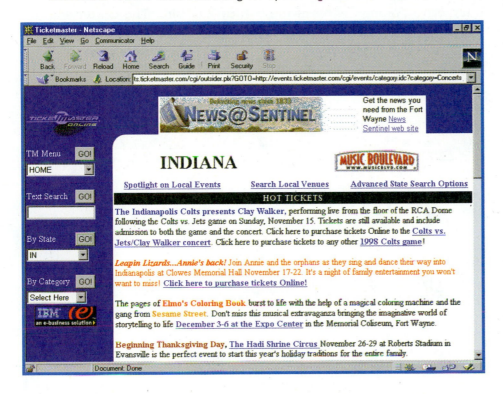

Figure 6.7
Ticketmaster's local events results

Use the "Search By Name" feature to locate performances of Phantom of the Opera. Click the state nearest to you to find details. Explain how this information helps Ticketmaster sell more tickets. _____

_____

THINKING ABOUT TECHNOLOGY

Do you think that people who use the Internet are more likely to be the kinds of buyers who are willing to spend money for flowers, gourmet food, and entertainment? Which do you think is higher, the proportion of the general population who send fresh flowers, or the proportion of Internet users who send fresh flowers (by any method). Does your answer help explain why so many retailers of these kinds of products have an online presence?

ACTIVITY

6.3

Objective:

In this lesson, you will learn how to configure big-ticket purchases.

Would You Buy a Car from This Site?

It is not surprising that computer manufacturers make it easy for their buyers to configure systems and buy online. After all, that is their business. It may surprise you, though, that you can shop for a car online. Car manufacturers' Web sites will help you understand models and options, but won't sell a car to you. Figure 6.8 shows the Interactive Pricing Center at the Saturn Web site. The center shows you how to determine the car you want and how much it will cost. The site reminds you, though, that you can't figure the value of a trade-in online, nor can you take a test drive! To actually purchase the vehicle, you will have to work with a dealer.

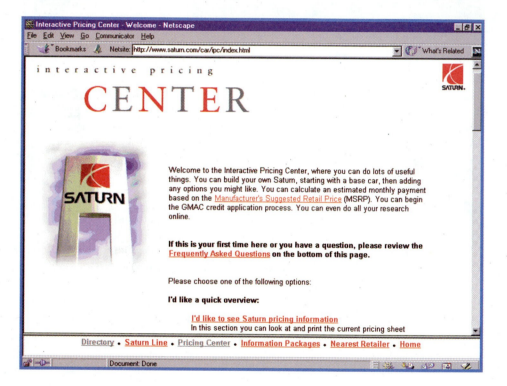

Figure 6.8
Saturn's Interactive Pricing Center

Web sites from car dealerships list their inventory and let you determine whether or not you want to visit the showroom. Car purchase sites will search for the best price and availability for a model you specify. In this activity, you'll follow several different paths to obtain information about a 1999 Pontiac Grand Am.

1 Begin by visiting the Pontiac site. Click the Grand Am button to learn more about features and options for this car.

How can you use this site to get information about the car? _____

_____

How can you order a brochure?_____

_____

Use the Dealer Locator button to find the name of the dealer closest to you. If the dealer has a Web site, visit the site. (If your dealer does not have a Web presence, visit *Fusonth.com*.) Which of these actions can you do from the dealer's site?

☐ Link to the manufacturer.
☐ Find the dealership location and hours.
☐ Find out about rebates.
☐ See a new car inventory.
☐ See a used car inventory.

What else would you, as a prospective customer, like to see at the dealer's site? _____

_____

_____

2 Next, visit a site that helps you shop. Go to the Autobytel site. After reading the opening material, click Help. Go on to find the answer to the question, "So who are you guys anyway?" Describe the process that a user of the site would follow to find a new car. _____

_____

_____

3 Microsoft has also established a site to help you shop Car Point is a full-service car-buying site that provides just about anything you need to help you select, buy, insure, and maintain a car. As you can see from Figure 6.9, there are many links to help you. Look around all you like. When you are ready, click the New Car Buying Service. Describe the process that a buyer would use to find a new car. _____

_____

_____

How do car manufacturers benefit from sites like this? Will these kinds of sites eventually replace their own sites? _____

_____

_____

NET TIP
Build It Your Way

To configure a new car, go to Pontiac's Shopping section, and click Pricing. Then click Configure. Follow the steps of the Build Your Own Grand Am section to configure the car of your choice. This does take some time to complete, and you need to have a good understanding of what you would like to have. Most options are explained for you.

Net Ethics Just Looking

All of the car-buying sites operate by sending your specifications to a member dealer. Although you are under no obligation to buy, each site asks you to put the dealer who spent time preparing your quote at the top of your list when you get ready to buy. Is "just looking" while you are online any different that "just looking" at a dealership?

Figure 6.9
Car Point car information site

④ Is buying a used car different from buying a new car? Investigate used-car purchasing at *autoweb.com*. What different options do you have in shopping for a used versus a new car? _____

_____

THINKING ABOUT TECHNOLOGY

New-car buyers can now see dealer cost information online. In the past, a buyer needed to "know someone in the car business" or do extensive leg work to find invoice prices. How has the availability of this information influenced the way dealers quote prices and work with customers? If you were running a car dealership, how would you prepare your sales force to work with customers who brought Web site printouts along when they came to buy a car?

When a Business Is the Buyer

ACTIVITY

6.4

Objective:
In this lesson, you will learn how to locate business suppliers.

Because it is easy to find consumer goods online (and get distracted as you follow interesting links!), you may not realize how much business-to-business buying and selling there is on the Internet. Many businesses sell merchandise to other businesses, which then resell the merchandise to other businesses or to consumers. Selling merchandise to other businesses for resale is called selling **wholesale**. A sale is considered to be "retail" if the buyer doesn't resell the item. The determination of what is "wholesale" and what is "retail" selling depends on the buyer's intention.

Businesses also purchase items that enable them to operate. Things such as office supplies, machinery, transportation, uniforms, and maintenance services are necessary for the day-to-day conduct of some businesses.

If a business is involved in production of some sort, it will need raw materials or component parts. Plastics manufacturers need to know where to find materials, farmers need to know where to buy seed and fertilizer, and pharmaceutical firms need to know where to get chemicals. Car companies buy sub-assemblies, computer companies buy chips, and plumbers buy pipe.

All of these business-to-business transactions can occur with the help of the Internet. In this activity, you'll visit businesses that sell exclusively to other businesses, and see how they use the Internet.

1. One way to search for a business that will support your business is to go through Yahoo's Business and Economy section and click on Companies. This will give you a list of categories, and from there you will be able to search for what you need. It is not unusual to see thousands of hits from these searches. The search engine will supply a sentence or two of description for each link, but a business would certainly want to examine the Web sites to see what the business has to offer.

   Assume you work for a chemical business, and you are looking for products or services that will help your company's compliance with clean-air laws. One topic that appears in the Companies category of Yahoo's Business and Economy section is Environment. When you click that link, and then the Business-to-Business link, you will see a list of categories and companies, similar to the one in Figure 6.10.

NET TIP

SOHO

*Look for business-to-business links for SOHO. What is **SOHO**? The letters stand for "small office/home office." Many entrepreneurs start at home, and SOHO sites offer products and services that fit this market.*

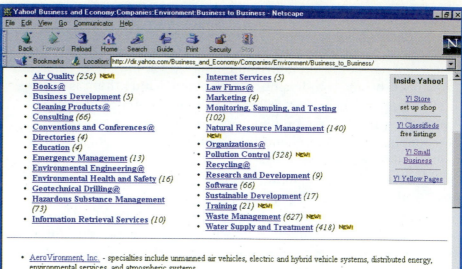

Figure 6.10
Yahoo's Environment Business-to-Business links

To see the kinds of products and services in this business-to-business section, visit the three air-quality businesses listed below. Does the site provide a product or a service, or both? Is the site's purpose informational, or can you buy products or schedule services online?

Purafil _____

CK Environmental _____

Lucas Process Systems _____

2 To see the operation of an online warehouse with many different items, visit the Barnhill Bolt's Secure Fastener Warehouse, shown in Figure 6.11. How could this site support business-to-business sales to a construction company that is building an apartment complex? _____

_____

_____

Net Business *E Business Magazine*

   In November of 1996, the Hewlett Packard company launched *E Business*. This magazine was intended to be a "high-quality independent web zine." (**Zine** is Net-speak for "magazine.") This monthly magazine is neither printed nor sold, but is available online for no charge. Articles don't especially feature Hewlett Packard products. You can find subscription information at www.hp.com/Ebusiness.

   Regular features include E-commerce topics, the home office, new developments, and tools, tips, and techniques. There are regular columnists, and some of their columns are funny.

   Figure 6.12 shows a selection of covers from back issues of *E Business*. As you can see, the magazine has covered some of the topics in this chapter—auctions, online shopping, and retailing—and from other chapters of this book—jobs and online real estate.

Figure 6.11
Barnhill Bolt's
Fastener Warehouse

❸ The ultimate source for American and Canadian manufacturers is the Thomas Register. This free service lists over 150,000 companies and has links to Web pages of over 1,000 advertisers. Go to the Thomas Register site and read about the TPN Register. If you were a buyer searching for a component part, would you prefer to work with a company that was registered with TPN? Why? _____

_____

_____

Figure 6.12
Back Issues of E
Business magazine

Are you surprised that at least 80% of online transactions are business-to-business? Do you think search processes for consumer products are easier to use? If you answered yes, think about how familiar you are with consumer products. Would a business be just as familiar with the products it needs?

Creating a Business-to-Business Site

For an excellent set of principles for establishing a business-to-business Web site, refer to the July 1998 back issue of *E Business* for the article by Laurie Windham and Jon Samuel entitled "Raising the Bar." Here is an outline of their nine principles:

- Know the audience.
- Identify topline content objectives.
- Leverage existing content.
- Build dynamic environments.
- Create a whole structure access system.
- Test the interface.
- Unify vision, style, and theme.
- Write for the Web.
- Give something back.

Sold to the Highest Bidder!

Internet users are finding a new way to shop online. An online **auction service** allows anyone to offer an item for sale to the highest bidder. Like other auctions, buyers learn about the merchandise, place a bid, raise their bid if necessary, and eventually either buy the item or drop out of the bidding. For years, art, antiques, and livestock have been sold at auction. Now with online auction services, you can bid on just about anything that anyone wants to sell. You'll find everything from Beanie Babies to Hummers. Figure 6.13 shows one of the more popular auction sites.

ACTIVITY
6.5

Objective:
In this lesson, you will learn how to participate in an online auction.

Figure 6.13
Home page for eBay.com

In this activity, you'll visit several of the auction services. You'll learn how to offer an item for sale and how to bid. You'll also learn how auction companies make their money and why search engines want to participate.

1 Over 100 companies offer online auction services. One of the best known is eBay. Site statistics are updated frequently, but at one time eBay had 895,305 items for sale. Over its life, eBay has had over 47 million items for sale and users have placed over 176 million bids. The site receives over 600 million views per month. Go to the eBay site.

Does the home page tell you whether or not there is a charge to place a bid? _____

The home page shows items you can buy and tells you how many auctions are available. Why do you think the page is designed this way?

_____

_____

2 Click a sales category that interests you. Follow the links until you get to the item list. Choose an item, read its description, and look at its picture, if available.

What is the current bid for your item? _____

When does the sale end?_____

Do you think this is a good price, or would you place a higher bid?

_____

How does this site and this method entice you to bid on this item?

_____

3 Both Yahoo and Excite have recently established auction services. Yahoo's began on September 14, 1998. Open Yahoo, and click Yahoo! Auctions. Notice that there is a large display that says "It's Free." Why would Yahoo be willing to offer a free home to auctions?_____

_____

4 Use the Yahoo! Auction search to see if you can find the same sort of item you examined in step 2. If not, then use the links to work your way toward a similar item. Click on an item name to read more about it. Figure 6.14 shows the item list for Mark McGwire memorabilia, and Figure 6.15 shows the auction details for one of the items.

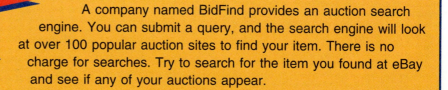

A company named BidFind provides an auction search engine. You can submit a query, and the search engine will look at over 100 popular auction sites to find your item. There is no charge for searches. Try to search for the item you found at eBay and see if any of your auctions appear.

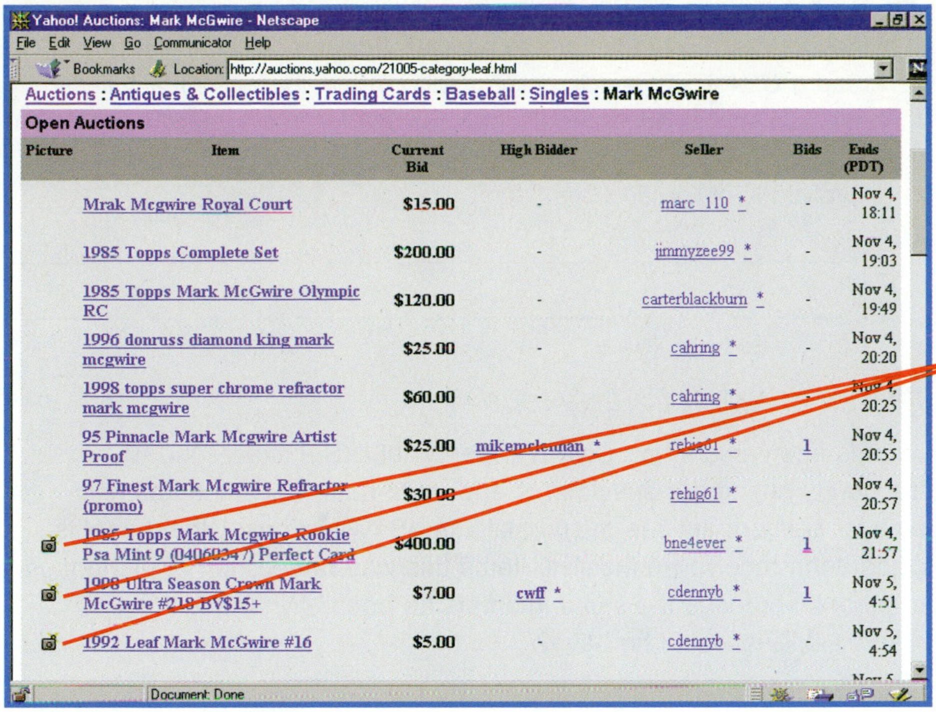

You can see a picture of these items.

Figure 6.14
Mark McGwire items at Yahoo! Auction

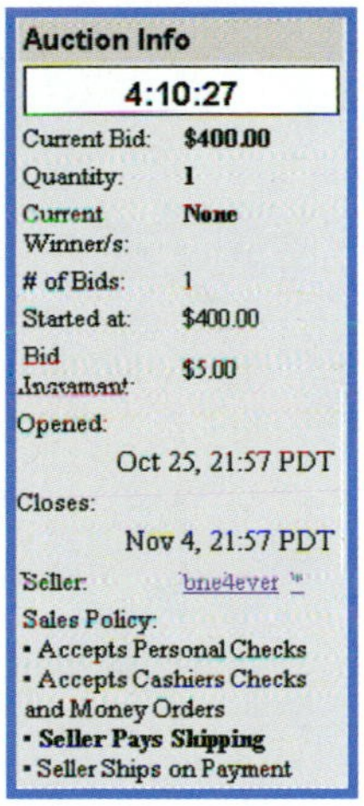

Figure 6.15
Detail of the auction information for a McGwire trading card

What is the current bid for your item? ____________________________

When does the sale end? ____________________________________

Do you think this is a good price, or would you place a higher bid?

____

How does this site and this method entice you to bid on this item?

____

5 You've seen two of the many different online auction services and thought about why they are so popular. For an additional viewpoint, read a *USA Today* article online. Go to *Internetnews.com*, a collection of press articles about the Internet. Search for "Excite auction" to find an article from June 10, 1998. Why would Yahoo and Excite want to be involved in online auctions? _____

_____

_____

THINKING ABOUT TECHNOLOGY

John is interested in the Civil War period of U.S. history, and he frequently attends re-enactments and visits battlefields. He has sold several items of antique memorabilia in eBay auctions. What benefits could John receive from selling items this way rather than at gatherings of others who have the same interests he does? What additional responsibilities would he have?

CHAPTER REVIEW

NET VOCABULARY

Define the following terms:

1. auction service

2. cookie

3. online mall

4. SOHO

5. wholesale

6. zine

NET REVIEW

Give a short answer to the following questions:

1. Why would you use an Internet shopping service when you can use a search engine?

2. Name three important things to consider if you are ordering groceries online.

3. How has the Internet changed the way customers bargain with car dealers?

4. Which is responsible for more online transactions: sales of consumer goods or sales to businesses?

5. How do auction sites make money?

6. Name three features that a business Web site should exhibit.

NET PROJECT

COMPARISON SHOPPING

Choose several items and compare their prices in your local store to their prices online at two different locations. Check prices for a dozen roses, a bag of Puppy Chow, and a two-liter bottle of Diet Coke. Be sure to include delivery costs. Was one source consistently priced lower than the others? Why do you think this is so? What else are you paying for at each location?

NET PROJECT TEAMWORK   Small Business Assistance

Through personal contacts, or with the help of your instructor, learn about a small business in your area. After you understand what this business does, go to the Thomas Register to look for suppliers whose products might be useful for this business. Visit Web sites of companies that have these products, and prepare a report that details sources of supply. Present your report to the small business and, if necessary, demonstrate how to conduct an online search of the Thomas Register.

WRITING ABOUT TECHNOLOGY   It's a New World of Shopping

Imagine that you are shopping for a tent to take on a camping vacation. How has the Internet changed the way you can shop now versus the way you would have shopped five years ago? Use about 100 words to explain the differences.

PORTFOLIO PROJECT

Making Online Purchases

Chapter Objectives:

After completing the activities in this chapter, you will be able to

1 place a secure order for a consumer product and track its delivery status.

2 use an online gift service to send a present and create an automatic reminder.

3 explain the kinds of ordering, payment, and delivery information required for online business purchases.

4 purchase a subscription for an online periodical and specify delivery.

Net Terms

electronic shopping cart

security

I'll Take It!

Your window-shopping is done. You've searched the Internet for just the right item, and you've found it. It might be a book for your little brother or a box of chocolates for your boss. It could be a shipment of fan blades for your air conditioning company or software for your new computer. If the company selling it will take your order online, you are only moments away from completing your purchase.

What do you need to know to buy online? The hardest part, if only because there are more and more online alterna-tives every day, is to decide what you want to buy. Once you make that choice and you are at the store's Web site, you just need to understand how to place your order.

Many online stores offer an **electronic shopping cart**, a small program at the site that keeps track of your selections as you shop. Like its physical counterpart, an electronic shopping cart allows you to continue browsing until you have made all your selections, so that you can pay for them all at once. If you change your mind about a selection, you can take it out of your cart at any time. Figure 7.2 shows the contents of an electronic shopping cart at eToys. Notice that it even keeps track of your bill as you go along.

Once you have selected the items you want to purchase, you need to tell the store how you are going to pay for them. Figure 7.3 shows a portion of the purchase form you would use to order from eToys. Consumers generally pay with a personal credit card. Other billing arrangements are usually established for online business-to-business sales.

Before you give your credit card number to a site, be sure that the site has **security** measures in place, to guarantee than no one else can gain access to your credit card information. A small lock in the lower left corner of the screen is a common indicator for security. When the lock is closed, security measures are in effect. You'll learn more about security in upcoming

Net Business *eToys*

On October 1, 1997, eToys was launched online in time for holiday shoppers. The company had been founded the previous March. As its press release says, its founders "saw the need to bring the power and convenience of Internet shopping to the toy buying experience, and created this ultimate toy retail site that combines superior selection, high quality, and reasonable price."

Although the industry first thought eToys would have trouble competing against stores like Toys "R" Us, that has not been the case. In June of 1998, the interactive edition of The Wall Street Journal said, "But in its first eight months, the Santa Monica, Calif, on-line retailer has proven its critics wrong, expanding steadily, striking an aggressive series of deals with popular portal sites, and establishing itself as an increasingly well-known brand in cyberspace." Visitors to the site will also find a friendly, helpful, and easy-to-navigate online store. The goal of the company is to combine the selection of a discount store with the service available at a small specialty toy store. You can see some of the services in Figure 7.1, which shows the eToys home page.

Look at some of the links in Figure 7.1. Shoppers have the ability to search for any toy they might have in mind, but they can also benefit from recommendations for certain ages, interests, or occasions. You can look by product, such as Barbie, or by category, such as action figures. You can enter contests or buy a gift certificate. You can search by price. A prospective recipient can even register for the toys he or she wants!

Customers who order from eToys can fill a shopping cart, arrange for payment, and specify delivery instructions right at the site. The company addresses the issues of ordering, secure payment, and delivery in its FAQs. Answers are only a click away.

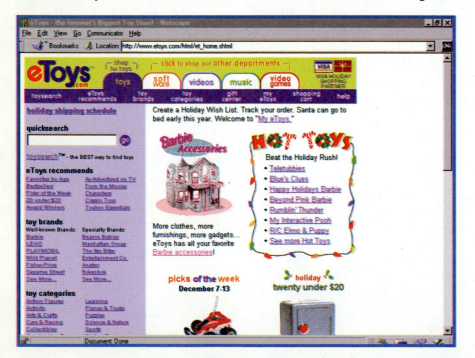

Figure 7.1
The home page for eToys.

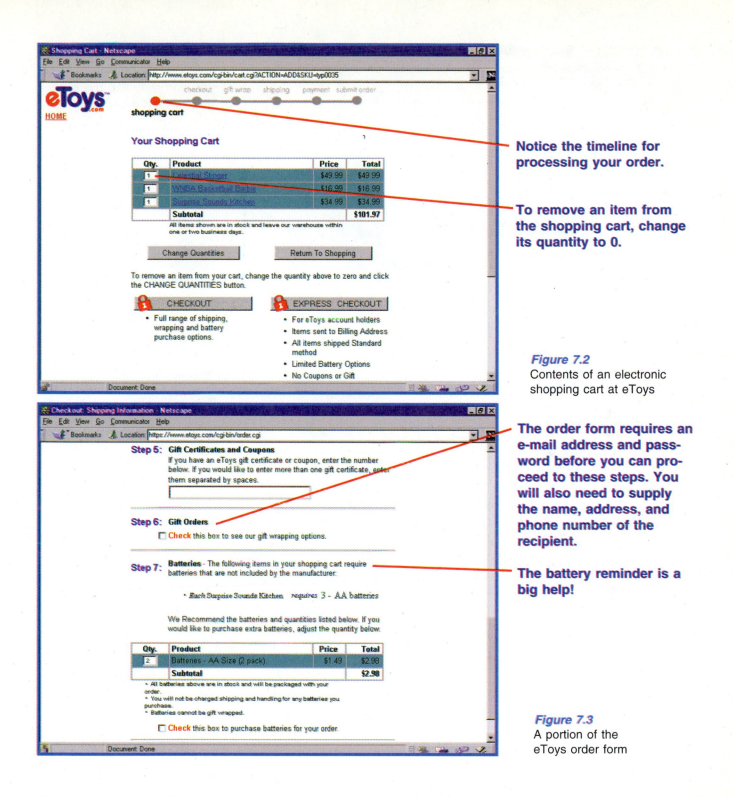

Notice the timeline for processing your order.

To remove an item from the shopping cart, change its quantity to 0.

Figure 7.2
Contents of an electronic shopping cart at eToys

The order form requires an e-mail address and password before you can proceed to these steps. You will also need to supply the name, address, and phone number of the recipient.

The battery reminder is a big help!

Figure 7.3
A portion of the eToys order form

chapters. Figure 7.4 shows the credit card section of the eToys order form.

As you complete your purchase, the site will tell you when and how delivery will occur. If you need the item in a hurry, you may be able to up-grade the shipping choices by paying a premium. Some sites provide ways for you to track the progress of your order. Most will provide some sort of e-mail confirmation of your order, and some will inform you when delivery has occurred.

This is particularly reassuring if you have ordered a present online.

In this chapter, we'll look at four different online purchases and see how each buyer would place the order, make payment, and take delivery.

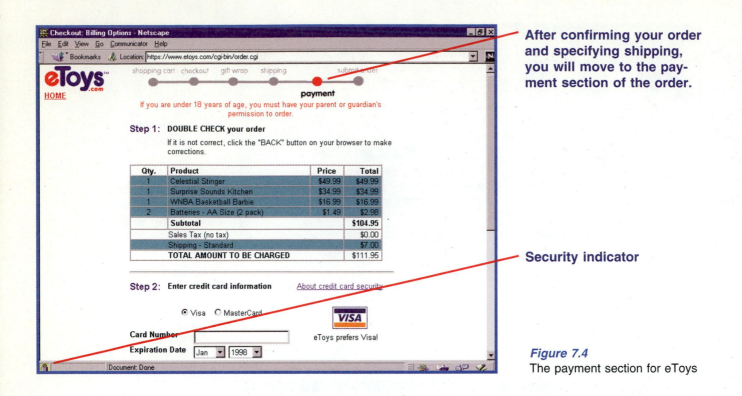

After confirming your order and specifying shipping, you will move to the payment section of the order.

Security indicator

Figure 7.4
The payment section for eToys

Web Producer

If you search for Web-related jobs at a site like Career Mosaic, you'll see a long list of available positions. Although many will use the same terminology, you really do need to read the position descriptions, because titles have different meanings to different companies.

One interesting title is Web producer. Both Toys "R" Us and WEEK-TV, a station in Peoria, Illinois, have listed openings for a Web (site) producer. At Toys "R" Us, the Web producer plans and schedules the creative content of new business and strategic areas for the company's Web site. The person who will fill the job needs to have at least one year of Internet experience, plus tremendous management, organizational, and interpersonal skills. For WEEK-TV, the applicant needs to have more technical skills (Internet and Web design, HTML coding skills, and many programming languages) in addition to being an excellent problem solver and detail person.

Think about the different goals for these companies' Web sites and the sizes of their IT departments. Does this explain why employees with the same titles might do very different kinds of work in different organizations?

Bring the Music Home

ACTIVITY

7.1

Objective:
In this lesson, you will learn how to place a secure order for a consumer product and track its delivery status.

In Chapter 6, you saw how to look for music CDs at online music stores. In this activity, you'll see how to place an order with CDnow and follow your purchase until delivery.

1 Go to the CDnow Web site and find at least two albums you'd like to order. Note: To complete this activity, you will not have to complete the order form. Click the price to add the album to your shopping cart. Remember that if you are not sure which album you want, you can read reviews and find out what songs are on which album. Figure 7.5 shows the CDnow shopping cart. Notice that the site is not yet secure.

CDnow : Shopping Cart - Netscape

File Edit View Go Communicator Help

Bookmarks Location: ww.cdnow.com/cgi-bin/mserver/SID=169845433/pagename=/RP/CDN/ACCT/cart.html/lcc=7863+67634+2/distcod

Switch to Secure Mode

Shopping Cart
All of your account information can now be found in My CDnow.

Cart Contents

Ready to continue shopping? Go back to the CDnow home page.

Click here for an explanation of our inventory information.

To change item quantities or move items to your Wish List, click here.

qty	CDnow price	list price	description
1	**$ 11.88**	$ 16.97	Jewel : Spirit
	CD		In stock Shipping Ctr A
1	**$ 11.88**	$ 16.97	Third Eye Blind : Third Eye Blind
	CD		In stock Shipping Ctr A
1	**$ 11.88**	$ 16.97	Natalie Imbruglia : Left Of The Middle
	CD		In stock Shipping Ctr A

Account Login

New customers: Click on Create New Account. You can then place your order or continue shopping.

Create New Account

Returning customers: Please enter your name and password in the spaces provided below, and click on the Login button.

If you do not remember your password, please visit our Contact CDnow page.

Document: Done

Figure 7.5
CDnow shopping cart

If you see music at CDnow that you'd like to own, create a Wish List. When your birthday comes and your family and friends want to know what you want, you'll be able to refer them to this list!

2 When you have all the items you want in your shopping cart, scroll down to read the rest of the order form. If you are working in a computer lab, answer as many of the questions as you can without logging in.

What is autologin? _____

Why would a customer want to use autologin? _____

How does using autologin help the store?_____

Why does CDnow warn against using autologin on a public computer?

_____

Continue reading the order form. Examine the shipping, invoice, and gift wrap choices. Stop before entering credit card information or clicking the Process Order box.

3 Remember that for this activity, you don't really have to buy the merchandise. If you were going to buy the items in your shopping cart, what other payment methods could you use besides typing a credit card number in the online order form?_____

_____

Return to the CDnow home page and click "Safe Shopping Policy." What is SSL? _____

_____

You will learn more about security issues by reading Appendix C.

4 To see the progress of your order, you can click Order History. This choice is always available through Help's Order Status. You can expect to receive an automatically generated e-mail message immediately after your order is placed. In this message, you'll find a confirmation of the titles you ordered, your order number, the shipping address, and the total charge. The message also provides links to a credit card sponsor, your order history, payment information, and customer service. Finally, you get a thank you for placing your order online with the company.

THINKING ABOUT TECHNOLOGY

Do you think that online retailing tends to increase the number of purchases customers make? Do you like to walk through a music store and read the album covers? Or did you discover that you liked having the choices, recommendations, and ease of access provided by shopping online?

Flowers for All Occasions

The immediacy of the Internet and its ability to reach customers and suppliers in any location makes it particularly useful when you want to send a present to someone. While you are online in your home or office, you can make arrangements for delivery to another location at any time you specify. You can visit an online gift store, purchase a place setting of china from the store's inventory, and have it mailed to the bride and groom. You can join a fruit or cheese of the month club, and the food will be sent regularly to you or your recipient. When you place an order, floral companies ship products from their own warehouses or contact a member florist in the recipient's community. In this activity, you'll see how one Internet floral site does business.

1 Go to the Excite Web site and follow the links to its floral services. Excite's store directory for flowers shows a wide range of sources, as you can see in Figure 7.6. Some deliver worldwide from their warehouses; others contact a florist in your community. Click the link to 1-800-FLOWERS, whose home page is shown in Figure 7.7, or go there directly. List two of the Popular Occasions that might offer a suggestion for an arrangement for your neighbor's 80th birthday.

1. _____

2. _____

Figure 7.6
Excite's floral links

Figure 7.7
Home page for
1-800-FLOWERS

NET TIP
Seasonal Sites

As you know, organizations frequently update their Web sites. This is particularly true when the company has a new product or model. Car manufacturers would not want to show pictures of last year's models on their opening screens! Companies also update their site to market a seasonal product. The screens that you will see from 1-800-Flowers may show Valentine's Day, an autumn bouquet, or spring bulbs, depending on the season, instead of the Christmas arrangements you see in Figure 7.7. And eToys doesn't always display candy canes! These decorations serve the same purpose that in-store decorations do by contributing to the shoppers' desire to make a purchase.

2 This site provides a pictorial catalog of the arrangements they offer. Browse through the birthday floral arrangements, as shown in Figure 7.8. Why is it critical for this Web site to have a catalog with pictures?

Figure 7.8
Some birthday arrangements
available at 1-800-FLOWERS

For this exercise, find an arrangement that you like, and click on it to place it in your shopping cart.

Can your order be delivered today? _____

Does the site guarantee that your order will look just like the arrangement in the picture? _____

_____

3 You will not really be ordering this arrangement, but proceed with filling out the order form. When you have finished, click "Add Then Checkout." Browse through the payment form to see what information is required, but don't enter any information.

This is as far as you can go in the order process without actually placing an order. At any time during the process, you can click My Basket to see what is in your shopping cart. When you have completed the order form, you will be asked for delivery information. You can specify a delivery date and special instructions. You'll also be asked if you want to be reminded of any upcoming occasions for which flowers would be appropriate. If so, you'll be notified by e-mail, the same way you will receive confirmation of the order you've just placed.

4 As you saw in Chapter 6, you can receive an automatic reminder from the florist for those occasions that you shouldn't forget! You won't be prompted to create one of these unless you complete the order form, but you can go there directly by clicking My Flower Shop and then My Flower Shop Benefits. Would it be possible for one person to have a reminder sent to another person? Investigate to see if this feature is password protected.

THINKING ABOUT TECHNOLOGY

You learned about cookies in Chapter 6. 1-800-FLOWERS uses cookies to save your order information and any reminders you want to receive. After seeing how much information you had to supply to place an order, do you think cookies help make sales transactions more efficient?

Net Fun

You may reach sensory overload, but if you're a chocolate lover, follow the links from Yahoo Shopping to Food and Drink | Sweets | Chocolate. Links here let you order everything from a box of two chocolate horses for $2.75 to a gift box of truffles for $49.95.

Objective:

In this activity, you will learn about the kinds of ordering, payment, and delivery information required for online business purchases.

Downloading an Online Image

You've seen many examples of personal use of the Internet—for career searches, financial planning, booking travel, and buying a present. Remember, though, that by far the largest E-commerce use of the Internet comes from business-to-business activities.

Running a business requires both personnel and materials. If you are involved in production, you will need to secure raw materials to make your product. If you are involved in a service, you will need the supplies to make your organization work.

Think for a moment about the business of running an orthodontist's office. Professionally trained personnel are certainly needed for work with patients, but the office also must have equipment, orthodontic materials, and office supplies. Some orthodontists take before and after pictures of their patients' mouths, so supplies might include film as well as wires, elastics, and material for impressions. The practice would also need to contract for janitorial and maintenance services. The orthodontist, or the office manager, might work with a diverse group of suppliers. Think about how efficient it would be to be able to make these purchases online!

In this activity, you'll see how a company that deals in photographic images sells those images to other businesses.

1. Stock photographs are pictures that are sold or licensed for use in publications or advertisements. The publisher of a computer book might need a picture of a chip, and the editor of a cookbook might be looking for a picture of a perfect apple pie. A travel company's Web site might need a photograph of a tropical sunset, and a company that sells party goods might want a picture of happy children at a birthday party. Instead of hiring a photographer to shoot the required pictures, it is easier to take advantage of professional shots that are in a photo bank.

   Many companies offer such collections online. To see one of them, go to *www.picturequest.com*. Although there is no charge to register, you will be able to work with PictureQuest without registration. Click "About Picture-Quest" and read about the services and products the company offers.

2. How might you use PictureQuest if you were the proprietor of the Seaside Shop, a gift shop and restaurant specializing in nautical gifts and cuisine? One way would be to choose an image to use for your logo. By placing this image on your Web site, your letterhead, your business card, your gift bags, and your menu, you would be able to strengthen your shop's identity.

   Begin by using PictureQuest to locate an image. Return to the home page and click Sample Search. Search for a lighthouse, a sailing ship, or a beach. Figure 7.9 shows some of the lighthouse pictures that are available. Decide on an image that you would like to use for the Seaside Shop's logo. Record the PNI Object ID for your picture._____

NET TIP

Registration Information

To avoid frustration, determine a single user name and password to use for all of your E-commerce registrations. Although some sites provide a way for you to retrieve a password you've forgotten, why not make it easier on yourself by standardizing your selection? If you find that your choice is not available at some site, then change it systematically by adding a 1 or an A or something easy to remember. And write it down!

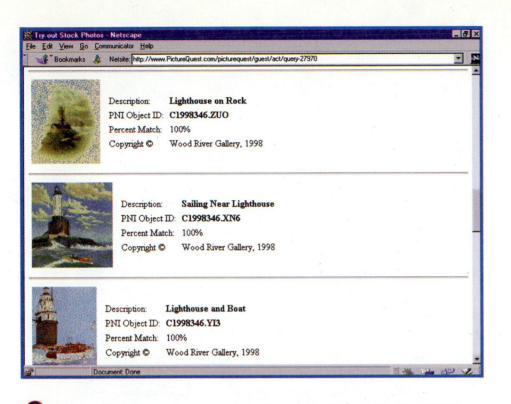

Description: **Lighthouse on Rock**
PNI Object ID: **C1998346.ZUO**
Percent Match: 100%
Copyright © Wood River Gallery, 1998

Description: **Sailing Near Lighthouse**
PNI Object ID: **C1998346.XN6**
Percent Match: 100%
Copyright © Wood River Gallery, 1998

Description: **Lighthouse and Boat**
PNI Object ID: **C1998346.YI3**
Percent Match: 100%
Copyright © Wood River Gallery, 1998

Figure 7.9
Lighthouse images available from PictureQuest

3 To actually order an image, you must register and set up an account with PictureQuest, which we will not do for this activity. However, you can find out general information about purchasing the images without going to a shopping cart.

How much would it cost to buy the rights to use the image you chose? To find out, return to the home page and click Products and Providers. Then click License Types and Prices. Click "Most Uses" under "Royalty Free Images."

Will Seaside's use be "Products For Sale" or "Products Not For Sale"?

_____

If Seaside decides that the lower resolution will be sufficient for this use, how much will it cost to license an image? _____

Will Seaside have to make multiple payments if it uses this image on multiple pieces? _____

4 Return to the "License Types and Prices" page and click the "click here" box.

How are images delivered to the customer? _____

_____

How quickly can they arrive, and what are the delivery costs?_____

_____

5 You've seen how the music and flower companies provide online suggestions for their customers. PictureQuest provides less online advice but has a sales force. How do these differences reflect both the products and the buyers who purchase them? _____

_____

_____

THINKING ABOUT TECHNOLOGY

When a sales representative calls on a business in person, the rep can show the business client samples, discuss product specifications, and be sure that the client understands how the product will fill the needs of the business. If this relationship is at a distance, how can the sellers convince the buyers that the products will meet their needs?

Rewrite Net Fun

Some stock photo sites provide pictures with specific themes. For pictures of food, see Great American Stock or Foodpix. For pictures of emergency services, try 911 Photo. Striking Images specializes in pictures of lightening. For pictures from around the world, see China Span, CyberPix (for England), Photo Rack India, Don Sutton (for Ireland), or Asia Pix. You can download photos of architectural sites around the world by visiting Archivision. Figure 7.10 shows the instructions for educators to sample and order one of over 200 images.

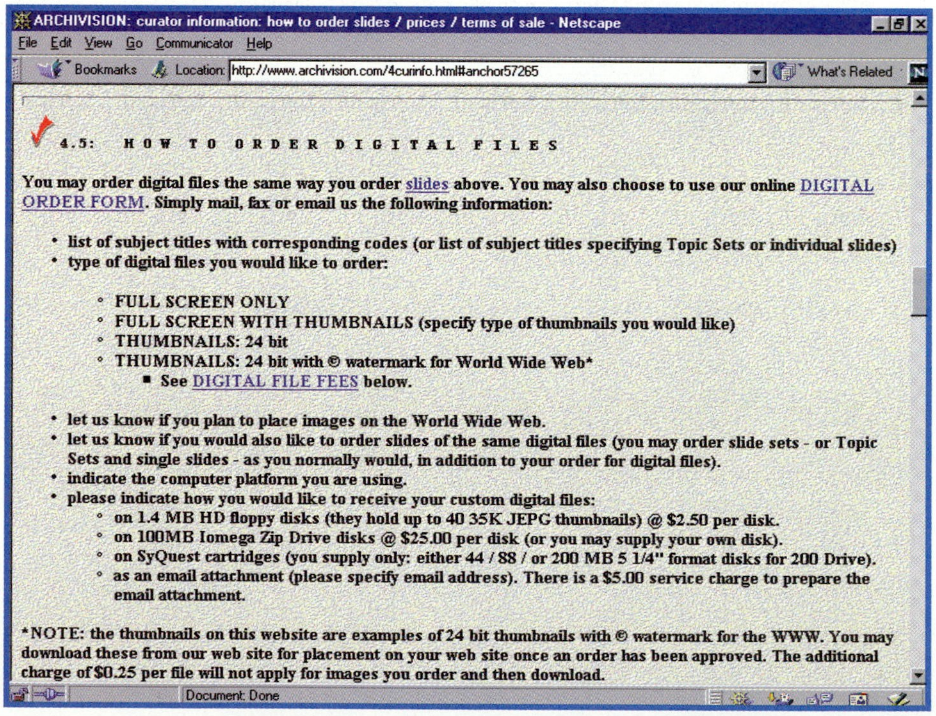

Figure 7.10
Ordering instructions for photo images from Archivision

Online Subscriptions

ACTIVITY
7.4

Objective:
In this activity, you will learn how to purchase a subscription for an online periodical and specify delivery.

The activities in this chapter have shown you how to put items you'd like to purchase online into a shopping cart, how to complete the order and specify delivery, and how to track your purchases. You've seen how CDs can be ordered online and delivered to your door, how flowers can be ordered online and delivered anywhere, and how photographic images can be purchased and then sent to you in a variety of formats. In this activity, you'll see how you can subscribe to an electronic magazine.

1. Although periodicals from your local newspaper to the big national papers may have Web sites, they usually don't put their entire paper online. Magazines are the same. Both *Time* and *Newsweek* have Web sites that show both features and breaking stories, but neither furnishes its entire magazine on its Web site.

   Visit the Web site for *The Wall Street Journal*, shown in Figure 7.11. The printed version of the *Journal* is published daily, Monday through Friday. Scroll down to find information on subscribing to the Interactive Journal.

   How much does it cost? _____

   What special features do online subscribers receive? _____

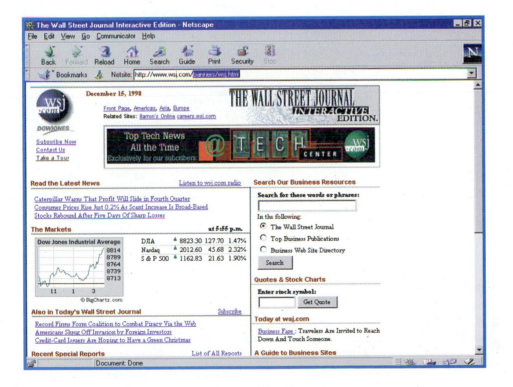

Figure 7.11
Home page of The Wall Street Journal

2 *The Wall Street Journal* offers potential subscribers the opportunity to take a tour of the Interactive edition. Do this by visiting *http://public.wsj.com/tour/.* Click "…or see the big picture." Now click the "2" at the top of the page to read about company information online. Click "3" to learn how you can personalize your online subscription.

Who do you think would have more interest in subscribing to the Interactive Edition, a banker or a manufacturer? Why?_____

_____

3 Click Subscribe at the bottom of the page to see instructions for subscribing. The instructions begin with security options. Figure 7.12 shows the options. Subscribers are given even more assurance later in the form, and may phone in their payment information if they prefer.

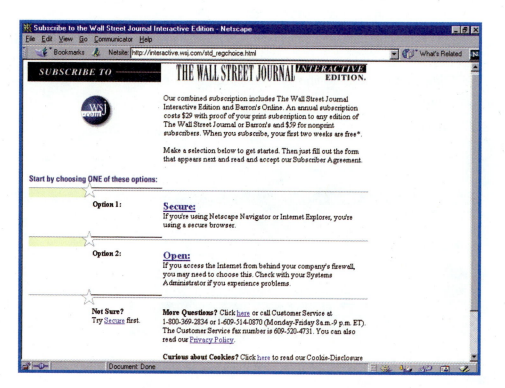

Figure 7.12
Subscription security information

Want the inside information on your favorite college sports team? Many schools offer online subscriptions to their publications. Check out *Blue and Gold Illustrated* or *IrishInsider* if you support Notre Dame. Other fans might want to subscribe to *Aggie Station, Huskers Illustrated,* or the *Wildcat's Lair.* To find your favorite team, search for "online subscriptions" in your search engine's sports category.

Click Secure, and then scroll through the subscription form to see what kinds of information are required. There are five sections of the form, separated by stars, to complete. Give the name of each section, describe the kinds of information it requests, and tell why it is important for *The Wall Street Journal* to have that information.

Section	Information	Why is it important?
1.		
2.		
3.		
4.		
5.		

4 Go back to the *wsj.com* home page. Find a topic in the menu list that interests you. Highlight it, and click Go.

THINKING ABOUT TECHNOLOGY

Online subscriptions allow readers access to more information than they can get from printed versions of the publications. Online versions can be updated more frequently, and there are articles and services that are too specialized to appear in the general editions. Do readers have enough time to make use of all of this information? How has technology changed the role of publishing in our society?

NET TIP

Online Does Not Mean Free

The Ziff Davis Company publishes eCommerce Alert, a subscription newsletter that provides information, statistics, case studies, and new developments. This service costs $265 for a year's subscription. What other business-related subscriptions can you find? How do their costs compare?

CHAPTER Review

NET VOCABULARY

Define the following terms:

1. electronic shopping cart
2. security

NET REVIEW

Give a short answer to the following questions:

1. *Is online ordering more convenient than dialing a toll-free phone number? Why or why not?*

_____

_____

2. *What do you need to have available before you can complete an online order form?*

_____

_____

3. *How can a lawyer's office use the Internet to make business-to-business purchases?*

_____

_____

4. *How can an online subscription give a manager access to the most useful information available?*

_____

_____

5. *Why do online stores want their customers to register before they complete an order form?*

_____

_____

6. *How can a buyer be sure that a site has security measures in place?*

_____

_____

EQUIPPING THE PIZZA RESTAURANT

How could you use the Internet for your business if you were starting a pizza restaurant? At a minimum, you would need ingredients such as flour, cheese, and sauce; equipment such as pans, knives, plates, glasses, and silverware; furnishings such as tables, chairs, and linens; and office supplies. Which of these could you find, and purchase, online? Make a chart with each of these categories and include the URL of a company that provides each of the items listed above.

NET PROJECT TEAMWORK   The *Good Sports!* Store

Jim Newton likes to play softball. For years, he has played in summer leagues, on intramural teams, and on a team at work. And every team he's played on has bought T-shirts and hats with the team name on them. Jim has a closet full of old team shirts and hats.

Jim is also looking for a business opportunity. He and two partners feel that they have the time and resources to start a small business. They have decided to combine their sports knowledge and their business knowledge to start a team apparel store. Their plan is that the store will stock licensed college and pro sports logo items and will custom-print shirts and hats for local school and league teams. They've decided to name the store *Good Sports!*

Jim and his partners are experienced Internet users, and they'd like to take advantage of online business-to-business opportunities. The first site they visit as they begin to investigate how they can purchase supplies for the printing side of their business is the Fruit of the Loom Activewear site, a portion of which is shown in Figure 7.13.

Figure 7.13
Business-to-business choices from Fruit of the Loom Activewear

With your team, investigate what Fruit of the Loom offers to small businesses like Jim's. Prepare a report that would recommend a basic T-shirt and sweatshirt for Good Sports! to use for printing. Be sure to tell Jim how many colors are available in each. Include in your report the names and addresses of three wholesalers that carry this product and are located close to Jim, who lives in northern Florida. Examine new product development, and make a suggestion for another product that Jim should consider ordering for his store. As an appendix, include an explanation of terminology that Jim will need to know when he works with suppliers and customers.

WRITING ABOUT TECHNOLOGY   Customer Information

Some of the sites you've visited in this chapter ask the purchaser to provide much more information than is necessary for purchasing the product and arranging for delivery. If you were running an online store, what would you like to know about your customers, and why? Do you think it is reasonable to ask this information of your customers? Use about 100 words to answer these questions.

CHAPTER 8

Consumer Issues

Chapter Objectives:

After completing the activities in this chapter, you will be able to

1 evaluate the security and privacy of a site you visit.

2 report any dissatisfaction with a site to the appropriate agency.

3 find product comparison and safety information online.

Net Terms

recall

lemon

The Savvy Online Buyer

Whether you are buying for yourself or for your company, you want to know before you buy that the online store will deliver what it promised. As a buyer, you want to be certain that the product or service is as described, that your purchase information is secure, and that you have some recourse if you are dissatisfied with the purchase. You should also be able to determine if the information you provide when you complete an online registration form will be shared with someone else. It is critically important to be aware of these issues when you are buying or offering information online.

With its wide access to information, the Internet can help you become a better consumer. You don't have to be an online buyer to find online help with consumer issues. The Internet can give you access to product safety information, to consumer news, and to product ratings. You can see if a product is subject to a **recall**, which is the manufacturer's request to return a product because of severe risks to health or safety. You can also use the Web to learn the specifications and prices of items you want by comparison-shopping electronically before you make a purchase decision.

All of the major search engines provide links to topics of interest to consumers. When you search for the word "consumer" with Infoseek, you find over 5 million references!

Figure 8.1 shows Snap.com's Consumer Information Center. By following the links found here and at other sites, you can learn how to find all kinds of product information and become a savvy online buyer.

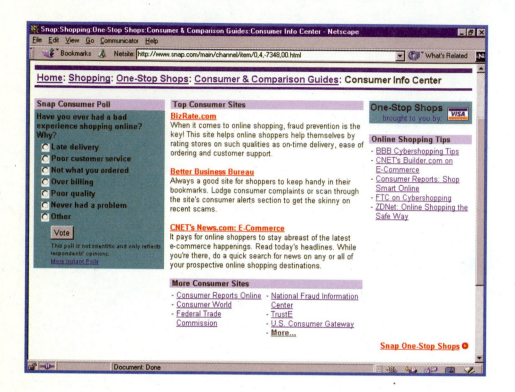

Figure 8.1
Consumer Information Center at Snap.com

Internet Lawyer

Advising online stores about tax issues and developing privacy statements for Web sites are two of the tasks that commonly fall to Internet lawyers. A business with an online presence—and that means most businesses—must be certain to adhere to technology laws.

A large corporation needs to have lawyers in its legal department who understand issues of privacy and access, and smaller companies need to retain the same kinds of expertise. The relatively new specialty of Internet law attracts attorneys who are experienced Internet users, who can develop electronic contracts, and who understand the policies, procedures, and regulations of E-commerce. Those with some technical experience can provide even more benefits to their clients.

You can find links to Internet law through your search engine. You'll also find sites devoted to helping law offices make the most of the Internet. If you are interested in a possible career in Internet law, you might want to start your search for information at the American Bar Association's Web site, or visit the home page of a law school like the University of Nebraska's College of Law. There is also an online journal titled The Internet Lawyer.

Safeguarding Security and Privacy

ACTIVITY
8.1

Objective:
In this lesson, you will see how to evaluate the security and privacy of the sites you visit.

Privacy and security are not new topics. In earlier chapters, you examined a site use statement and learned to look for a closed lock or other security symbol before you place an order from an online store. In this activity, you'll take a closer look at privacy policies and visit a site that guarantees security.

1 You've visited sites that offer services and sites that sell products. Go now to the four sites listed below and examine each home page for a statement of privacy. This is usually found near the bottom of the home page. You may need to look under Legal Information. What does each site tell you about the issues listed in the table?

Site	Security	Privacy	Responsibility
Career Mosaic			
Quicken			
Amazon.com			
CDnow			

2 Career Mosaic offers services at no charge. Amazon.com and CDnow sell products. Quicken does both. How do the security and privacy statements of these sites reflect their business? _____

_____

3 Not all sites have security and privacy statements, and some companies are better than others at upholding what they say they will do. How can you be confident that a site will operate according to appropriate guidelines? One way is to look for accreditation by an agency that evaluates online operating principles.

"Building a Web you can believe in™" is the slogan of TRUSTe, an organization founded in 1996 to certify the privacy and security operations of Web sites. Go to the TRUSTe home page and read The TRUSTe Story, How TRUSTe Protects Privacy, and the FAQs for Users.

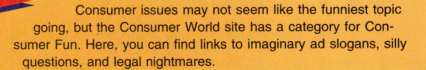

Net Fun

Consumer issues may not seem like the funniest topic going, but the Consumer World site has a category for Consumer Fun. Here, you can find links to imaginary ad slogans, silly questions, and legal nightmares.

What are the two basic principles of the TRUSTe program? _____

_____

_____

What are the four privacy principles of fair information practice? _____

_____

_____

What does "Click-to-verify" mean, and how does it guarantee safety?

_____

_____

TRUSTe participants come from all areas of E-commerce. Figure 8.2, Figure 8.3, and Figure 8.4 show the TRUSTe trustmark at an information site, a corporate service site, and an online store.

TRUSTe trustmark

Figure 8.2
The TRUSTe trustmark at CBS Sportsline

TRUSTe trustmark and other certifications

Figure 8.3
The TRUSTe trustmark and other certifications at Northwestern Mutual Life

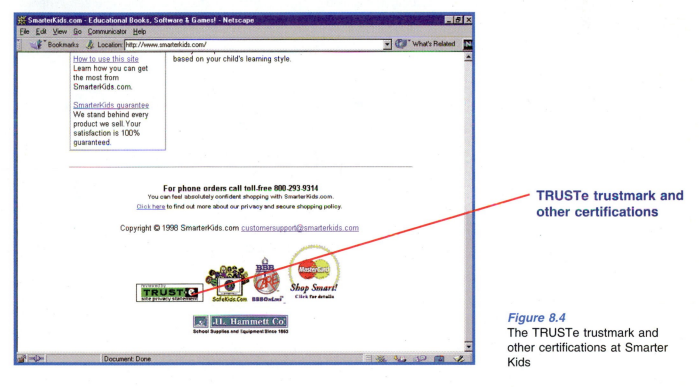

TRUSTe trustmark and other certifications

Figure 8.4
The TRUSTe trustmark and other certifications at Smarter Kids

THINKING ABOUT TECHNOLOGY

Would you make an online purchase from a company you had never heard of if it displayed the TRUSTe symbol? Would you purchase from an established company's Web site if it did not offer you a privacy statement whose terms you could accept?

ACTIVITY
8.2

Objective:

In this lesson, you'll learn how consumers can report any dissatisfaction with a site to the appropriate agency.

Speaking Up

Just as the Internet enables companies to reach an ever-expanding number of Web consumers, it also enables these users to react online to their experiences. A buyer can contact the company's customer service department by e-mail and expect to get a quick response. There are professional organizations and Web businesses that gather ratings information from users and publicize the results online. In extreme cases, a user with a complaint about a product or service can launch a Web page to air a grievance, making it simple for search engines to help other buyers find the site and add their opinions.

In this activity, you'll look at some of the avenues available to you if you want to make responsible comments about a product or service.

NET TIP

Financial Watchdogs

There are Web sites that support ethical financial behavior. You can report problems with Internet banking to the FDIC and see a broker scorecard at Gomez Advisors.

1. The Federal Trade Commission sponsors the Consumer Line site at *www.ftc.gov/bcp/conline/conline.htm*. Go there, and read one of the online consumer documents that is interesting to you. You'll find documents on subjects ranging from indoor tanning to car leasing, including one called "Cybersmarts: Tips for Protecting Yourself When Shopping Online."

   How did you choose which document to read? _____

   _____

   Do you think that putting these documents online will encourage significantly more people to read them? Why or why not? _____

   _____

   Click the FTC Complaint box at the bottom of the Consumer Line site. Is there anything in these dialog boxes that you are surprised to see, or not to see? _____

   _____

   What does the FTC do with your complaint? To see, click the Privacy link, and Talk To Us. _____

   _____

NET TIP

More Places to Air Your Complaints

You can find other online avenues for complaints at the Netcheck Commerce Bureau, Internet ScamBusters, and your state's Attorney General or consumer affairs sites.

2 You can submit your own review of a book to Amazon.com or of a product to Consumer Review. Figure 8.5 shows some of the golf clubs that have been reviewed by users at the Consumer Review site. Visit this site and read the submitted reviews of a product you know well.

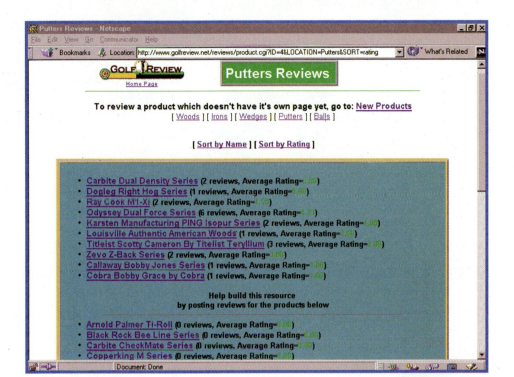

Figure 8.5
Golf clubs reviewed at Consumer Review

Do you agree with the reviews you read? _____

Are any of the reviews moderate, or do they all express strong opinions? _____

Do you think that people who are dissatisfied are more likely to write a review than those who are happy? _____

How seriously should buyers take unscientific ratings like these? _____

_____

_____

If you were the manufacturer of this product, how much attention would you pay to reviews like these? Why?_____

_____

_____

What action would you take if you found a negative review of your product?_____

_____

3 If a serious situation of fraud occurs, users can make a report to the National Fraud Information Center's Internet Fraud Watch site. Figure 8.6 shows a description of the site. Go to the site, and click the Online Incident Report Form. Scroll through the form to see the kind of information a user would report.

Why do you think the form has special instructions for problems encountered during online auctions? _____

_____

Why does the form urge a user to be clear and concise? _____

_____

Why would the IFW want your credit card company but not your credit card number? _____

_____

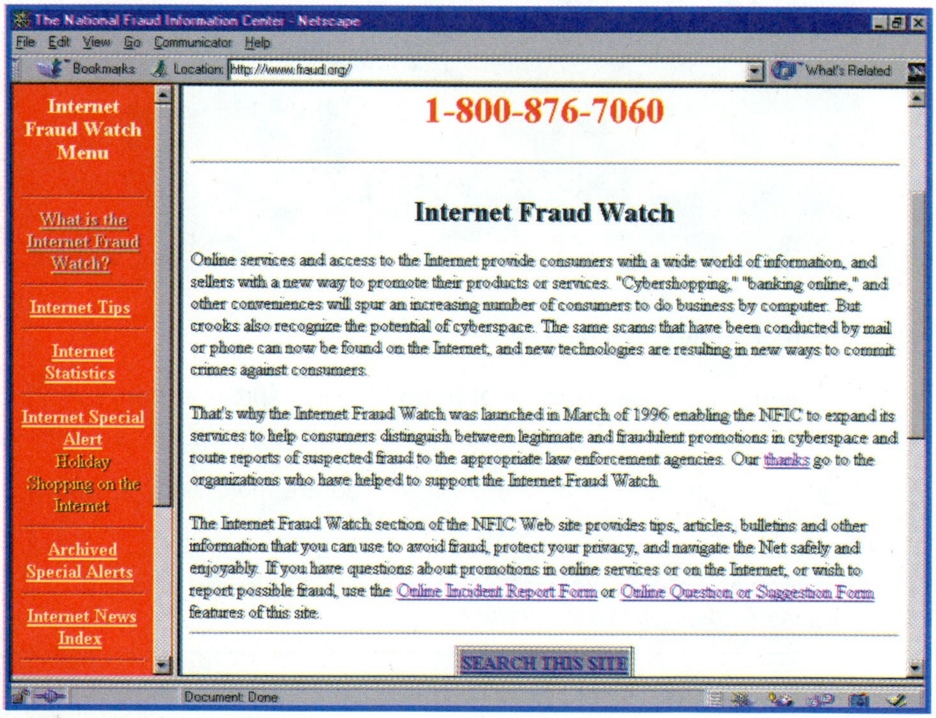

Figure 8.6
The Internet Fraud Watch home page

THINKING ABOUT TECHNOLOGY

How has the Internet changed the way companies and individuals can exchange information about products and services? List three positive factors and three negative factors that can be traced to Internet technology.

Net Business *BizRate*

Binary Compass, a company that prepares marketing research for other companies, is the creator of BizRate, an independent rating system for on-line stores. Binary Compass was founded in June, 1996, with a mission "to facilitate widespread acceptance of electronic commerce by providing both consumers and merchants important information about one another." Its BizRate Guide gathers information from online customers and makes that information available to the public. Figure 8.7 shows some of the categories of BizRate information.

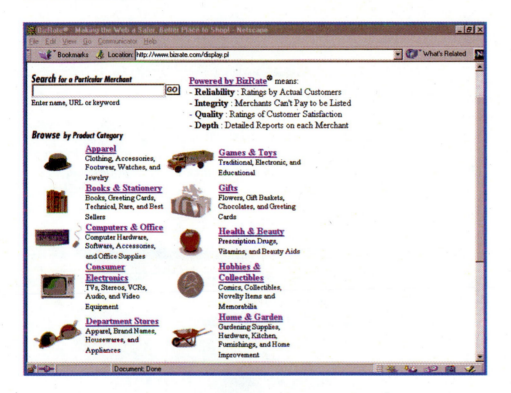

Figure 8.7
The BizRate home page

How does BizRate gather the information? If you order flowers online from 1-800-FLOWERS, BizRate will contact you and ask you to complete a survey. The florist has been accepted as a participating merchant, a "Gold Site," agreeing to allow BizRate access to its customers. BizRate does not charge the merchants, and does not accept advertising from them. BizRate also evaluates stores that have not been listed. These "Silver Sites" are rated by BizRate employees who purchase from them and then fill out a 40-item rating. Member merchants receive customer comments and can purchase other marketing research reports from Binary Compass Enterprises. Figure 8.8 shows the evaluation form sent to a 1-800-FLOWERS customer.

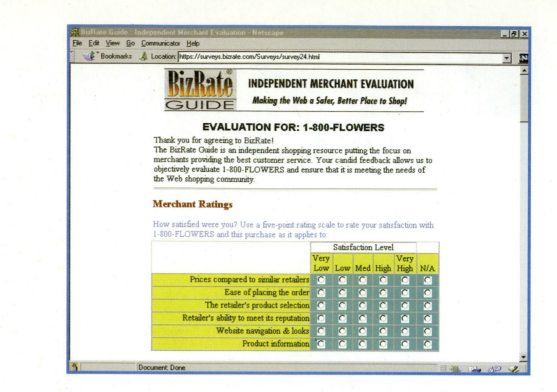

Figure 8.8
BizRate customer evaluation form

You can read ratings results for any participating company. From BizRate's home page you can search for a company, look at those in the "Buyer's Best" category, or follow the links to a category of your choice. Figure 8.9 shows the summary of customer ratings for 1-800-FLOWERS. Note the icons that tell you what the site supports.

Searchable site

Live customer support available

International shopping supported

Shopping cart system

Secure ordering is supported

Overall rating

Link to the company

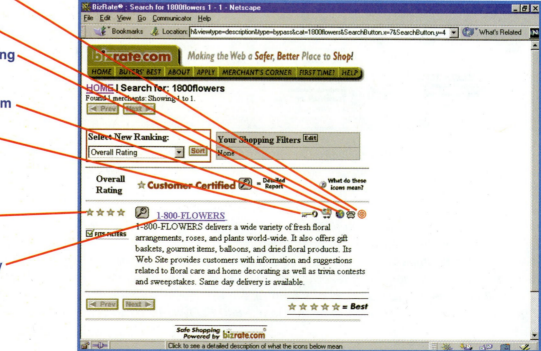

Figure 8.9
Rating results

To read the company's score on 10 qualities, click the magnifying glass. Figure 8.10 tells you how 1-800-FLOWERS scored with 3,302 customers during the fall quarter of 1998

Figure 8.10
Scorecard for 1-800-FLOWERS

Net Fun

Are you stuck with a car that you call a lemon? Legally, a **lemon** is a car with so many problems that the manufacturer repurchased it. Vehicle Identification Numbers of lemons have to be reported to the state. You can check to see if your clunker is really a lemon by submitting its VIN to the Carfax Lemon Check. This check is free. The company also sells information about your car's history.

ACTIVITY

8.3

Objective:

In this lesson, you'll see how to find product comparison and safety information online.

Wise Consumerism

When some people hear the word "consumer," they automatically think of publications like *Consumer Reports* that provide ratings on consumer products. Others think of issue-oriented campaigns for product safety or fair pricing. The Internet is home to online versions of a number of sites that serve exactly these purposes.

1. Begin your Web tour by visiting the online version of *Consumer Reports* magazine. To read ratings of products, you must purchase a subscription to the online magazine. But there are features you can access without subscribing. Links to selected articles and topics from the current month's issue appear. Figure 8.11 shows the link to "Consumer Report's Guide to Shopping Online." This article may or may not be available when you visit the site. Choose a featured article that is interesting to you and read it.

Why do you think the magazine chose to include this article? _____

_____

Do you think that after reading it a person would be more interested in subscribing to the magazine? Explain. _____

_____

_____

_____

_____

NET TIP
Decision Making

Comparison-shopping is a smart thing to do when you have a major purchase or decision to make, but most sites simply provide you with tables of information without helping you make any sense of it. For real assistance, based on some theoretical decision-making principles, visit Personalogic. By answering a series of questions about what is important to you, Personalogic will narrow a list of items to those that best fit your specifications. You can use the system for everything from cars to colleges.

Figure 8.11
Consumer Reports Online

Visit two other large consumer sites. Go to Consumer Review and Consumer World. How would you use these two sites if you were buying a portable CD player? _____

_____

2 Corporate Web sites can provide a wealth of product information if you are trying to learn the specifications for different models of similar products. If your business needs to buy a new copier, you can visit manufacturers' sites to learn sizes, speeds, and features of the models in each line. Independent Web sites also exist to help you make comparisons between models and manufacturers. You can find reliability ratings, price comparisons, and feature reviews at a number of comparison-shopping Web sites.

Begin by visiting Compare Net Interactive Shoppers' Guide. Figure 8.12 shows you some of the product categories in the comparison database.

Figure 8.12
Compare Net home page

Use the Compare Tool to conduct a comparison of tents, found in the Sports and Leisure category. Once you reach tents, do a comparison by Price and Feature. Search for a tent that has a retail price between $200 and $400. Your tent should hold 3 or 4 people, be usable in three seasons, and have a vestibule. For this activity, you don't have to be able to buy online. Watch the green line at the bottom of the screen as you add constraints to your selection. The number of matches will decrease. After your list appears, pick three tents you like and click the Add button to add them to the Compare Tool. When they all appear in the list, click Compare. You should see a list of features similar to the ones shown in Figure 8.13.

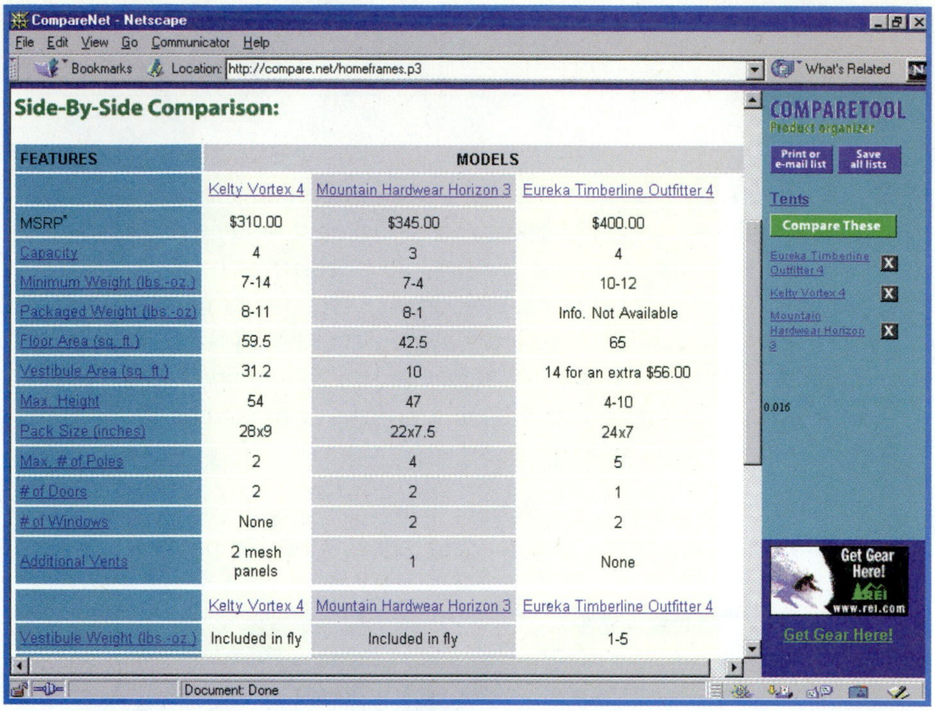

Figure 8.13
Side-by-Side comparisons
from Compare Net

You may not know much about tents, but do you feel that this site provides enough information to help you begin to make a decision?

_____

What else would you like to see?_____

_____

Would you like to have a link to the tent manufacturer? _____

_____

3 The immediacy of the Internet makes it particularly useful for posting safety bulletins. Four federal government agencies have joined to create the U. S. Consumer Gateway at *www.consumer.gov*, shown in Figure 8.14. Here, consumers can find information on product recalls, tips, warnings, and research. Visit this site and follow the link to Children.

What kinds of information did you find there? _____

_____

_____

Net Fun

The Internet Coupon Directory site lets you print coupons for brand name grocery items or link to manufacturers who offer coupons on their Web sites. Follow the ValuPage link to find coupons acceptable at a grocery within your Zip code. A typical week's coupons totaled $42.75 and covered Jell-O, Velveeta, Pepsi One, and Snackwell Crackers, among many other products.

Figure 8.14
The U.S. Consumer Gateway

Some online stores also have links to safety information. Figure 8.15 shows the Product Recall list from Toys "R" Us. Notice that this site has a link back to the Consumer Gateway.

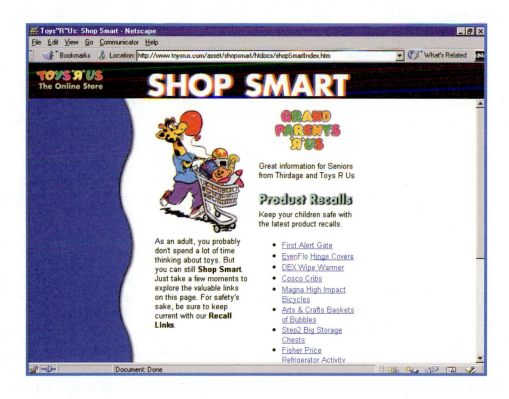

Figure 8.15
Product recall information at the Toys "R" Us site

How else could you find general information about product recalls? One way would be to do a general search for "product recall" with your search engine. Do this, and record below the names of three companies that have posted recalls of their products.

1. _____

2. _____

3. _____

Other than to comply with the legal requirements to post recall notices, why would a corporation use the Web for this purpose?_____

_____

_____

THINKING ABOUT TECHNOLOGY

Consumer Reports reminds visitors over and over again that they accept no advertising. Compare Net, on the other hand, puts their advertisers on the home page. What effect do you feel these strategies have on the attitudes of the consumers who visit these pages?

Net Ethics — The Better Business Bureau Online

When you visit company sites on the Internet, you may see the Better Business Bureau Online icon displayed. To find out about ethical standards on the Web, visit the BBBO and follow the link to Good Practices for Ethical E-Commerce. According to the BBBO, you can expect any company displaying the BBBO icon to follow these five principles:

- Provide an authentic company profile with complete information.
- Conduct business according to all applicable laws and provide details on company policies.
- Inform customers about links to other sites, but not link to questionable sites nor give improper information about other sites.
- Use a secure payment system.
- Respect customer privacy and security, and prominently disclose any access to adult-oriented material.

NET FACT

Sales Tax

A question sure to receive attention from state legislators and Congress is how to collect taxes on sales that are made online. In the early days of E-commerce, the White House suggested the states not place a tax burden on this emerging market. However, with the current and potential size of electronic sales transactions, states are worried about loss of tax revenue. Online stores follow the same rules that traditional mail order houses use, which allows them to collect tax from customers who live in those states where the company has a store. But these rules may not be adequate for E-commerce. Watch in the future to see if Congress passes legislation that will allow the states to establish new taxation policies. Do you think that some states will develop more favorable tax plans than others do in order to attract businesses?

NET VOCABULARY

Define the following terms:

1. *recall*
2. *lemon*

NET REVIEW

Give a short answer to the following questions:

1. *Why is online information security important, even when a sales transaction is not conducted?*

2. *Where would you look for a company's statement on user privacy?*

3. *What would you look for at a corporate site if you had a problem with the company's product?*

4. *What does the BizRate company do?*

5. *Why are state governments concerned about online sales made by a store in their state to a customer in another state?*

6. *If you were buying a large-screen television and needed to know how the features and prices of different models matched up, what kind of site would give you the information?*

THE BABY SHOWER

You are hosting a baby shower for friends who will make the world's most protective parents. The other guests know how concerned the parents will be, and so they want to make sure their presents are safe. They've asked you to check for ratings information and product safety bulletins for pacifiers, strollers, baby carriers, and educational toys. They'd also like you to recommend an online store for baby things. Using BBBO, BizRate, and any other online resources, determine what products in these four categories the other guests should avoid. Find three online stores that carry baby merchandise and that you would feel comfortable recommending.

NET PROJECT TEAMWORK   How Much a Minute?

Your team has been hired to recommend long-distance telephone services for your consulting client. Use the Internet to comparison-shop. Determine a customer profile (business? individual? family?) and the amount of usage (weekday? weekend? evening?). Be sure the carrier provides access to the Internet. Find the five best plans for your customer. Your customer has heard the phrase "routing calls over the Internet" and would like you to provide an explanation of it. Don't forget to investigate to see if there are any complaints about the phone companies or plans you recommend.

WRITING ABOUT TECHNOLOGY   Savvy Shopping

In this section, you've visited many online stores to see how they work, and you've learned some of the strategies buyers should follow when they shop online. In about 100 words, develop and explain *your* five principles for online purchasing.

Doing Business on the Web

In Sections 1-3, you learned about e-commerce from a consumer's perspective. In this section, you will begin to see e-commerce from the business's point of view. You will learn why and how companies use the Internet for business purposes.

Your work in this section will take you through the typical business marketing cycle. In Chapter 9, you will examine how your company can provide pre-sale service, accept orders electronically, deliver some goods electronically, and provide post-sale follow-up and customer service. You will see how a shipper can track packages electronically using the Internet. You will configure a customized personal computer through a Web page.

Businesses have found that e-mail based newsletters provide an inexpensive way to deliver their messages directly to the consumer. Chapter 10 includes a thorough discussion of digital advertising, including use of targeted advertising and banner ads. You will learn how an advertiser can achieve both richness and reach with Internet advertising. You will find out how to promote your Web site, including how to get it into the search engine listings.

If you're planning a visit to another country—or looking to open a business facility in another country—the Internet can help you learn the customs of that country. You can visit Web sites of global companies and access information originating in other countries. Chapter 11 covers the global perspectives of the Internet and electronic commerce. You can even look up jobs available in other countries.

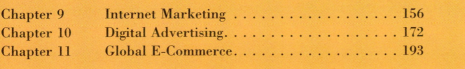

Chapter 9   Internet Marketing 156
Chapter 10   Digital Advertising. 172
Chapter 11   Global E-Commerce. 193

Internet Marketing

Chapter Objectives:

In this chapter, you will learn about ways that you can use the Internet to market your company's products. After reading Chapter 9, you will be able to

1 explain how your customers can find out about you and your products through Internet advertising.

2 discuss how to sell products through online catalogs and order systems.

3 describe how to track and deliver products using the Internet.

4 describe the kinds of post-sale services that you can give your customers electronically.

Net Terms

encryption

hit counter

embedded hyperlink

banner ad

MP3

FAQ (frequently asked questions)

PDF (portable document format)

NET TIP
Why Use the Net for Business?

For a good presentation of reasons to do e-commerce, see "The Original 20 Reasons to Put Your Business on the WWW," by Stormy Knight, at www.net101.com/reasons.html.

Marketing Through a New Medium

Companies have been marketing products to consumers through traditional media—TV, magazines, billboards, etc.—for decades. Marketing managers take advantage of the characteristics of each medium in implementing their marketing plan. Now marketers have a new medium with its own unique qualities: the Internet.

Marketing products to consumers is a four-phase process:
1. Providing pre-sale information
2. Taking the order
3. Delivering the product
4. Providing post-sale customer service

The Internet offers some unique advantages for marketers in each phase of the marketing process.

Pre-Sale

Let's say that you are the owner of a small company, and you would like to start using the Internet to grow your business. The first thing you must do to market to your customers is to advertise your products. On the Internet, your main advertising tool is a Web site with lots of product information. Because customers look for vendors with search tools like Yahoo or Lycos, make sure your Web site is located in the search tool catalogs. Another advertising possibility is to send e-mail messages to targeted customers with a Web link to your Web site. You can also place ads in other companies' Web sites, with links to your own site.

Taking the Order

Once the customers reach your Web site, they can browse through your online catalog to locate the product they want. You might want to catch their eye by featuring sale items on your home page. Once customers make their product selection, your Web site can take their order or direct them to your telephone number or to your retail store. Most electronic commerce sites encrypt or code personal information, such as a credit card number, for security.

Delivering the Goods

After customers place their orders, they can track the progress of their orders by visiting the customer service section of your Web site. If you sell products like software, maps, or research data, you could even deliver the product itself through the Internet.

Post-Sale

After your customers receive their products, they might want to learn more about the product or ask a question about its functions. To give your customers good service after the sale, you could place common questions and answers on your Web site. You could also provide directions at your site for returning or exchanging the product. To answer more technical questions, you could include a link to the manufacturer's Web site.

Gathering feedback from your customers is always important for helping you improve your products and marketing effort. To gather feedback, you could include a follow-up questionnaire on your Web site to find out about your customers' satisfaction with your company's product and service.

As you can see, the Internet offers some valuable marketing opportunities in all phases of the marketing process. Doing business online is less costly than handling customers at a retail store or through a catalog operation. It is also an inexpensive way to distribute your product information and gather information from and about your customers. With information you gather about customer interests, you can then use the Internet to target individuals with a unique message based on their interests. ■

NET TIP

Home Page

Access the E-Commerce: Business on the Internet *home page through the following URL:* e-commerce.swep.com. *Remember that a Web address may change at any time. An address given in this book as an example may no longer be valid. If so, either access the home page* (e-commerce.swep.com) *for the current link or do a search to find a similar site.*

ACTIVITY 9.1

Objective:
In this lesson, you will learn how your customers can find out about you and your products through Internet advertising.

Phase I: Pre-Sale

The Internet offers many opportunities for conveying your advertising message to your customers. You can set up an electronic showroom for your customers to browse. Your site can make it easy for customers to order product literature, comparison-shop, or "test drive" your product's features. You might even offer free sample products. Not only is the advertising cost per customer much less than with printed catalogs, but you can provide multimedia features in your online product displays.

You can also gather information about potential customers. A Web **hit counter** is an electronic device that keeps track of the number of customers that visit your site during a particular time period and provides limited identity information about them. You can learn what Web pages visitors have navigated and even what Web sites they came from when they arrived at your site. In fact, some advertising rates are based on the number of people that click on an ad to go to the advertiser's Web page.

By offering giveaways to entice customers to fill out a brief electronic survey, you can update your customer database and mailing list. Once the customers are in your database, it is easy to send periodic e-mail messages about special offers. Your message can refer customers to your storefront Web site with a built-in hyperlink. Unlike radio and television advertising, you can target messages to a particular consumer.

Let's take a look at some of the types of advertising you can use to let your customers know about your company and products. You will learn more about Internet advertising in Chapter 10.

1 A **banner ad** is a large, splashy advertisement that appears on a Web page and often has a hyperlink to the advertiser's own Web site. You can use a banner ad to target customers with a particular interest in your type of products. To see how this works, open Yahoo and search for "basketball" as the key word. What banner ad does Yahoo display at the top of the page of matches to basketball Web sites? _____

_____

Why do you think this advertiser chose to place a banner ad on this page? _____

_____

_____

How does this banner ad "target" customers who might have an interest in the advertiser's product? _____

_____

_____

NET TIP
Embedding Hyperlinks in E-Mail

*Does your e-mail program support embedded hyperlinks? An **embedded hyperlink** is a link between one object and another that, when clicked, opens your browser and loads the linked document or Web site. Some e-mail programs automatically create or "embed" a hyperlink when you type a URL. All your e-mail receiver needs to do is click on the embedded hyperlink to go to the linked site. This is a great way to encourage potential customers to visit your Web site. If your e-mail program doesn't give you this capability, you might consider switching to a program like Eudora, Outlook, or Netscape Messenger.*

2 Now search using the key words below. What product did the banner ad feature at the top of the list of search matches? What customer interest does each ad target?

Search Key Word	Advertised Product	Targeted Interest
1. Hawaii	_____	_____
2. Computer	_____	_____
3. Newspaper	_____	_____
4. Hepatitis	_____	_____
5. Indiana	_____	_____

3 Many companies use sweepstakes or giveaways to gather information about customers. Visit the OfficeMax Web site shown in Figure 9.1. If OfficeMax is no longer offering giveaways, go to the text's home page at *e-commerce.swep.com* for a link to a site that is offering them. Follow the links to the sweepstakes details.

How is the company gathering information about its customers through the sweepstakes?

_____

What kinds of information is it collecting that will help the company market to customers?

_____

What incentives is it offering to customers to provide this information?

_____

Web Site Sweepstakes and Giveaways

Figure 9.1
OfficeMax home page

4 Many Web sites keep information about customers in a small text file called a "cookie" located on the customer's own hard drive. As you learned in Chapter 6, a cookie allows the Web site to identify a previous visitor and quickly display information about that customer. Figure 9.2 shows the home page of CDnow. Notice that my name and links to my account appear at the upper left. When I registered at CDnow, I provided the requested information about myself, and the site stored the information in a cookie on my hard drive. Then when I returned to the site, the site retrieved this information from the cookie and used it to "personalize" their Web page for me.

Go to the CDnow Web site at *www.cdnow.com*, and read about "My CDnow." If you want, follow the instructions to create an account.

In what ways will CDnow "personalize" the Web site for you?

_____

What kinds of information about you do you think the company would store on the cookie to be able to personalize the site for you?

_____

How does personalizing benefit the company?

_____

Personal Information Retrieved from a Cookie

Figure 9.2
CDnow online store with personal information

THINKING ABOUT TECHNOLOGY

Are you likely to click an embedded hyperlink in a company's e-mail to visit its Web site and view its products? When would you consider an e-mail "junk" and not read it? What would you do in an e-mail to encourage customers to visit your company site?

Phase II: Taking the Order

Once your customers have made a selection, you must give them a painless way to order it. Some Web sites are designed to funnel customers to a salesperson at a retail store or on a toll-free telephone line. For complex products, this approach may work best, because customers are likely to have questions about such products. Even for simpler products for which online ordering is easy, you might want to provide an option for customers to talk to a salesperson. For people who are uneasy about providing credit card or other personal information online, talking to a live person might spell the difference between making and losing the sale.

Of course, customers have to pay for the goods. For ordering online, you can provide a secure Web site that scrambles credit card numbers so that others cannot read them. The closed lock in the toolbar of Figure 9.3 indicates a secure transaction; an open lock means a normal session. You must verify that the credit card number is authentic and your customer has sufficient credit limit to support the transaction. You'll learn more about electronic payment systems in Appendix C.

ACTIVITY

9.2

Objective:
In this lesson, you will learn how to sell products through online catalogs and order systems.

NET TIP
Encryption

*The process of scrambling credit card information for security purposes is called **encryption**. You'll find out more about encryption in Appendix C.*

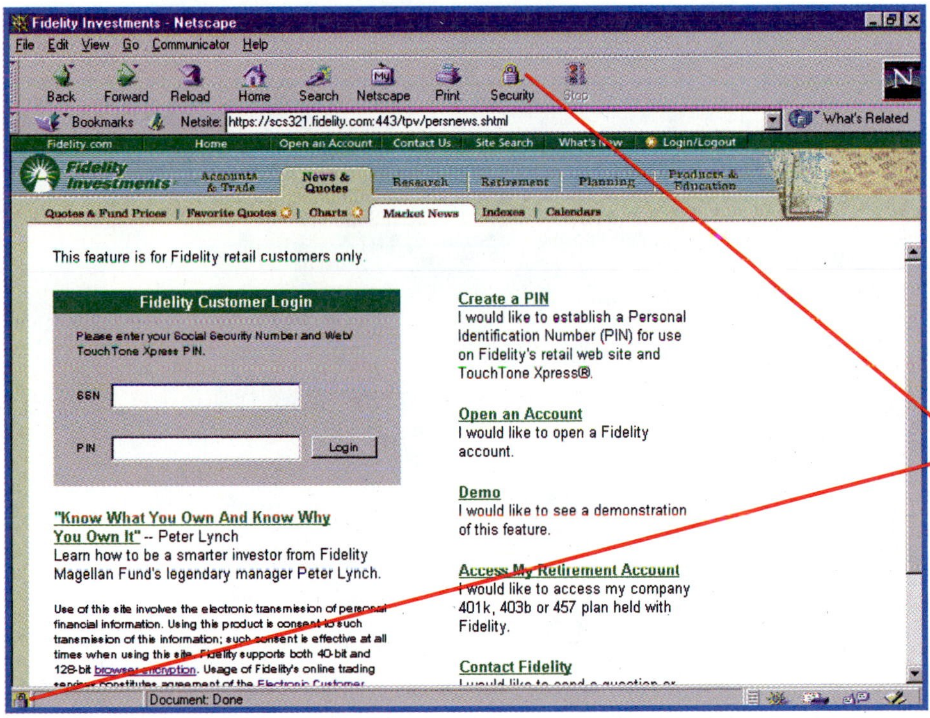

Icon Indicating a Secure Transaction

Figure 9.3
Secure transaction in Netscape browser

NET TIP
Secure Your Credit Card

Never enter your credit card information unless your browser displays the secure transaction indicator. Some browsers use a key to indicate security: a broken key means not secure, and an intact key means secure.

To make electronic ordering easy for your customers, your Web site can display a form on the screen. In Chapter 7, you saw an electronic shopping cart used at Amazon.com and other online stores. Customers use the electronic shopping cart to "hold" their orders until they are ready to check out, just like the shopping cart in a grocery store. A cookie keeps track of customers' selections as they shop. Then the selections appear on their order form when they are ready to check out.

The order form should also gather shipping information. Customers can specify the type of shipping and provide a shipping address and an e-mail address. Many companies send an e-mail message to confirm receipt of the order and to give an estimated shipping time. For out-of-stock products, another e-mail message can notify the customer when the product is ready to ship.

1 Connect your browser to the PC Connection Web site pictured in Figure 9.4. Search the catalog for "virus." Pick one antivirus product. What kinds of information does the catalog give for that product? What other information about that product would you like to see in the PC Connection online catalog? _____

_____

_____

View/Checkout Button

Figure 9.4
PC Connection home page

2 Add the antivirus product to your shopping cart. Select another kind of product and add it to your cart. Then click the View/Checkout button, as shown in Figure 9.4. Notice that the selections are conveniently listed and totaled. Now click Order (Secure). *Unless you want the* *products, don't fill out or submit the order form!* What kinds of information does the order form collect? How can this information help the business market to this customer again later?

_____

_____

3 Visit the CDnow Web site and look for an album by Garth Brooks or your favorite artist. What information does the CDnow online catalog provide for that album? What other information would you like to have as a consumer? _____

_____

_____

4 Go to the Gateway Web site at *www.gw2k.com.* Click the button for Solo portable computers. Then click the Customize It button on one of the models, and configure an affordable notebook computer for a college-bound student. Notice that the configuration sheet shows both the Web ordering link and the telephone number to speak to a salesperson. Would you prefer to purchase this product through the Internet or by a toll-free telephone number? Why?

_____

_____

THINKING ABOUT TECHNOLOGY

You have looked at several online catalogs in this activity. From what you have seen, what characteristics make an online product catalog effective? How would you improve upon the ones you've seen?

Net Fun

Did you know that you can buy and sell Beanie Babies on the Internet? There are many virtual auction sites out there, led by eBay. Need to complete your collection, or want to know how much it is worth? Then search the Web for the key word "eBay" to find an auction site.

ACTIVITY

9.3

Objective:
In this lesson, you will learn how to track and deliver products using the Internet.

Phase III: Delivering the Products

Most products and services cannot be delivered electronically over the Internet, so this marketing phase usually means tracking the progress of goods shipped by conventional means. But products like software can be delivered instantly over the Internet by downloading the files.

One of the most popular products delivered online is information, like custom newsletters, specialized news stories, personalized stock prices, legal cases, and the like. For information products, the Internet saves customers significant time, because they don't have to visit the library or wait until the information is printed and mailed. Refer back to Figure 9.3, which is a Web page from Fidelity Investments. Financial sites like this deliver information in the form of stock quotes, financial news, and educational materials about investing.

Some companies promote their products by delivering free samples over the Internet. For example, CDnow offers free sound bites of the music it sells, so you can "hear it before you buy it." Let's take a look at some of the products now being delivered electronically.

1. Suppose you are planning to do some hiking and need U.S. Geological Survey topographical maps. Visit the REI Web site at *www.rei.com.* Follow the links to the map download section, shown in Figure 9.5. What does the map viewer software cost? _____ How much does each map cost? _____ How long does it take to download the sample maps with a 28.8 modem? _____ What states are available at this time? _____

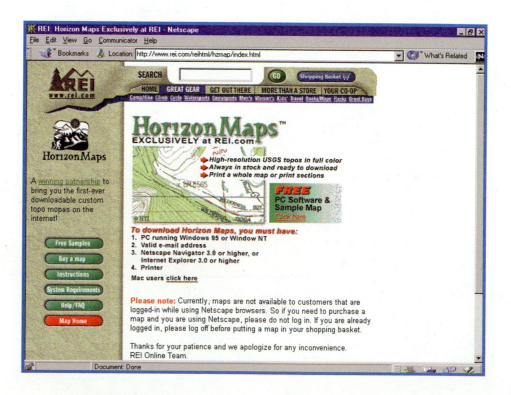

Figure 9.5
REI Horizon Maps

2 In Chapter 4, you learned about the kinds of information that some financial sites offer to subscribers. At some financial sites, you can get specialized financial research reports delivered online by becoming a member. Figure 9.6 shows online growth fund prices from Fidelity Investments. You can also subscribe to popular periodicals online. Visit Business Week Online to see how to order an online subscription. What does the subscription cost?_____

_____

_____

How would the online magazine differ from what is delivered to your physical mailbox? _____

_____

_____

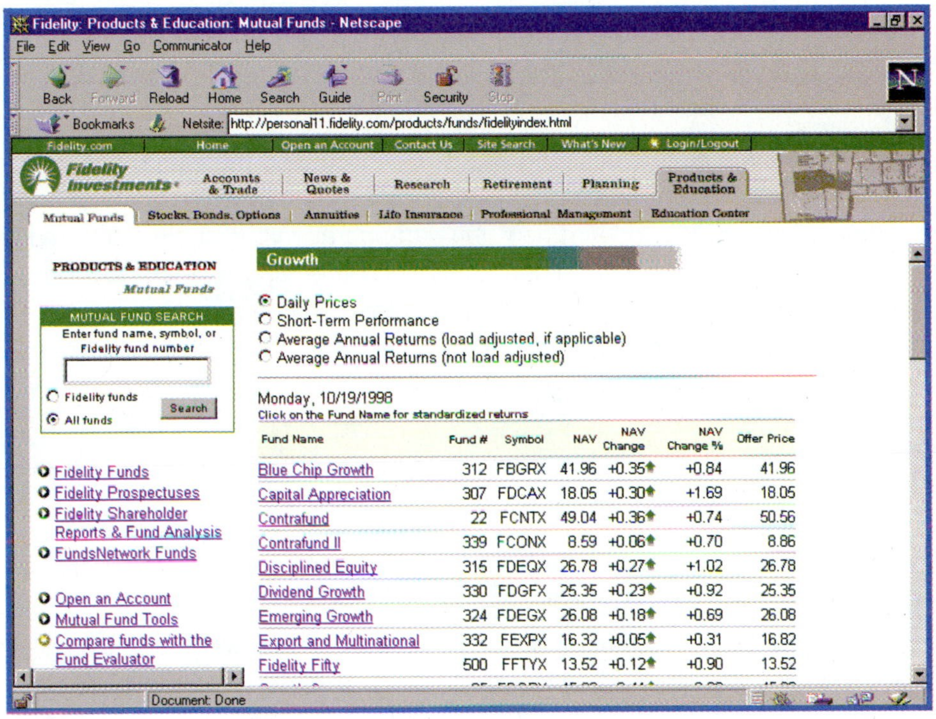

Figure 9.6
Fidelity Investments growth fund prices

3 Both UPS and FedEx have extensive online Web sites for providing customer services. The FedEx tracking page is shown in Figure 9.7. Visit the UPS site and locate the nearest drop-off point for your package. Use your home or school address. Why is it better for the customer to use the Web site than other ways of finding this information?_____

_____

List three other services for shippers at the UPS Web site. _____

_____

_____

Figure 9.7
FedEx tracking page

④ Suppose you have purchased a U.S. Robotics 33.6 modem and want to upgrade it to the 56K V.90 standard. Visit the 3COM Web site at *www.3com.com,* and learn how you can upgrade your modem by simply downloading a software patch. Would you rather upgrade your current modem by downloading a patch or buy a new modem that contains the 56K capability? Why?

_____

_____

_____

THINKING ABOUT TECHNOLOGY

Using a FedEx or UPS package tracking number, you can track a package's shipping details from pickup to delivery at the company's Web site. From the perspective of the shipping company, why would you want to have an online package tracking service? How does this online system benefit your company?

Net Fun

Some radio stations have placed their broadcasts on the Web. Sporting events are especially popular for fans. Visit the Broadcast.now site at *www.broadcast.com* and select a radio station to hear.

Phase IV: Post-Sale

Marketing doesn't end with the delivery of the products. After the sale, you need to provide customer service. E-mail and a friendly form on your Web site are easy tools for communicating with your customers. When customers order a book from Amazon.com, they receive, several weeks later, a friendly letter from the company president, thanking them for their order and suggesting other books by the same author or on a similar subject.

Often after customers receive their products, they have questions about product features or how to use the products. Rather than fielding all customer questions by phone, you could post an online FAQ list. A **FAQ** (frequently asked questions) list provides answers to common questions that customers ask. In many cases, your customers can find out what they want to know from the FAQs, and you don't have to pay the cost of having enough employees to handle every customer question personally.

Sometimes customers misplace their instruction manual or configuration guide. You can deliver a replacement to them as quickly as browsing the Web and printing it out. Not only is this less costly than working through a human customer service agent, but it is also quicker and certainly less trouble than faxing the missing documents.

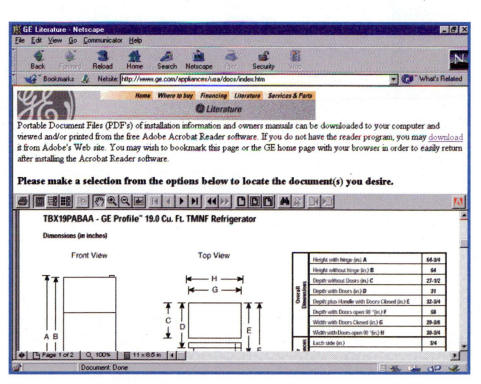

Figure 9.8
Refrigerator installation sheet in PDF

ACTIVITY

9.4

Objective:
In this lesson, you will learn about the kinds of post-sale service that you can give your customers electronically.

NET FACT

Portable Files
PDF (portable document format) is a file format generated by the Adobe Acrobat program that makes it possible to download and read the files on different computers. To read PDF files on any machine, users need the Acrobat Reader program. This program can be downloaded free from the Adobe Systems Web site at *www.adobe.com* or at many sites that feature PDF documents. Using PDF, companies can make even complicated technical drawings available for customers to download, view, and print out. For example, Figure 9.8 shows technical information about installing a refrigerator, delivered as a PDF file. PDF files can be very large so there could be delays in downloading them.

You can also use your online customer database for additional product surveys and questionnaires delivered via e-mail, often with a link to an easy-to-answer Web site form. Your customer database serves as an e-mailing list to send promotional messages, starting the marketing cycle again.

1 Maxtor is a manufacturer of popular hard drives for personal computers. Maxtor drives are frequently used to upgrade a computer to a larger hard drive, purchased after the original. Open the Maxtor Web site at *www.maxtor.com*. Switch to the Service & Support page shown in Figure 9.9. What kinds of support services are available at this Web site?

_____

_____

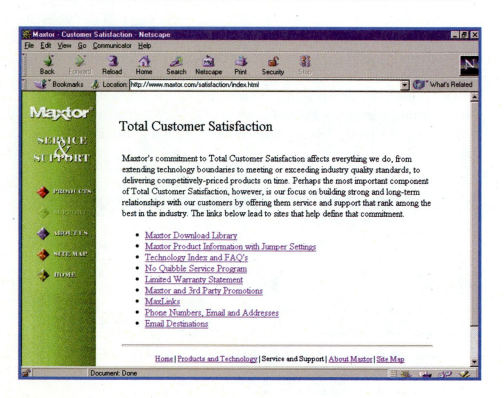

Figure 9.9
Maxtor Service & Support home page

2 Suppose you need to return your Maxtor drive for repair. What information must be included with the packing slip inside the box?

_____

_____

3 Assume you are selling a nontechnical product, like a compact disc or book, via e-commerce. Brainstorm with a friend about the sorts of post-sale customer service features you could add to a Web site or accomplish through electronic mail. _____

_____

_____

List three ways these post-sale efforts could be used as the pre-sale phase of someone's *next* purchase:

1. _____

2. _____

3. _____

4 List five ways that your school or business could do its business on the Internet.

1. _____

2. _____

3. _____

4. _____

5. _____

THINKING ABOUT TECHNOLOGY

Think of a situation in which a thoughtful customer service representative solved a problem for you after you bought a product, and convinced you to buy another product from that company. How can the Internet be used to provide good customer service?

Net Ethics   *Support Your Local Salesperson?*

Some customers use the Internet to locate products of interest, and then visit a local store to examine the products carefully and ask questions of the salesperson. Is it ethical for them to turn around and order the same product from a Web site, depriving the local store of its revenue for that item?

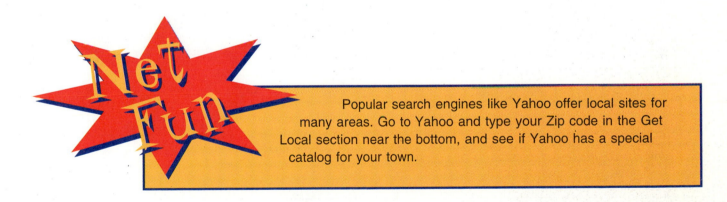

Popular search engines like Yahoo offer local sites for many areas. Go to Yahoo and type your Zip code in the Get Local section near the bottom, and see if Yahoo has a special catalog for your town.

NET VOCABULARY

Define the following terms:

1. *banner ad*

2. *embedded hyperlink*

3. *encryption*

4. *FAQ*

5. *hit counter*

6. *MP3*

7. *PDF*

NET REVIEW

Give a short answer to the following questions:

1. *What are some of the activities in the pre-sale marketing phase?*

2. *Give four reasons why a company would want to sell its products online.*

3. *Why would a company use an online sweepstakes giveaway through its Web site?*

4. *What types of products would be difficult to sell through the Internet? Why?*

5. *Why should you have an e-mail program that supports embedded hyperlinks?*

6. *How can companies use cookies to "personalize" their Web pages?*

7. *Why is PDF useful for distributing files through the Web?*

Net PRoject

THE FOUR PHASES OF MARKETING ONLINE

Go to the Dell Computers Web site and analyze the way Dell accomplishes the four phases of marketing. For each phase, record what the site shows or asks you to do. What are your reactions? Would you, as a customer, feel comfortable buying this way? If you were a Dell marketing manager, how would you improve the site to better market your products?

NET PROJECT TEAMWORK   Comparing E-Commerce Web Sites

Each member of your team should examine the home page of a different sort of online seller. You might include an apparel company (The Gap), a computer company (Gateway), a consumer products company (GE), a services company (Marriott), and a gourmet coffee company (Starbucks). Each group member should write down at least five features that the site uses to market to consumers. Also analyze how each feature contributes to the company's marketing efforts.

Compare your lists. Although these sites offer diverse products, what similar features do they have? How are they different? Why do you think these differences exist? Make a presentation that summarizes your findings.

WRITING ABOUT TECHNOLOGY   Invasion of Privacy?

How do you feel about cookies? Write a 100-word summary that a business could use to justify its use of cookies to a user who thought cookies were invasive.

PORTFOLIO PROJECT

Digital Advertising

Chapter Objectives:

In this chapter, you will see how digital advertising can be used for electronic commerce. After reading Chapter 10, you will be able to

1. subscribe to e-mail services and discuss how to use e-mail effectively for advertising your business.

2. describe types of banner advertising on the Web and discuss the benefits and drawbacks of each type.

3. discuss ways to promote your company Web site and get your site in a search engine's catalog

Net Terms

richness

reach

demographics

e-mail ads

mailing list service (LISTSERV)

HTML-enhanced e-mail

pixel

static ad

animated GIF ad

alt-text lines

cooperative ads

portal sites

dynamic ads

CPM (cost per thousand)

rotation ad

pop-up ads

web spider

Richness and Reach on the Internet

Advertising traditionally requires a tradeoff between richness and reach. **Richness** is the degree to which the ad content can be designed for a specific market segment. **Reach** refers to how many people view the ad. Television as a medium has great reach, in that many people view TV ads, but the ads are the same for everyone. A personalized letter or a sales call have great richness, in that the message can be tailored specifically to the needs of the person addressed, but it reaches only that person. In the past, advertising could have either richness or reach, but not both.

The Internet age brings a new way of communicating with potential customers. Most companies doing e-commerce advertise their products through targeted e-mail and banner ads that appear when customers search for certain keywords. Ads can have both richness and reach. Creating and placing these messages in banner ads and e-mail is a way to draw customers to the company's Web site.

Demographics are characteristics of human populations, such as age, gender, income, and ethnic background. Advertisers collect demographic information to help them target their ad messages to particular types of customers. For example, if your company sells baby clothes, your advertising would be most effective if you could send it to just parents with babies.

You can collect demographic information for your customer database through various methods, including surveys, sweepstake giveaways, product registrations, or even buying the information from other companies. Along with typical demographic information, like age and gender, you would probably also want to collect e-mail addresses and interests. Once you have captured your customers' information in your database, you can target your advertising message to particular customer groups. For example, if you run a sporting goods store, you can write an e-mail message promoting your camping equipment to all customers between the ages of 18 and 30 who like to camp. Your message will have richness, because it is specifically tailored to customers with an interest in what you are selling. It also has reach, because you can send an e-mail to many customers at once.

In this Chapter you will examine various types of advertising and learn ways to promote your company's Web site, so that it will appear in search engine lists of potential sites when someone searches.

Many companies generate interest in their Web sites by offering contests and sweepstakes. Check out PC Connection's site to see if they are still giving away a computer each day.

ACTIVITY
10.1

Objective:
In this activity, you will learn how to subscribe to e-mail services and use e-mail effectively for advertising your business.

E-mail Advertising

The most common type of Internet advertising uses electronic mail messages sent to individuals maintained in a database. **E-mail ads** are inexpensive, easy to send, and hard to ignore in the recipient's inbox. The ads describe the company's products and services, and usually include a link to the company's Web site.

You can add customer names to your company database in several ways:

- purchase the names from another company
- have customers add their names and information through online surveys when they visit your Web site
- pick up the names when customers make a purchase
- pick up the names when customers enter a sweepstakes

E-mail ads can be complete as sent or can contain an embedded hyperlink to a Web site with more information. In fact, most e-mail ads are linked to a Web server with much more information. Figure 10.1 shows an e-mail ad from Office Max, notifying customers of weekly specials and linking to the company Web site for full details. This ad also contains a special sale for first-time online buyers.

What type of customer do you think Office Max is targeting in this e-mail ad?_____

Embedded hyperlink to the company Web site

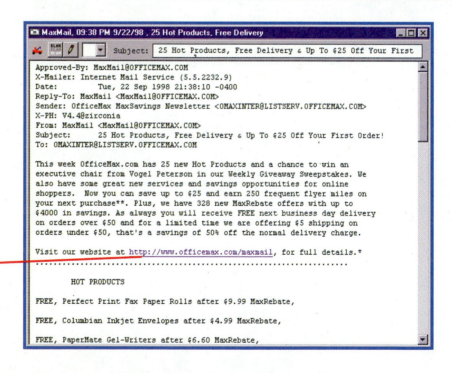

Figure 10.1
Office Max e-mail advertisement

Online Privacy Codes

Many online companies subscribe to a privacy code that states that they will not share customer information with any other organizations without the explicit permission of the customer. InfoBeat asks subscribers at the time of registration whether they will allow their names or e-mail addresses to be used outside InfoBeat. Customers can change that election at any time.

NET FACT

You can electronically group customer e-mail addresses in your database according to common demographic characteristics. For example, you could group together all customers who have purchased ski equipment from your sporting goods store or expressed interest in skiing in a survey. Then when you have a sale on ski accessories, you can send an e-mail to these customers, and not send it to other customers who have not shown an interest in skiing.

Another way to target specific customer groups with an e-mail ad is to advertise with an Internet mailing list service. A **mailing list service** is an automated e-mail system on the Internet, maintained by subject matter. Internet users subscribe to the service if they are interested in the service's subject, such as sports news, reports of snow conditions in the mountains, or any of thousands of subjects offered this way. New users generally subscribe by sending an e-mail with the word "subscribe" in it, and then automatically receive all e-mail reports sent to the list of subscribers. Such a service is often called a "LISTSERV" after the popular software used to maintain mailing lists. Such a service is also called a discussion group because participants can discuss issues online.

For your sporting goods store, a mailing list service identifies potential customers for you and gives you a way to reach them. People who have subscribed to receive reports about snow conditions in the mountains would likely be interested in your ski equipment. If you advertise with this mailing list, then your ski equipment ad will be placed on the e-mail reports that go to the list's subscribers. Again, you get the benefit of both richness and reach in your e-mail ad.

One popular mailing list service is InfoBeat. Its e-mail reports are free, and the ads pay for the cost of providing the service. InfoBeat delivers customized e-mail messages to over two million subscribers each day.

Some of the InfoBeat services work best with **HTML-enhanced e-mail** programs, which are capable of displaying messages with embedded HTML commands that link to Web pages. Eudora, Netscape's Messenger e-mail client, and Internet Explorer's Outlook Express support HTML mail. You will learn more about HTML in Chapters 12 and 13.

NET FACT

Unsubscribing

Because members of mailing lists might want to discontinue the service at some time, virtually every e-mail message to subscribers has a section at the end that explains how to remove your name from the mailing list. This is known as "unsubscribing" from the mailing list. In general, you can send an e-mail message to the mailing list processor to unsubscribe, or visit a Web site and discontinue your subscription by using a form there.

① Go to the InfoBeat Web site at *www.infobeat.com*, shown in Figure 10.2. Name three mailing list subjects available at this site, besides the snow report. What types of products might a retailer promote to each mailing list?

Mailing List Subject | Products to Promote to this List

1. _____ 1. _____

2. _____ 2. _____

3. _____ 3. _____

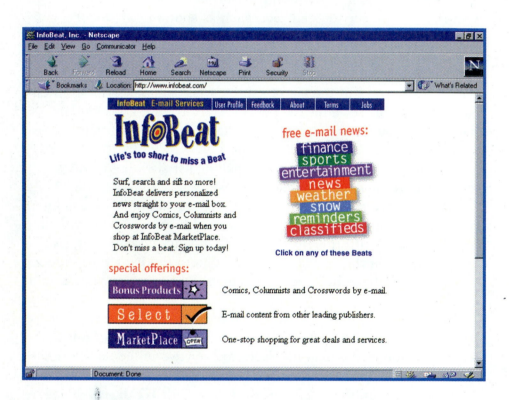

Figure 10.2
Main InfoBeat Web site

② From the InfoBeat home page, select the Entertainment service. Describe the entertainment services available at this section. What advertisers might be interested in using this section for promoting their products?_____

_____

_____

③ Subscribe to the TV Tonight Edition service at InfoBeat. You must have a valid e-mail address to subscribe. Notice the kinds of information the site is collecting about you in the subscription form, illustrated in Figure 10.3.

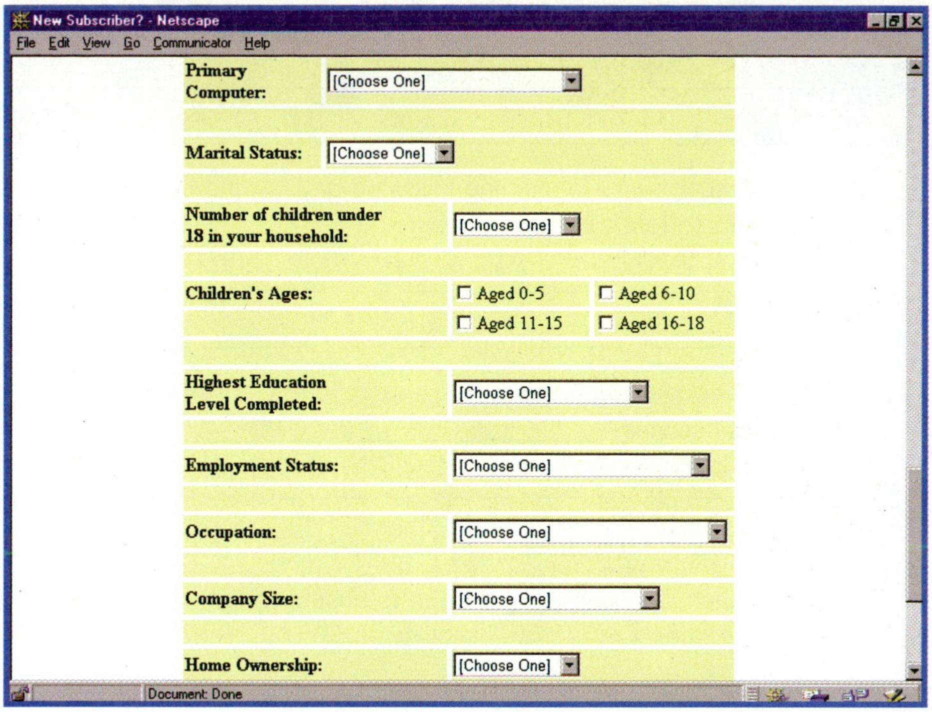

Figure 10.3
InfoBeat's form to collect customer information

How can advertisers benefit from having this information about potential customers? _____

_____

_____

Print a copy of an actual e-mail message from this service when it arrives in your e-mail inbox. Then follow the directions to unsubscribe if you no longer want to receive the messages.

What advertisement(s) appear in the message you received? _____

_____

_____

Do you think the ads at the bottom of the e-mail message are less effective than the ads at the top of the message? Why or why not?

_____

_____

Does your e-mail program support the embedded hyperlinks to the advertisers' sites? _____

4 At the InfoBeat home page, select the Sports service. Add your own e-mail address and follow the instructions to subscribe to the College Basketball report. Select the following conferences for the Daily Standings report:

Big Ten, ACC

What information is provided for each conference in this report? _____

_____

_____

When you receive your e-mail the following day, list the companies who advertise in InfoBeat's e-mail newsletter. _____

_____

_____

What types of companies would you expect to advertise in the InfoBeat sports e-mail service? _____

_____

_____

Follow the instructions in the message to unsubscribe.

THINKING ABOUT TECHNOLOGY

InfoBeat offers its mass e-mail services to corporations, as mentioned on its Web site. Why would a company want to use the services of a firm like InfoBeat? How could a college benefit from having regular e-mail messages go out to prospective students?

You can follow your favorite top college or pro team with InfoBeat. Go to *www.infobeat.com* and select Sports. Then choose your favorite team. Select box scores or game recaps. InfoBeat will send you an e-mail message after each game.

Banner Advertising

Banner ads appear on Web pages usually as a rectangular image. Most banner ads contain a link to the advertiser's Web site for the viewer to click. Unlike print advertising, banner ads can not only grab the customers' attention, but also in seconds they can supply customers with detailed information about the ad's contents—right on their own computers!

Objective:
In this activity, you will examine different types of banner advertising on the Web and learn the benefits and drawbacks of each type.

1 Go to the CNN Interactive Web site at *www.cnn.com*. What banner ads appear on this home page? Don't forget to scroll down to the bottom.

Static ads are advertisements that always appear in a given location on the Web page, similar to an ad in a magazine or newspaper. These ads appear regardless of the key words used to arrive at the site. Advertisers pay rates based on the number of hits on the Web page containing the ad, with a bonus if the viewer clicks on the ad. Check out the URL of a hyperlink in a Web ad, and you will usually see extra codes at the end that tell the advertiser where the user came from and/or where to search. The advertiser can use this information to make decisions about future advertising placement. Ad rates for some ads are based on how many hits came from a specific location. Figure 10.4 shows a banner ad at the Lycos site. When the pointer is over the banner ad, as in the illustration, the hyperlink shows in the status bar. Notice the extra information at the end of the URL.

URL of ad hyperlink, with code showing how viewer arrived.

Figure 10.4
Hyperlink for banner ad

Some banner ads are animated, drawing your eye and increasing the likelihood that you will click on the ad to find more information. These **animated GIF** (graphic interchange format) **ads** are often much larger and take longer to load than do nonanimated ads. Although not depicted in the restricted environment of the printed page, the ad in Figure 10.4 is animated on the Web, flipping between two different messages.

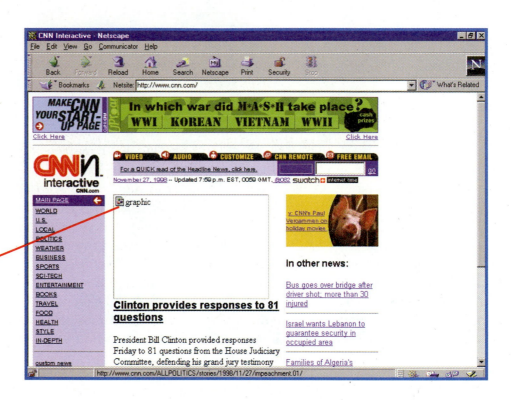

Alt-text line

Figure 10.5
CNN site with alt-text line in image location

NET FACT

Pixels and Ad Rates

Banner ads are sold by size, measured in pixels. A **pixel** (PIX [picture] ELement) is the smallest element on a video display screen. A screen is broken up into thousands of tiny dots, and a pixel is one or more dots that operate as a unit. The most popular ad size is full-banner, which is 468 pixels wide X 60 pixels high, or about 6 inches wide and 1 inch high. Other common sizes are 392 pixels X 72 pixels (5 inches X 1.2 inches), 234 pixels X 60 pixels (3 inches X 1 inch), 125 pixels X 125 pixels (1.6 inches X 2.1 inches), and 120 pixels X 240 pixels (1.5 inches X 4 inches). Because of the geometry of a computer monitor, pixels do not measure the same way horizontally and vertically. Roughly, 78 pixels equal 1 inch horizontally and 60 pixels equal 1 inch vertically.

CASIE (Coalition for Advertising Supported Information and Entertainment) is an advertising industry organization that established standards for Web ad size and for measuring the viewing audience for online ads.

Companies choose to advertise on Web sites that draw the types of people who would most likely be interested in their products. A computer hardware company's Web site might contain ads by software firms that produce products that run on those computers. In some cases, companies have reciprocal agreements that allow each to put advertisements on the other's Web site. These **cooperative ads** are pairs of ads placed in complementary sites. Viewers at one site would likely be interested in products at the other site. For example, the PC Connection home page highlights Compaq computers. When you get to the Compaq Web site, you will find PC Connection listed first among the online sellers.

Search engine sites are often called **portal sites**, because they are natural starting points for users. A portal site contains links to other sites, acting as a doorway or portal. Because popular sites like Yahoo and Netscape Netcenter are in the top three sites for Web activity, they are popular among advertisers who want to capture more viewers.

In the last chapter, you saw how entering subject keywords in a search engine brings up an advertisement related to that subject at the top of the search results. These ads are called **dynamic ads**, because they only appear when users select a particular subject. Advertisers prefer dynamic advertising, because they know the viewer is already interested in topics that pertain to their products.

2 Go to the Excite Web site and look up information about advertising at this site. The online media kit is found at *http://corp.excite.com/MediaKit,* shown in Figure 10.6.

NET TIP
Alt-Text Lines

*One way to improve the effectiveness of your advertising message is to use alt-text lines with the ad. **Alt-text lines** are short text phrases that appear in an image's location while the image is downloading. Larger images take longer to download, particularly when using a phone line connection to the Internet. The alt-text lines are replaced by the image when it has finished loading. But for Internet users who have a text-only browser, the alt-text lines are the only way to display information about a graphic image. Figure 10.5 shows alt-text lines in the CNN site just before the large graphic image in the center loaded.*

Figure 10.6
Figure 10.6 Excite media kit page

What is the basic rate for general rotation ads? _____

How much do keywords cost? _____

What is a keyword package, and why would an advertiser want a package of keywords? _____

_____

_____

What other Web sites appear in the Excite network? _____

What is the market coverage of the Excite network? _____

_____

Advertising rates are usually based on **CPM**, or cost per thousand impressions. On the Web, the number of "impressions" is the number of hits, or times the page has been accessed. CASIE recommends that a third party, rather than the site owner, measure the number of hits a Web site receives. Media Metrix is one of the leading companies that measure Internet audience. Nielsen Media Research, which has been rating television programs for many years, has also begun to track online users.

The more targeted the audience, the more expensive the ad rates. To minimize the cost of advertising, two or three companies might share a rotation ad on a given Web page. A **rotation ad** is a banner ad that rotates between advertisers. Each time the page comes up, the advertiser changes. Usually the sponsors of the rotation ads are all named at the bottom of the Web page.

One popular search engine site charges $24 CPM for general rotation ads that appear at the top of pages on the site. Advertisers can reserve keywords for a certain period of time at a rate of $70-85 CPM. A reserved keyword means that whenever the viewer searches for that keyword, one advertiser's ad appears. Advertisers receive daily reports about hits on their ad site.

Each Web site has its own advertising rates. As a potential advertiser, you can negotiate with the provider for favorable rates.

Figure 10.7 shows the Lycos Business Guide site. See if you can identify the four dynamic ads on this page. Each is related to the content on the page. Because dynamic ads can target potential customers with relevant interests, they sell at a premium rate. Advertisers may compete for a prime spot in a popular Web site like Yahoo or ESPN's Sportszone.

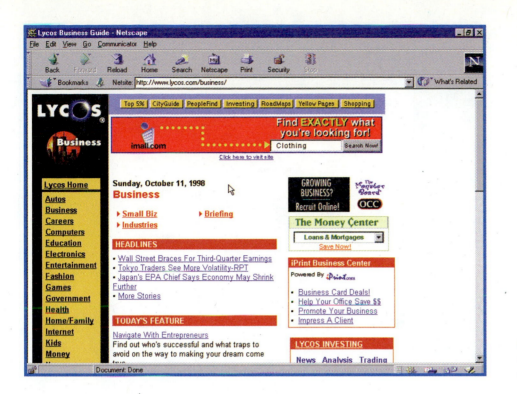

Figure 10.7
Lycos Business Guide
dynamic ads

③ Go to the Business section at the Lycos site shown in Figure 10.7. Examine the current ads there.

What companies are represented in the ads? _____

_____

How do these companies relate to the Lycos Business Guide? _____

_____

Now go elsewhere and then return to the Lycos Business Guide. Have the advertisements changed? If so, why? _____

_____

ZDNet has introduced a new kind of advertising called a "sponsored link" at the bottom of some of its pages. These hyperlink ads are text-only and less expensive than banner ads with images. Figure 10.8 shows some of the sponsored links on the ZDNet Web site.

Net Ethics   Net Privacy

Some companies have a checkbox to let customers choose whether they want their names shared with other companies. Others, like Office Max, use a pledge of privacy for all information gathered about a customer at a Web site. For an example of a privacy pledge, go to the Office Max site at *www.officemax.com*, and follow the links through Customer Service to Privacy Policy. What is the responsibility of a company to protect customers' identities, once they get into the company's database?

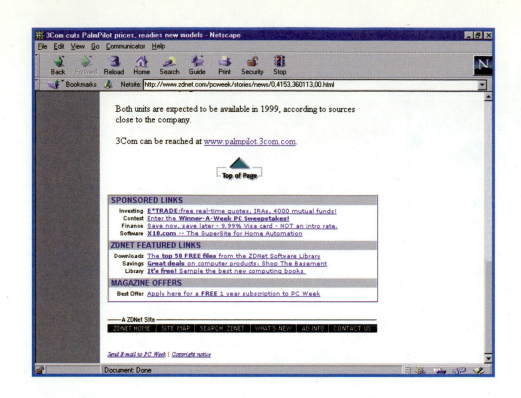

Figure 10.8
ZDNet sponsored link ads

④ Go to the following portal sites and search for the same keyword, camping. Use Lycos, Yahoo, Metacrawler, Hotbot, and Infoseek.

What large banner ads appear at the top of the search results from each search engine?

Lycos banner ad: _____

Yahoo banner ad: _____

Metacrawler banner ad: _____

Hotbot banner ad: _____

Infoseek banner ad: _____

Which do you think is the most effective? Why? _____

_____

Are the ads that are not located at the top of the listing as effective? Why or why not? _____

_____

⑤ **Pop-up ads** are ads that appear in a different browser window on top of the base Web page, which remains open in the background. A pop-up ad can grab a viewer's attention more than a normal banner ad within a Web page, and therefore earns a premium advertising rate. To remove the ad from view, users must close the extra window by clicking the Close button, probably causing the ad to remain in users' minds longer

than other types of ads. Figure 10.9 shows the pop-up ad for
Netscape's new browser found at *www.netscape.com*. Go to the
Netscape site and see if a pop-up ad is still there. It may take a few
seconds for the ad to appear. Netscape rotates the contents of this
ad, so when you open the page something else might appear.

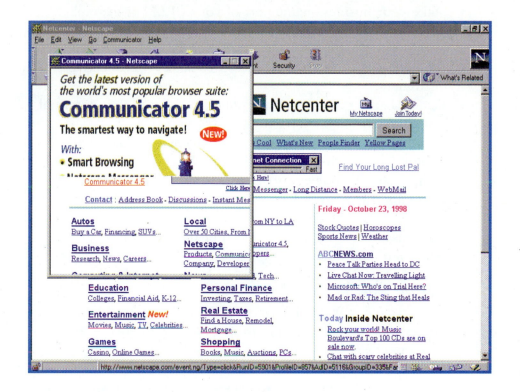

Figure 10.9
Netscape pop-up
ad in separate window

THINKING ABOUT TECHNOLOGY

How do you think companies select locations for their print advertising?
Should the process be any different for digital ads placed on the Internet? Why or why not?

ACTIVITY
10.3

Objective:
In this activity, you will learn how to promote your company Web site and get your site in a search engine's catalog.

Promoting Your Site

You need to deliver your message to potential customers. Most companies doing e-commerce try to lure buyers to a Web site. So, how do you get that URL out to the world? Consider the following:

- Make your business name part of your URL. For example, *cnn.com*, *www.unitedway.org*, and see *www.washingtonpost.com.*
- Include your URL in e-mail messages sent to prospective customers.
- Place a banner ad on another popular Web site that potential customers are likely to visit.
- Submit your URL to the major search engines, like Yahoo, Excite, Lycos, InfoSeek, and Hotbot. When customers search using keywords relevant to your business, your site should come up in the list of Web sites that match their search criteria.
- Advertise your Web address in other media, such as print, television, and radio.
- Include your Web address on your business cards, stationery, and other documents.
- Advertise your Web address on billboards, trucks, and other places visible to potential customers.
- Use a paid service to promote your Web site.
- Hire an advertising agency to promote your site.
- Do nothing and hope that the search engines' web spiders will find your site and catalog it. A **web spider** is a robotic search tool that is constantly examining sites around the Web and adding them to a search engine's catalog or index.

It is particularly important to make sure that your Web site contains appropriate keywords that web spiders can pick up. Select good descriptive words that will be programmed into the home page file by a Web developer. Make sure the title of your site is a good description of the site. The site title appears in the title bar of the browser when customers visit your site and is frequently listed in the search engine search results. A Web developer can place the title text into your site's home page file. We will discuss creating a home page later in this book.

Web Developer

A Web developer creates the computer files necessary to maintain a Web site. Most advertising firms now offer Web development services to their clients. In fact, some print advertising materials can be converted for use in Web pages. Although the Web developer must have some programming skills, many also have artistic talent, an abundant skill at an advertising agency. Chapters 12 and 13 will focus on the details of developing Web pages.

1 To get an idea of the kinds of titles used in Web sites, visit the following sites and write down the title from the title bar of your browser. Is each one a good description of the site?

www.ge.com _____

www.nytimes.com _____

www.real.com _____

www.nike.com _____

www.intel.com _____

2 Suppose you are building a Web site for your retail sporting goods store. Use a search engine to find the Web sites of three sporting goods stores.

How did you find the sites? _____

What keywords would you submit to a search engine to make your store's site easy to find? _____

_____

3 Refer to the USA Today Web site (www.usatoday.com) shown in Figure 10.10. In your opinion, are the banner ads in the Marketplace section effective? Which ones are most interesting to you, and why? _____

_____

Open the current USA Today page and compare those ads to the ones in Figure 10.10.

Figure 10.10
USA Today Marketplace banner ads

4 Visit the Northwest GIF Shop shown in Figure 10.11, a repository for free animated GIF files, at *http://www.nwgifshop.com/*. Also search Yahoo using the keywords "animated GIF" to find other GIF sites. List the names of three animated GIFs that would enhance the Web site for your sporting goods store. How would you use each one?

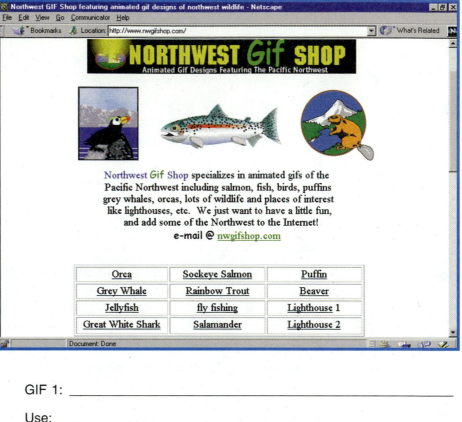

Figure 10.11
Web site for free GIF files

GIF 1: _____

Use: _____

GIF 2: _____

Use: _____

GIF 3: _____

Use: _____

Why would you want to use animated GIFs in your business Web site?

_____

_____

What are some possible disadvantages of using animated GIFs? _____

_____

5 Visit the Lycos page and click on the "Add Your Site to Lycos" link at the bottom of the page.

How can you tell if a site is already in Lycos?_____

_____

How long does it take to get your site listed in Lycos? _____

_____

What is the cost to list your page in Lycos? _____

_____

How long does it take for an inactive (missing) site to be removed from
the Lycos catalog? _____

_____

⑥ Submit-It is a paid service that promotes Web sites. It will send your
Web site's URL to over 400 search engines and other online indexes for
one fee, increasing the likelihood that someone will come across your
site when searching. Open the Submit-It site at *www.submit-it.com*,
shown in Figure 10.12.

Figure 10.12
Submit-It Web site

How could Submit-It help you promote your sporting goods store? _____

_____

What is the cost for this service to announce one or two URLs? _____

_____

How long does it take to get your Web site into the search engine databases? _____

Companies can hire advertising agencies to promote their company Web sites. Why do you think this might be a good idea for a company just getting into electronic commerce? Can an agency offer advantages, even though a large array of tools for "do-it-yourself" Web publishing is available to companies?

Net Business   *Aureate Media*

Aureate Media (www.aureate.com) is a Web development company that specializes in placing targeted advertising into Internet-based software applications. The firm gathers important demographic data from users and offers highly qualified buyers to the advertiser. Aureate differs from normal advertising companies because the ads are placed in software programs, not on other Web sites. When the user runs the program for the first time, he or she is asked to provide demographic information like gender, age, location, and so forth. That information is stored and can be provided to the advertiser.

When the user clicks an ad in the application, a browser opens and the user will see the advertiser's Web site. The software developer receives ongoing cash flow from advertisers every time a user runs the program. Users get to use a "free" program, provided they view the ads. The content of the ads can be changed to match the advertiser's needs.

Do you like Italian food? Check out Mama's Cucina Web site at *www.eat.com* where you can find recipes and coupons for good dishes. This site is sponsored by Ragu, and you can subscribe to an e-mail newsletter there.

NET VOCABULARY

Define the following terms:

1. alt-text lines
2. animated GIF ad
3. cooperative ads
4. CPM (cost per thousand)
5. demographics
6. dynamic ads

7. e-mail ads
8. HTML-enhanced e-mail
9. mailing list service (LISTSERV)
10. pixel
11. pop-up ads

12. portal sites
13. reach
14. richness (advertising)
15. rotation ad
16. static ad
17. web spider

NET REVIEW

Give a short answer to the following questions:

1. How do the names and e-mail addresses for customers get into a company's database?

2. Why are portal sites popular places for advertising?

3. Why do advertisers have to pay more for keyword or dynamic advertising?

4. In the advertising business, what is CPM?

5. What does a web spider do for a search engine site?

6. Why is it important to select appropriate keywords and titles for your Web pages?

CONCERT TICKETS

Suppose you are in the business of selling tickets to popular band concerts. Give your company a name. What keywords you would use to describe your Web site? Where would you put these keywords on your site? Why?

Think of ways to promote your Web site. What companies would you consider approaching to share cooperative ads? What major Web sites would you consider for placing your ads? Why? What are some other good ways to promote your kind of business? Explain why you chose these particular ways.

NET PROJECT TEAMWORK: Preparing Web Ads

Assign each team member a type of online advertising for promoting your team's concert ticket business. Each person should write an advertisement for the business, designed to work well for the assigned ad type. Be creative! Find ways to capture your customers' attention and lure them to your site. Use the unique features of the Internet to help you promote your product.

The team should then prepare a presentation of your company's ads for the class. Your presentation should explain why each ad was designed as it was. How does each ad contribute to promoting your business? How does each ad use the capabilities of the Web to advantage?

After all teams present their advertisements, discuss the features that seemed to work best.

WRITING ABOUT TECHNOLOGY: Creative Minds

How would you go about creating an online advertisement for a company that sells sporting goods? What kinds of information do you want to put into the advertisement? How is it different from a print ad for the same firm? How is it different from an online ad for concert tickets?

Global E-Commerce

Chapter Objectives:

In this chapter, you will learn how companies can use the Internet to do business around the world After reading Chapter 11, you will be able to

1 discuss how companies use the Internet to do business virtually anywhere in the world.

2 explain how the Internet can get customers and sellers together, even though they are not in the same place at the same time.

3 find international business information on the Internet.

4 describe how a company can take advantage of its own "private Internet" to manage business around the world.

Net Terms

multinational corporation

packets

mirror site

image map

Internet

intranet

extranet

authentication

Doing Business Anywhere, Anytime

Today, business is a global activity. **Multinational corporations** have branches, plants, and business partners all over the world. They may gather raw materials in one country, transform them in another, assemble them into finished goods in yet another country, and sell their finished products virtually everywhere. And although English is the dominant language in North America, the United Kingdom, and a few other countries, most multinational firms must be able to conduct business in many languages. As you will see in the activities in this chapter, larger firms offer versions of their Web sites in several languages, available by clicking a link. Some search engine sites have international versions that highlight sites in that particular country, often in the country's language.

The Internet lowers geographic barriers by supporting low-cost communications between suppliers, employees, business partners, and customers. You are likely to see television commercials that tout a tiny eastern European company's presence on the Internet. Through the Internet, it can sell products in the U.S. as easily as larger firms can.

In fact, the Internet permits business partners to exchange information through e-mail and Web sites without ever meeting face to face. For instance, as an author, I have never met (face-to-face) with any of the editorial or production staff associated with this book. Virtually all our communications have taken place through e-mail, with attachments for document files.

If you were an international business person, you could access critical information about other countries through the Internet. You could learn about the culture and business practices of a particular region along with demographic statistics, transportation capabilities, industrial resources, and so forth. You could begin to develop business relationships before you ever set foot in the country.

Net Fun

Visit the portal site *www.rahul.net/lai/companion.html* for all sorts of language translation information available on the Web. Just for fun, find a site that can help you translate English into Thai.

Lowering Geographic Barriers

ACTIVITY
11.1

Objective:
In this activity, you will see how companies use the Internet to do business virtually anywhere in the world.

In the past, a company operated by creating products, facilities to manufacture the products, a distribution system to deliver the products, stores to display the goods, and a sales force to promote the products. In most cases, the company's customers were primarily from the same geographic region.

But the Internet is reducing the need for some of these traditional business activities. If your company has an e-commerce site on the Web, customers can find you for free from just about anywhere. You don't have to have a retail store or salespeople to call on customers. You don't even have to accept sales orders in person any longer. Without these large expenses, small companies can compete with large corporations on the Internet.

The Internet is truly global–there are Internet connections and Web sites on seven continents. Table 11.1 shows country code domain names for a few countries that populate the Web. For instance, a URL ending in .DE refers to a site in Germany (Deutschland).

NET TIP

Finding A Country

Currently, there are more than 240 country code domain names, and the number is growing all the time. The Internet Assigned Numbers Authority (IANA) Web site contains complete details about country codes.

Table 11.1
Country Code Domain Names

Country	Domain Name
Australia	AU
Brazil	BR
Canada	CA
France	FR
Germany	DE
Hong Kong	HK
Israel	IL
Japan	JP
Korea (Republic)	KR
Russian Federation	RU
Spain	ES
United Kingdom	UK
Zimbabwe	ZW

Speed of Light

Data travel across the Internet at nearly the speed of light. Web pages, like most data that flow through the Internet, are broken up into segments and transmitted in blocks of data called **packets.** The packets are then reassembled at the receiver's end into the complete Web page.
The data packets often are delayed in handling as they pass across different networks. It will take noticeably longer for a Web page to download to your computer if it is coming from another continent. Some companies set up a mirror site in another country, so that users in that country can download its Web pages more quickly from a closer location. A **mirror site** is a Web site that contains a duplicate of the master site's contents.

Figure 11.1
Canon worldwide network home page

A URL that ends in *.com* refers to a commercial company or business. While most of these firms are in the United States or Canada, many are located elsewhere in the world. Although the domain name does not necessarily have the country code at the end, in many cases it does, and the next-to-last word is often *co*, short for "company." For instance, *www.thomson-directories.co.uk* is the URL for Thomson Directories Ltd., a company in the United Kingdom.

Figure 11.1 shows the home page the for Canon Web site. The large graphic images in the center are all animated GIF files, displaying different scenes. This site links to several Canon worldwide network locations and even has a link to a Japanese version in the text at the bottom of the page.

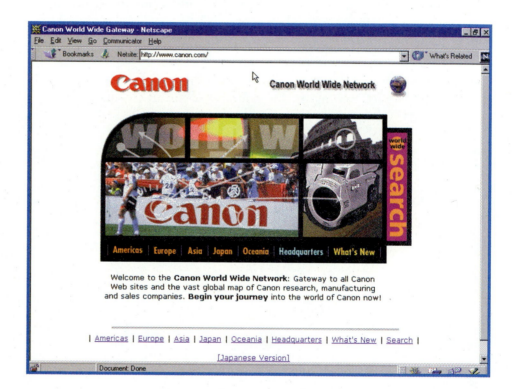

A company can translate the text on its Web site into a different language for users in other countries. The Netscape Web browser is available in 13 foreign languages. The English version can display many foreign characters.

1 Bring up the Canon Web site. Move your mouse pointer to the various text links at the bottom of the home page. As you linger on each one, note its actual URL in the status bar at the bottom of your screen. What country code appears for most of these links? That code means that the page is being sent to your browser from that country.

2 At the Canon site, select the Americas link.

What countries are available through this link? _____

_____

What countries are available through the Europe link? _____

Go to two of the Americas links. What main difference do you see?

_____

_____

Why do you think that Canon has so many different Web sites?

_____

_____

3 Suppose you are planning a trip to London and want to find housing. Open the Lycos home page and click the link to go it's U.K. site. From the URL, you can see that this page is being fed by a Web server located in the United Kingdom. Select UK and Ireland Sites in the Search box and search for the keyword "hotel," as shown in Figure 11.2.

What effect does this "Search in" setting have on your search? _____

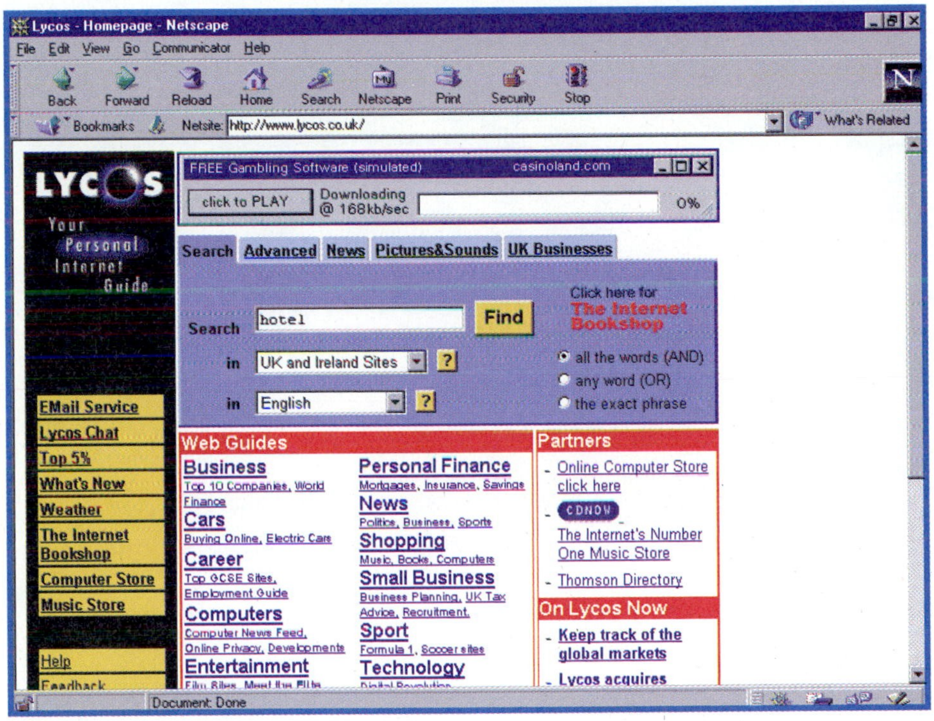

Figure 11.2
Lycos U.K. home page

_____

_____

Why would hotel owners want to have their Web sites in the Lycos U.K. version? _____

_____

Do the hotel owners anticipate that people who live outside the U.K. will

use the U.K. version of Lycos?
Why?_____

_____

4 Search for the Caterpillar home page and click the Global button, as
shown in Figure 11.3. Answer the following questions about Cat's global
businesses.

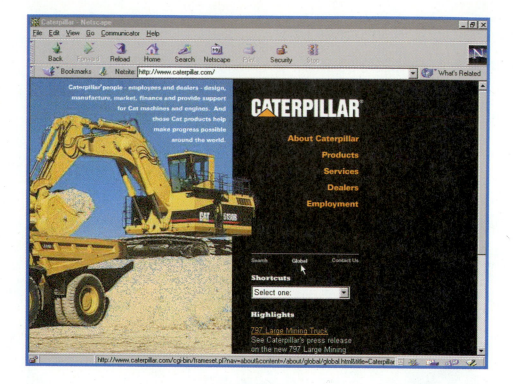

Figure 11.3
Caterpillar home page

What are Caterpillar's businesses? _____

_____

What proportion of Caterpillar's annual sales are outside the U.S.?

_____

How many dealers does Caterpillar have?_____ How many countries
does Cat serve?_____

What Cat facility is in Grimbergen, Belgium?_____

How does this Web site help Caterpillar sell tractors in Europe?

_____

THINKING ABOUT TECHNOLOGY

How would a multinational company like Caterpillar use the Internet to do
global e-commerce? For instance, comment on the navigation bar at the
top of the Caterpillar global page.

Asynchronous Business Activities

ACTIVITY 11.2

Objective:
In this activity, you will see how the Internet can get customers and sellers together, even though they are not in the same place at the same time.

Traditionally, a business transaction could occur only if the business and customer were in the same place at the same time. You would walk into a store, pick up the item you wanted, and pay at the cash register. You and the business were "synchronized" in time and place. To do business, the company facility would have to be near customers and open when the customers wanted to buy. If the company wanted to sell to a larger area, it would need multiple facilities.

Mail-order companies have taken advantage of the telephone to get around the problem of time and place to some extent. Still, customer service people must be available to take orders. Also, the companies have to get their catalogs into the hands of the customers, which is costly. Updated catalogs mean repeat mailings. Some companies mail catalogs 20 times a year.

On the Internet, business activities can be asynchronous—not synchronized in time and place. Internet companies can accept orders whenever customers want to place them, and online catalogs are always up-to-date. Customers and sellers can transact business at different times and in different locations. An airline customer can check flight schedules and make reservations online at any time, not just when the airline reservations center is able to answer the phone call from that customer.

The steps in this activity demonstrate the benefits of being able to do business almost anywhere at any time.

1. Open the Southwest Airlines Web site pictured in Figure 11.4. Notice the link above the main image that is used to add customers to the fare update mailing list. If you add your name to the list, sales and special promotion information will be sent to you via e-mail.

   Why would someone want to subscribe to this service? _____

   _____

   _____

   Using the Southwest Flight Schedule section, find at least two flights between Indianapolis and St. Louis on a date at least three weeks in the future.

Flight No.	Departs	Arrives	Cost
_____	_____	_____	_____
_____	_____	_____	_____

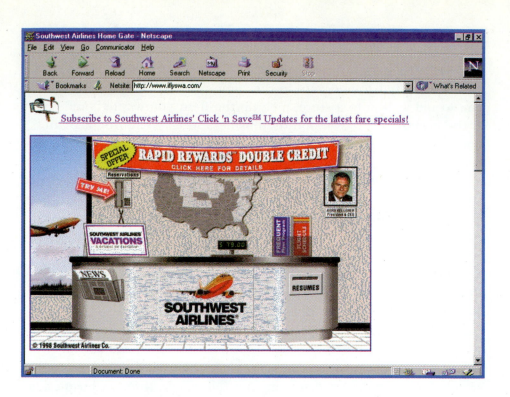

Figure 11.4
Southwest Airlines home page

2 Open an international airline Web site, such as Japan Airlines pictured in Figure 11.5. Write down information about a flight between a city in the United States and one in the country of that airline.

From	To	Flight No.	Departs	Arrives	Cost
_____	_____	_____	_____	_____	_____

How can an airline's Web site be helpful in making international business travel plans? _____

_____

Why should JAL provide an English language version of its Web site on the Internet? _____

_____

NET FACT

Image Map Links

The main graphic in Figure 11.4 is called an **image map.** It is a picture that is separated into sections. Each section contains a link that, when clicked, will take users to different Web locations. Watch the browser's status bar as you move the cursor over various parts of the Southwest Airlines image map. The numbers you see changing in the URL are actually (x,y) coordinates, like on a graph. When you click a section of an image map, the link associated with that (x,y) coordinate opens another Web page in your browser.

Figure 11.5
Japan Airlines English language
Web site

3 Find the Thomas Cook Web site from London, England. Select the currency converter, as shown in Figure 11.6. Use the currency converter in this Web site to convert $500US into the following currencies. Write down the amount for each currency.

British Pounds _____

French Francs _____

Japanese Yen _____

Australian Dollars _____

Malaysian Ringitts _____

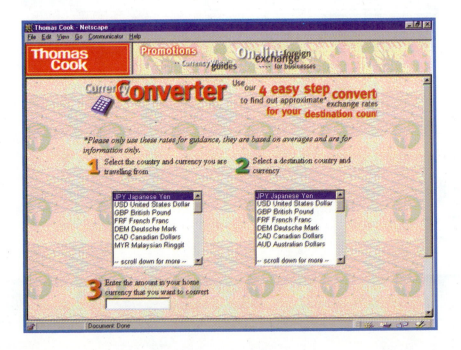

Figure 11.6
Thomas Cook
currency converter

4 Suppose you want to purchase Thomas Cook travelers cheques in local currency denominations for a trip to Shanghai, China. Locate the address and telephone number of the Thomas Cook office in this city. What are the opening times at this office?_____

_____

5 The Internet version of the World Travel Guide is available online at *www.wtgonline.com*. Select United Arab Emirates from the Middle East section, shown in Figure 11.7. Answer the following questions about this country with business profile information found at this site.

What industry is the main provider for the country? _____

_____

What country is the largest buyer of products from this industry? _____

_____

What is the appropriate dress for business meetings? _____

_____

What special office hours are observed during the month of Ramadan?

_____

What language is largely spoken in business circles?_____

Why is it important for business people to learn about local customs practiced in other countries? _____

_____

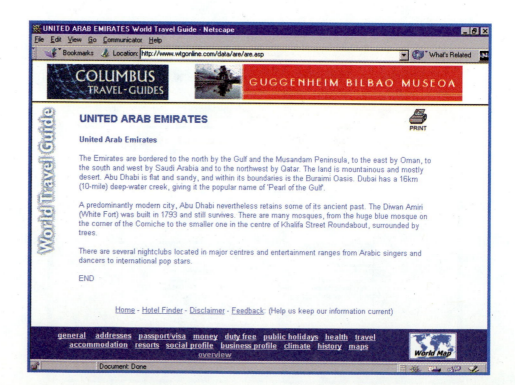

Figure 11.7
World Travel Guide Web site

THINKING ABOUT TECHNOLOGY

You used the Internet to plan a domestic trip in Chapter 5. How is the process of planning an international trip different than planning a domestic trip? What issues other than airline flights are important for international travel? How can you "prepare" for your international trip using the Internet?

Net Fun

The American Express site offers many services for the business traveler, including articles about travel to certain regions of the world. Check this site and look for warnings about travel to some parts of the world.

Net Careers

International Business

Do you enjoy working with computers and also enjoy foreign countries? As you saw from this activity, many organizations around the world have sophisticated Web sites. Some companies, like Yahoo and Lycos, have openings in other countries. Most positions require that you live in that country. For instance, at this writing, Yahoo lists openings for a public relations director in Australia, engineer in Germany, and assistant producer in Denmark. See Career Openings at the Yahoo site. Lycos lists an international business developer for Latin America. See the Jobs@Lycos link at the Lycos site.

ACTIVITY
11.3

Objective:

In this activity, you will learn how to find international business information on the Internet.

Online International Business Information

When you are planning to do business with someone from another country, there is much research to do. The Worldclass Supersite, pictured in Figure 11.8, is a useful portal site to begin your research. It contains links to 1,025 Web sites from 95 countries. It is divided into seven sections:

- Reference (guides to regions, countries, and world organizations)
- News (world business newspapers, business magazines)
- Learning (global MBA programs and notable business institutes)
- Money (stock quotes, news, international exchanges, foreign investment guides)
- Trade (business directories, cargo, business tools, contact information)
- Networking (industry associations, foreign business investment leads)
- World Beaters (manufacturing, service, and small/medium firms and trade services)

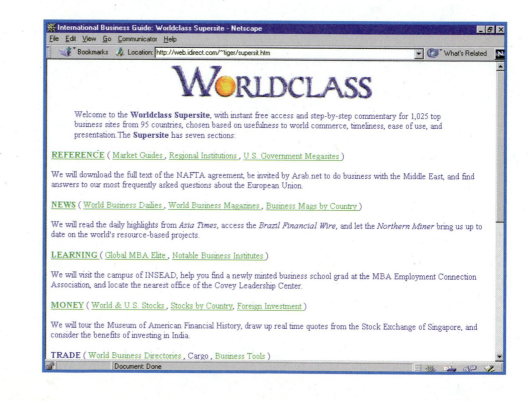

Figure 11.8
Worldclass Supersite

People around the world watch CNN to see what is happening during crises. Take a look at the CNN Interactive site and click the World link. You'll find news stories organized by region as well as the top stories. What other languages are available on this site?

Michigan State University operates CIBER – Center for International Business Education and Research. The index portion of the home page is shown in Figure 11.9.

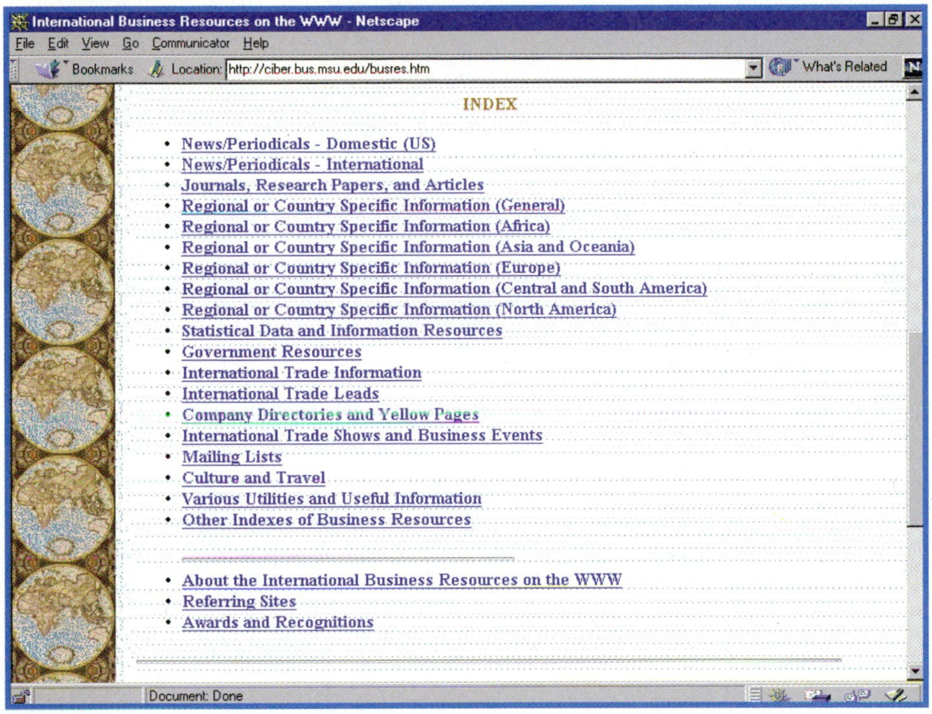

International Business Resources on the WWW - Netscape

File Edit View Go Communicator Help

Bookmarks Location: http://ciber.bus.msu.edu/busres.htm What's Related

INDEX

- News/Periodicals - Domestic (US)
- News/Periodicals - International
- Journals, Research Papers, and Articles
- Regional or Country Specific Information (General)
- Regional or Country Specific Information (Africa)
- Regional or Country Specific Information (Asia and Oceania)
- Regional or Country Specific Information (Europe)
- Regional or Country Specific Information (Central and South America)
- Regional or Country Specific Information (North America)
- Statistical Data and Information Resources
- Government Resources
- International Trade Information
- International Trade Leads
- Company Directories and Yellow Pages
- International Trade Shows and Business Events
- Mailing Lists
- Culture and Travel
- Various Utilities and Useful Information
- Other Indexes of Business Resources

- About the International Business Resources on the WWW
- Referring Sites
- Awards and Recognitions

Document: Done

Figure 11.9
Michigan State CIBER
international business resources

Like the Worldclass Supersite, much of the information maintained at the CIBER site is suitable for those interested in pursuing international business.

Assume that you work for World Ventures Limited, a company that does business around the globe. Your team needs to find answers to questions about commerce in a number of countries outside the United States. Using links found at these two sites, search the Internet for answers to the following questions.

1 Using CIBER, find information about doing business with South America. Select Brazil: Big Emerging Markets. What is the telephone number of the Brazilian Central Bank in Brasilia? What language is spoken in Brazil? What is a typical work week in Brazil? _____

_____

Net Business   *Mike Kuiack & Associates*

Mike Kuiack and Barbie Wu are co-founders and principals of the Mike Kuiack & Associates international management and marketing consulting firm. They developed the Worldclass Supersite in the fall of 1995 to help world business people take advantage of the Web. They chose sites based on their usefulness to world commerce, timeliness, presentation, and ease of use. Do you think this comprehensive world business guide site should be free of charge? Explain your answer. How can this firm use the Worldclass Supersite to attract consulting clients to the firm?

2 Check out the CIBER mailing lists hyperlink, and explain how to add yourself to *The Economist Newspaper's* Business and Politics summaries by e-mail. _____

_____

As an employee of World Ventures Limited, why would you want to subscribe to the world business summary news? _____

_____

_____

3 Many international newspapers and business digests are available on the Internet. Visit the Inside China Today Web site, available through CIBER and Worldclass Supersite and shown in Figure 11.10.

What does it cost to subscribe to the daily bulletin? _____

In what medium would you receive the daily bulletin?_____

Do you think this site is as sophisticated as U.S. or Canadian newspaper sites? Explain. _____

_____

_____

Figure 11.10
Inside China Today Web site

Global Language Statistics

According to the Global Reach Web site, English is the most popular native language on the Internet, with about 58% of the entire online population. Following English is Spanish at 8.61%, German at 8.57%, Japanese at 7.7%, French at 3.7%, Chinese at 2.6%, and Swedish at 1.7%. Portuguese, Italian, Dutch, and Korean have about 1% each. This site also offers translation services to convert a Web site from one language to another.

4 Suppose World Ventures wants you to relocate to Hawaii to pursue U.S.–Japanese ventures in the Pacific. Visit the Matson Navigation Company site and find out how much it would cost to ship your personal automobile from the U.S. mainland to Honolulu. _____

Should you drain your fuel tank before you leave the car at the Matson port facility? _____

What are the mainland ports of discharge (departure) for Matson auto cargo ships? _____

If a Matson container ship leaves from Los Angeles on Saturday, when does it arrive in Honolulu? _____

If the Web site were not available, how would you find out about transporting your car to Hawaii? _____

_____

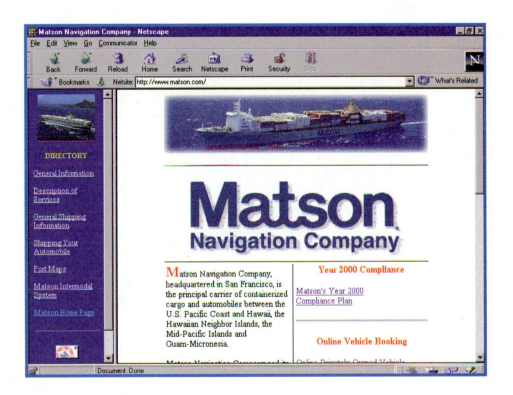

Figure 11.11
Matson Web site

THINKING ABOUT TECHNOLOGY

All the information that you retrieved in this activity was available free of charge. If global information were only available on the Internet for a subscription fee, would you still prefer to research the Internet for global information? In other words, is having this information quickly available worth the time saved? Explain your answer.

ACTIVITY
11.4

Objective:
In this activity, you will see how a company can take advantage of its own "private Internet" to manage business around the world.

Intranets, Extranets, and the Internet

You have been working with the Internet for most of this textbook. The **Internet** is a network of public networks, generally available everywhere. When information is placed on the Internet, it is usually considered public information and freely accessible.

But some companies want to make information available to employees only, not the general public. For this, a company can install an **intranet**, or internal network. An intranet is like a private Internet. Instead of being available to everyone, the intranet's cable that connects computers is only accessible inside the firm. Organizations put employee handbooks, company news and information, inventory status, internal job postings, FAQ's, and other internal information resources on an intranet. Information can be updated and distributed easily over the intranet, so companies prefer this online information tool over sending information updates to employees manually.

For organizations in which all users are in one central location, it is fairly easy to create an intranet. But for international companies with widely dispersed locations, it is not possible to install a private cable. In this instance, the company can implement an **extranet**, an intranet that uses the Internet to transmit private information beyond the firm's physical space. To keep the extranet private, companies install **authentication** software. It asks for a username and password before allowing a user access to the extranet's pages. With authentication, only the authorized user with proper knowledge can gain access to a particular site.

One advantage of creating an extranet is to be able to take advantage of inexpensive Internet connections from virtually anywhere in the world to connect to the firm's intranet.

1. Open the Fidelity Investments home page. Then navigate to Online Trading by clicking that link at the upper left of the page. You should see the authentication box shown in Figure 11.12.

   Why do you think that authentication usually requires two pieces of information instead of just one? _____

   _____

   _____

2. Suppose that a marketing organization maintains confidential price quote information on its intranet. Give at least three reasons why the company would want to have an extranet for use by the sales force.

   1. _____

   2. _____

   3. _____

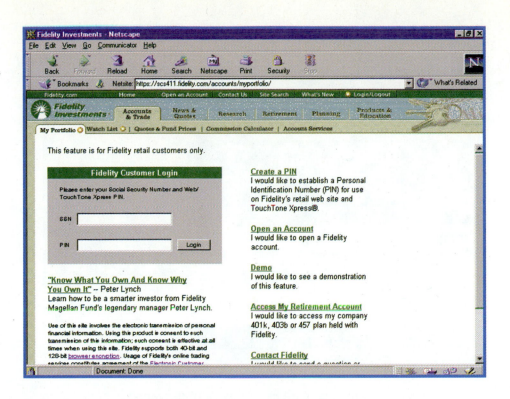

Figure 11.12
Fidelity Investments online trade authentication box

3. The Netscape Company sells intranet technology to other companies. One of its intranet customers is Litton Industries. Search the Netscape home page for the Litton Industries intranet customer profile. (Hint: Click Site Map. Then click Site Search, and search for "intranet." Select the Litton profile from the search results.) From this profile, answer the following questions about Litton's use of the intranet.

Why did Litton want to transform the paper- and phone-based repetitive tasks to an intranet? _____

_____

How did the intranet improve the development and analysis of capital forecast plans? _____

_____

Why would the Netscape company want to highlight Litton Industries in this profile? _____

_____

4. Search for the IntraMark Web site. Click Resources, and read the opening information. Then click Seminar and read the introduction. To begin the seminar "Building a Corporate Intranet," click Begin Seminar Now, as shown in Figure 11.13. Answer the following questions based on the lessons.

Figure 11.13
IntraMark corporate intranet seminar site

Begin Seminar link

List two disadvantages of traditional ways of delivering information to corporate users.

1. _____

2. _____

List three types of documents that could be placed on an intranet.

1. _____

2. _____

3. _____

List three types of documents that could be placed on an extranet.

1. _____

2. _____

3. _____

THINKING ABOUT TECHNOLOGY

Think about a company for which you have worked. What kinds of information would be appropriate and useful for this company to put on an intranet? Think about frequently requested items, or items that tend to change often for which a printed reference is needed. What sorts of information would not be appropriate for an intranet?

Net Fun

Visit the CoolSavings Web site to see how you can print real coupons with your own computer. What characteristics of an extranet does this site possess? (Hint: Think about the security issues associated with the login box.)

CHAPTER REVIEW

NET VOCABULARY

Define the following terms:

1. authentication
2. extranet
3. image map
4. Internet
5. intranet
6. mirror site
7. multinational corporation
8. packets

NET REVIEW

Give a short answer to the following questions:

1. Explain how the domain name for a particular Web site can identify the country where that site is located.

2. Why is having a mirror site particularly helpful for global companies with operations on more than one continent?

3. Why does a company place information in different languages on its Web site?

4. How does the Internet permit asynchronous business activities?

5. Explain how to convert U.S. dollars into foreign currency.

6. How can the Worldclass Supersite and the CIBER site help someone who does business overseas?

Net Project

WORLD VENTURES LIMITED

You have been assigned the task to research the best possible site for locating a new manufacturing facility in Malaysia. Use the Internet resources to find out the local currency, weather during October and November, geographic regions, major cities, population, head of the government, gross domestic product (GDP), major products or industries, and the inflation rate. In preparation for your visit the capital city, find a hotel and learn its street address, telephone number, and a Web site address, if available. Give the name of a local newspaper and its Web address, if available.

NET PROJECT TEAMWORK   Analyze Different Countries

Each member of the team should extend this project by examining possible manufacturing sites in a different country. For variety, look for countries in different parts of the world such as Zimbabwe, New Zealand, Rumania, and Chile. Write a report that compares the conditions in these countries. Where would your team recommend locating the manufacturing site? Why?

WRITING ABOUT TECHNOLOGY   Supporting Global Sales

You have visited many different international e-commerce sites in this chapter, and have seen some that are available in different languages. Write a 100-word summary that describes the sorts of customer support problems that might occur due to language or cultural differences.

PORTFOLIO · PROJECT

Developing an Electronic Commerce Web Site

In this section, you will learn the basics of how to establish your own business presence on the Web. Chapter 12 discusses the components of an e-commerce Web site. You will learn how a business Web site works and what methods of developing the site are available to you. You will even develop an online store in this chapter. Then you will learn how to register your domain name and submit your site's URL to the major Web browsers.

Chapter 13 will guide you through creating basic Web pages using Microsoft's FrontPage 98, the most popular Web development software on the market. You will learn the principles of good Web design and evaluate the design of some award-winning Web sites. Then you will actually create Web pages, edit them, and explore different design choices, including graphics.

Even if you don't have FrontPage 98, the discussion and illustrations in Chapter 13 will show you how Web development software works. When you are ready to create your own Web site, no matter which development software you buy, you will have a basic understanding that will make learning your new software easy...and fun!

Chapter 12   Creating a Web Site 214

Chapter 13   Developing a Web Site with FrontPage 238

Creating a Web Site

Chapter Objectives:

In this chapter, you will learn how to create a Web site. After reading Chapter 12, you will be able to

1 describe the components of a basic Web site, including some optional features on many E-commerce sites.

2 compare methods for developing a Web site.

3 register the domain name and promote your Web site.

Net Terms

domain name

InterNIC

hypertext markup language (HTML)

HTML tags

clip art

GIF

JPEG

Web editor

file transfer protocol (FTP)

Web server

24 by 7

publish

Webmaster

top-level domain name

What You Need to Make Your Web Debut

Creating a Web site is actually much simpler than most people think. Of course, building an *effective* Web site requires a touch of artistic creativity and some energetic work to keep it fresh. Simple Web sites are straightforward to build and publish on a Web server.

Here are the components of E-commerce Web sites that you will learn about in this chapter:

- Text files with embedded HTML commands
- Images, usually .GIF or .JPG files
- Web server computer and software to hold the text files and images
- Connection to the Internet or an intranet
- Database server (optional) supporting the online catalog
- Internal search engine (optional) to locate information in the Web site

Many organizations hire a consultant or advertising company to design and build the site. These individuals are called *Web developers*. If you have the technical knowledge and some artistic talent, you can do it yourself. The online stores at Yahoo make it easy to build your own Web site, which Yahoo will host for a low monthly fee. Or, you can purchase Web package software that helps you create an E-commerce site by simply answering a series of questions.

Before you can activate the Web site, you need to register

the domain name. The **domain name** is the last part of a URL that includes the organization's unique name followed by a top-level domain name designating the type of organization, such as .com for "commercial" or .edu for "educational." Most companies put the company name or trademark into the domain name. For example, our school's domain name is *indstate.edu*. The address of our main Web server is *http://www.indstate.edu*. In this chapter, you will learn how to check for available domain names at **InterNIC**, the organization that registers domain names.

As discussed in Chapter 10, you need to promote your site so that potential customers can find it on the Internet. We will look into ways to submit your site's URL to the major search engines, and other ways to let people know your site exists.

ACTIVITY

12.1

Objective:

In this activity, you will learn the components of a basic Web site and discover some optional features found on many E-commerce sites.

Components of a Web Site

Basically, a Web site consists of a few text files containing special HTML formatting commands and a Web server computer to host your site. The Web server runs special software that sends out the HTML files to users whose browsers request them. Your Web server will need a connection to the Internet or an intranet. An E-commerce site will also need software to process payment methods, such as credit cards. Let's take a closer look at each part of a Web site.

HTML Files

The language used to create most Web pages is **HTML**, or **hypertext markup language**. This simple language adds formatting tags to the basic text of the page. **HTML tags** are computer codes that tell your Web browser how to display information on your screen. HTML tags are used to indicate such features as bold, character size, font color, hyperlinks, and images. Each tag is surrounded by angle brackets. For example, <B> turns on bold for a phrase. The text remains bold until the matching </B> tag turns bold off. Thus,

<B> Organizational Department,</B> School of Business

would display as

Organizational Department, School of Business

Figure 12.1 shows a simple HTML file and the resulting Web page.

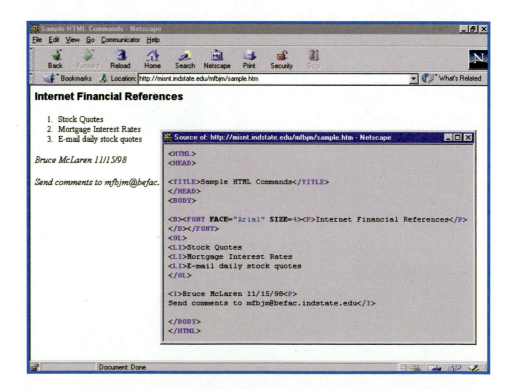

Figure 12.1
Sample HTML file and resulting Web page

Although it is possible to program Web pages manually using HTML tags, development software tools called Web editors can insert the tags for you, simplifying the task of coding home pages. There are many HTML primers available on the Internet.

1 Open your browser and go to the University of Illinois Beginner's Guide to HTML, shown in Figure 12.2. The URL is *www.ncsa.uiuc.edu/General/Internet/WWW*.

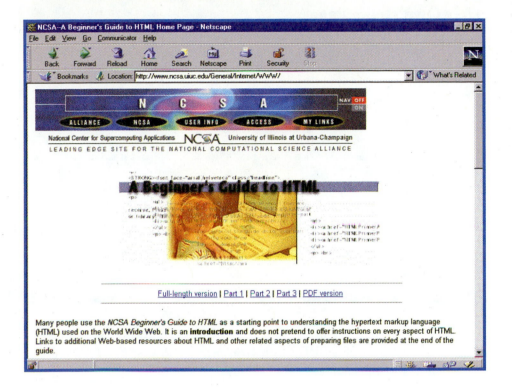

Figure 12.2
University of Illinois HTML online guide

Open Part I of the guide and scroll down to the section on Markup Tags. What do each of the following HTML tags do?

\<TITLE\>_____

\<H1\> _____

\<P\> _____

\</P\>_____

\<UL\> _____

2 Open the Web site at *misnt.indstate.edu/mfbjm/firstpage.htm*. To see the actual HTML source code that creates this page, click the View menu and then Page Source (in Netscape Navigator) or Source (in Internet Explorer). You should see the source code shown in Figure 12.3. You can close that window by clicking the Close button in the upper right corner.

NET FACT

Mosaic—The Original Browser

The University of Illinois was a pioneer in Internet development. Both Netscape Navigator and Internet Explorer descended from Mosaic, an early browser developed at the University of Illinois. The developers of Mosaic, graduate students at this university, co-founded the Netscape company in 1994.

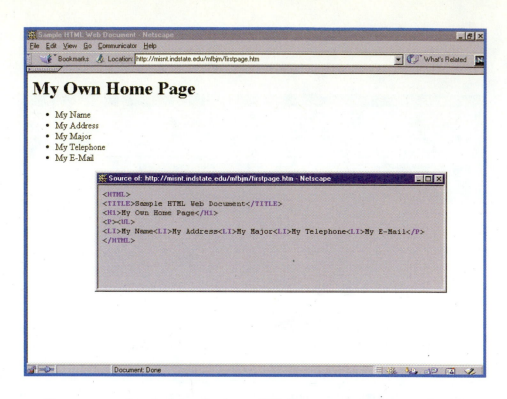

Figure 12.3
HTML source for Web document

For a more detailed book about HTML programming, see South-Western Publishing's *HTML Programming Concepts: Brief Course*, by Turner and Barksdale.

Image Files

As you have already seen throughout the Web sites featured in this book, most use graphic images to enhance the design of Web pages. These images come from a variety of sources, including clip art, photographs, and other software applications. **Clip art** is a collection of electronic drawings, pictures, and icons, created for use in Web pages and other documents. You can also purchase professional images from online sources, often simplifying the process of finding appropriate graphics for your site.

Many Web sites contain free clip art that you can use at your own site. Check out *http://clipartconnection.com* for thousands of clip art files.

3 Go to Yahoo's clip art directory at *http://dir.yahoo.com/Computers_and_Internet/Graphics/Clip_Art/.* Find clip art images for the following subjects, and print a copy of each image.

Basketball
Lawn mower
Computer
Family
Textbook

Once you have viewed an image in your browser, you can save a copy of that image by right-clicking the image and then choosing Save Image As (in Netscape Navigator) or Save Picture As (in Internet Explorer) from the menu, as shown in Figure 12.4.

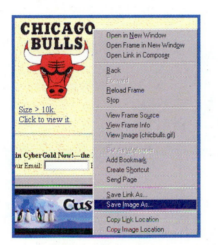

Figure 12.4
Chicago Bulls clip art with Save Image As command

4 You must convert an image into a compatible electronic format before it can be used on the Web site. Most sites use the .GIF or .JPEG graphic file formats. **GIF** (graphics interchange format) is the universal standard format for storing images for display in Web browsers. It is used for most lettering, small pictures, and animations. **JPEG** (for the Joint Photographic Experts Group, the photography committee that designed it) is the standard for compressing still images, such as photographs and art. JPEG files do not render lettering well.

If you have a photograph or artwork, use a scanner to convert the image to a file. If you have a digital camera, it can capture an image and save it as a .GIF or .JPG file directly.

NET FACT

JPEG Compression

The JPEG compression can reduce a 2 megabyte image file to 100 kilobytes or smaller. However, the compression "loses" some of the original image when it is displayed in your browser. The degree of compression is adjustable, providing a tradeoff between download time and image quality. The greater the compression you choose, the faster the image file will download, but the lower the image quality when displayed.

Web Editor

You can design your own Web site using a Web editor to create the HTML file. A **Web editor** looks like a word processing program. In it, you can type the contents of your Web page and then select various formatting options. You can choose such things as

- Font size and color
- Special formatting, like bold, italics, underline, and blinking
- Bullet and numbered lists
- Line alignment (left, center, right)
- Hyperlinks for text in your page
- Images
- HTML tables to create columns like you see in a newspaper

5 To see what these features look like on a Web page, open the User Services site at Indiana State University, shown in Figure 12.5. The URL is *web.indstate.edu/acns/user-serv/*.

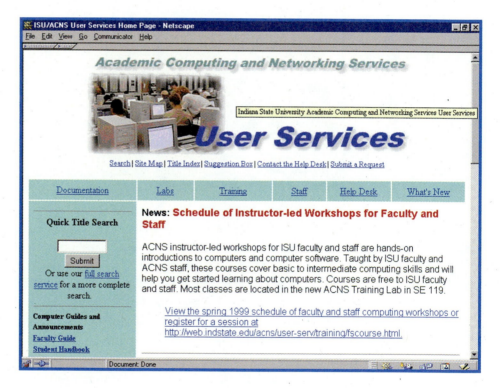

Figure 12-5
User Services Web page

Notice the use of several fonts sizes. Which ones draw your eye in this page? Why? _____

_____

_____

The page designer has used bold to emphasize certain items in this page, particularly in the table of contents that appears at the left side of the page. Which items appear in bold, and why? _____

_____

_____

Notice the many hyperlinks on this page. Most are the traditional blue underlined text phrases. Move your cursor to one of the hyperlinks. What happens to the mouse pointer when it reaches a hyperlink?

_____

_____

The Web designer has used tables on this page to organize the material. Notice the use of cells in the top row beginning with Documentation and ending with What's New. The table of contents at the left is one large cell in the table. The main content on the right side with a white background is also one large cell in the table.

The advantage of a Web editor is the ease with which you can build the features on your Web page. Advanced features like tables and forms are handled with ease with Web editors like Microsoft FrontPage or Netscape Composer.

When you are finished designing, you can save the HTML file with *.htm* or *.html* as the file extension. Then you can transfer the file to the Web server using **FTP (file transfer protocol),** a standard method for copying files from one computer to another over the Internet. We'll talk more about Web development in Activity 12.2 and in Chapter 13, where you will build a Web site with FrontPage, the most popular Web editor.

A **Web server** is a computer that stores the HTML files that make up a Web site. When your browser requests a Web page stored at the server, the Web server sends the appropriate HTML file over the Internet to your machine for display on your screen. When an organization "hosts" a Web site, it stores the Web pages on its Web server.

Internet Connection

Unlike your personal computer's occasional modem connection to the Internet, the Web server computer needs to have a full-time Internet connection. That is, the server must be available full time, **24 by 7** (24 hours a day, 7 days a week), whenever someone might request a Web page. Few companies host their own Web site unless they have a full-time connection, which can cost anywhere from $60 per month up to $1,000 or more, depending on the speed.

Most Internet Service Providers (ISPs) offer a limited amount of Web space for hosting personal Web sites as part of the monthly fee. You can also find other sources to host your Web site.

(6) Open the Geocities (*www.geocities.com*) site, pictured in Figure 12-6. Click the Free Home Page link at the top of the page. Find the following information about this service:

How much space is available for your home page in the basic program?

_____

What is the monthly GeoPlus membership fee? _____

What additional services are available in GeoPlus? _____

_____

_____

Can you perform commercial activities like E-commerce in the basic
GeoCities home page space? _____

Visit your own ISP's Web site and look around to see if it offers Web
hosting space. Does it? If so, how much space are you allowed? _____

_____

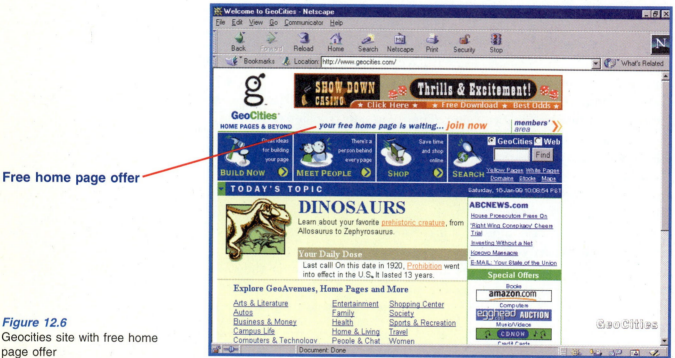

Free home page offer

Figure 12.6
Geocities site with free home
page offer

Internal Search Tool

Many Web sites include an internal search tool that can be used to look for materials on the Web site. They work just like the search engines you access at Yahoo and Lycos, with keyword searching capability.

Some search tools automatically catalog new material added to the Web site, constantly updating an index of addresses in the organization's Web site. Figure 12.7 shows a typical Search box found at a large Web site. Most internal search tools are constantly scanning the Web pages at the site for relevant keywords, building entries in a search database. When someone visits the site and searches for a keyword, pages containing that word can be found quickly.

7 Open the ACNS site at Indiana State University that was shown in Figure 12-5. In the Quick Title Search box on the left side, type the word *excel* and click Submit. You should see results similar to those shown in Figure 12-8.

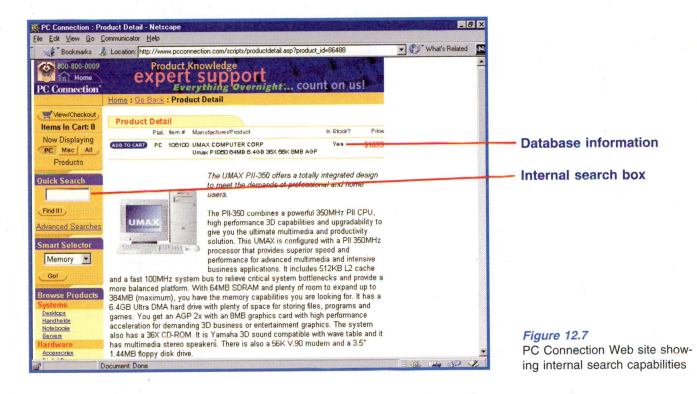

Database information

Internal search box

Figure 12.7
PC Connection Web site showing internal search capabilities

How many articles appear in your search? _____

Why is it useful to have an index of the documents available at this site? _____

_____

_____

_____

_____

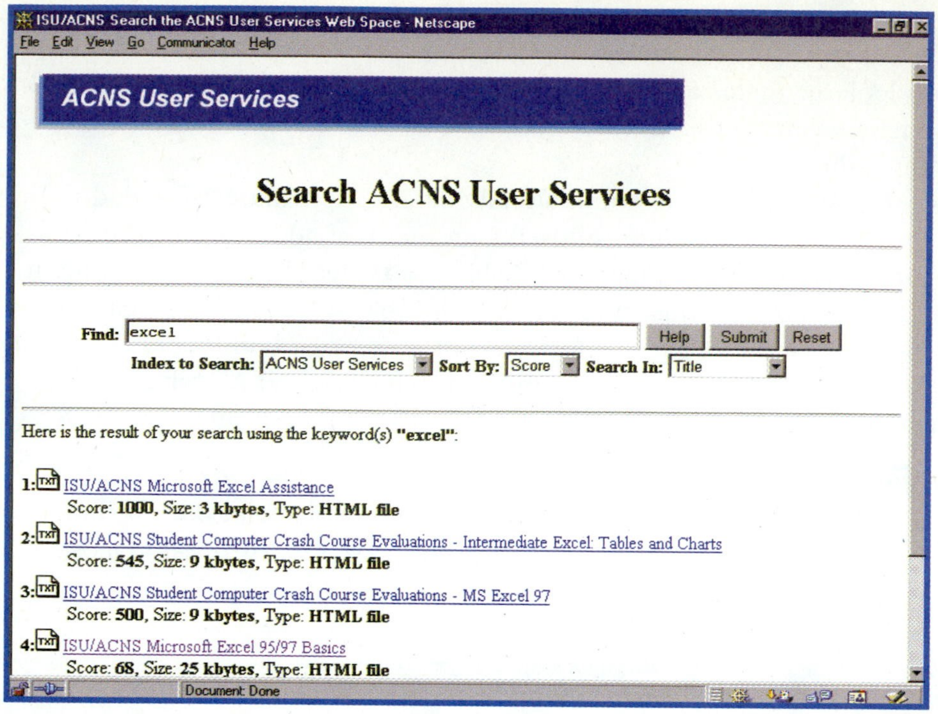

Figure 12.8
Results of internal search for "excel"

Database Server

Companies often store product catalogs and other useful information in electronic databases on a company server. When the company wants to add a product to the catalog or change a product's stock number, it simply makes the changes in the database. If the company Web site links to the database on the company server, then a customer can look up a product in the online catalog, and any changes will be there. The company doesn't have to make the changes on the Web site, too. When a customer requests something in the catalog, the Web site simply calls up the company catalog database, retrieves the desired information, and formats it for display on the customer's screen.

8 To see how data is retrieved from a database server, go to the Larry Helman Realtors site at *www.larryhelman.com*. Click the Our Listings button at the left side of the opening page. Click the Vigo County button to view a property selection form, pictured in Figure 12-9. Using this form, customers can search for particular properties in the company's database of listed properties. They can enter search criteria, such as type of house and price range, to call up just the properties they want to review.

Fill in the form with your own criteria. Click the Begin button to have the database server find properties that match your choices. When you see the search results, click the picture of one home to see the detailed information. List your property criteria here, and print the listing (including the photograph of the property) for at least one property that matches your choice.

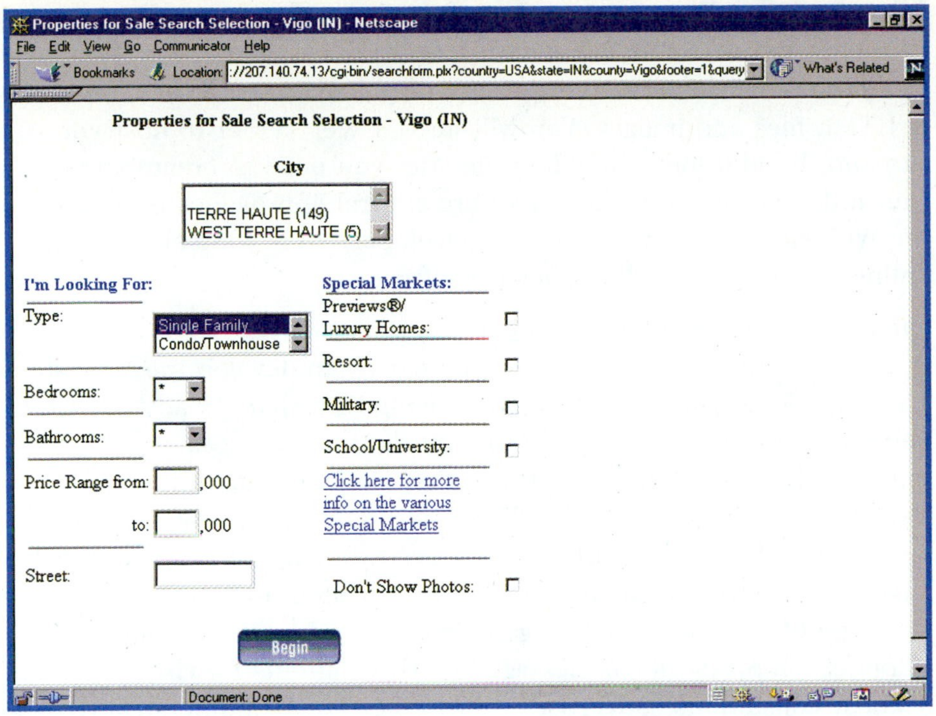

Figure 12-9
Realtor Web site database query form

City: _____

Type: _____

Bedrooms: _____

Bathrooms: _____

Price Range: _____ to _____

Street: _____

How many properties matched your selections? _____

_____

What is the address of one matching property? _____

_____

This site also features a mortgage calculator. Click a property in your search results to select it. Then scroll down to the bottom of the screen and select the Mortgage Calculator button. Using the default values in this form, what is the monthly payment for your property? _____

_____

THINKING ABOUT TECHNOLOGY

Why is it a good idea to use a professional firm to host your company Web site? What are the disadvantages of hosting it on your own computer?

ACTIVITY 12.2

Objective:
In this activity, you will compare methods for developing a Web site.

Methods for Developing a Web Site

In the previous activity, you learned that Web sites are composed of HTML files and images. You will need a Web server to host your site and, In addition to building the site, you need to create and register a domain name for it. There are several approaches to creating the Web site: You can hire a Web developer, do it yourself, use an online store, or use a Web package software.

Outsource: Hire a Web Developer

Most organizations hire an outside expert to develop the Web site. The Web developer is often an advertising firm that already has expertise in developing and delivering marketing messages to customers. This firm is able to put together the contents of the site as well as physically prepare the HTML files. Other kinds of Web developers would know how to build Web pages but would not necessarily have the expertise to create an effective promotional message. With this type of developer, your organization would be responsible for developing the promotional message and the contents for the Web site.

Most consultants "advertise" on the Web by including links to their home page on the sites they create. Like many other business services, word-of-mouth may be the best way to learn about effective Web developers.

Some organizations contract on a per-hour basis, while others offer one price for the entire Web site. Updates are necessary, so don't forget to include this expense in your organization's budget.

1 Go to the Broadmoor Hotel Web site shown in Figure 12.10. Follow the link near the bottom of the page to the developer's own Ardea Arts Web site. Follow the link from there to see her experience. List five of the roles she performs as a Web developer. _____

_____

_____

Do It Yourself

2 Rather than hire a Web developer, you could build the site yourself. This alternative is similar to the first one except *you* would be the Web developer! Before you panic, remember that building the Web page HTML files is fairly straightforward once you have the ideas for what you want to say. To build your own site, you would need Web editor software, like Netscape Composer or Microsoft FrontPage, and FTP software to publish HTML files on a Web server. **Publish** means to transfer a file from your computer to a Web server using FTP.
In Chapter 13, you will see how to develop a Web site with FrontPage.

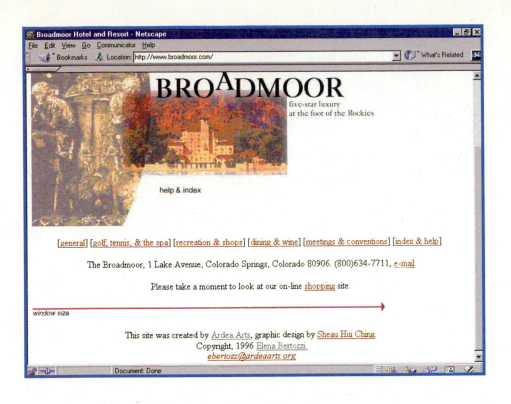

Figure 12.10
Web developer reference

What should you consider in deciding whether to do it yourself or hire a Web developer to build your site? _____

_____

_____

What skills do you need to be your own Web developer? _____

_____

_____

Use an Online Store

A few services will create and maintain a complete online E-commerce Web site for you. The best known of these is Yahoo!Stores. Your entire store would be hosted by Yahoo, including online catalog, order entry forms, and payment processing. You could add products, descriptions, prices, and even pictures of your products to your store. The process is simple, and there is a tutorial to get you started with a sample store. Your Yahoo!Store would offer your customers an electronic shopping cart and online payment methods, and would provide you plenty of management reports.

3 To access the Yahoo!Store as a shopper, go to *shopping.yahoo.com*. Figure 12.11 shows the Yahoo!Store site. Notice how the store categories resemble the Yahoo site opening page, listing categories with main headings and subheadings beneath them. In which Yahoo shopping category would you locate the following types of stores?

Sporting goods _____

Bicycle and outdoor recreation _____

Antiques and curios _____

Web development service_____

Figure 12.11
Yahoo!Store Web site

④ To see how a Yahoo!Store operates, visit Harrington's of Vermont. If you can't find it in the Food & Drink category, search for it with the search box. The opening page for this Yahoo!Store is pictured in Figure 12-12.

The advantage of an online store through a service like Yahoo is that everything is done for you once the store is created. You don't have to host the site or provide any hardware or software for the site. Yahoo stores the orders for you to check, or you can request the orders be e-mailed to you. Yahoo promotes your store along with its other online stores, and your URL can appear in Yahoo's main catalog and in other search engines.

NET TIP

Yahoo!Store
Requirements

To run an online store using Yahoo!Store, you will need a computer with a Web browser and Internet access. You need a Yahoo store account and a merchant account with a credit card processor.

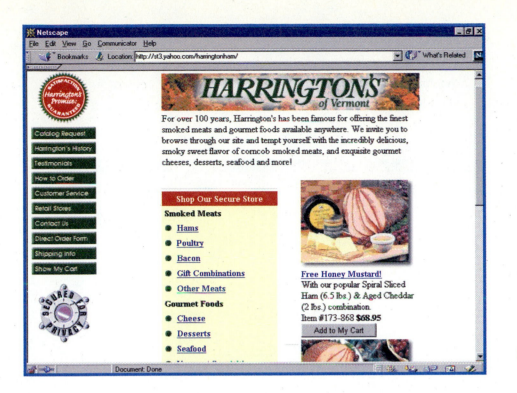

Figure 12.12
Yahoo!Store site

Locate the following information about Harrington's Yahoo E-commerce site:

How do you request a printed catalog? _____

What is the cost of the catalog? _____

Describe one of the current "website specials" and its cost. How much do you save over the catalog by ordering it from the Internet?_____

_____

How does Harrington's determine shipping charges for an order? _____

_____

What is the price of the smaller (6.5-7.5 lb.) spiral-cut smoked party ham? _____

5 Go to the main Yahoo page and click the Yahoo!Store link near the bottom right of the page. Then click the Yahoo!Store heading at the top of its advertising page. You will then see the Yahoo!Store opening page pictured in Figure 12-13. Answer the following questions about Yahoo!Store:

For a small store, how many items can be added to the catalog? _____

_____

What is the monthly cost for a small store?_____

What is the per-transaction cost for operating the store? _____

How is information protected when customers use a credit card? _____

_____

In what ways can the merchant receive orders from customers who
want to buy from the Web site? _____

_____

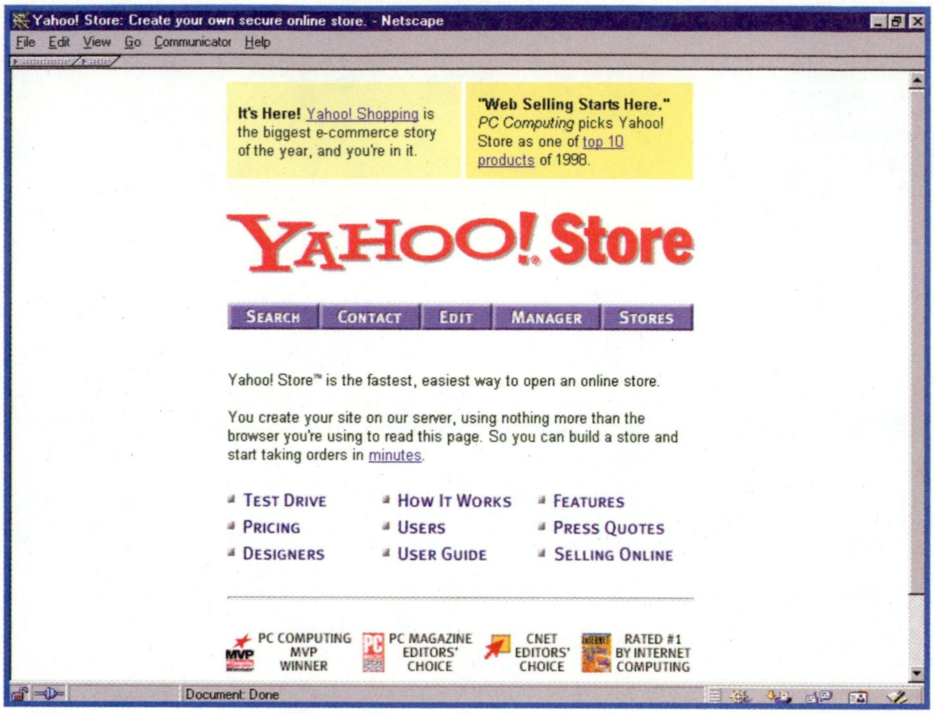

Figure 12-13
Yahoo!Store opening page

6 The project at the end of this chapter will ask you to create a Yahoo
sporting goods sample store. For now, you will choose a name for your
sporting goods store and go through the test drive at the Yahoo site.
You'll use this work when you complete the project. Don't create two different Yahoo sample stores.

Go to the opening Yahoo!Store page at *store.yahoo.com* and follow the
Test Drive link to create your own store. Figure 12.14 shows a portion
of the account creation form for the free 10-day trial version of the Yahoo!Store. You will have to provide the following account information:
unique account ID, full name of your store, account password (for management purposes), your name, and your e-mail address. Click the Create button to start building your store.

NET TIP

Yahoo!Store Test Drive ID

*When you create a sample store, it must have a unique account ID. Yahoo
will tell you if you have chosen a name already selected by someone else.
Remember that your test drive store is only good for 10 days. Save your
account ID and password in a safe place, because you will need it later to
enter products and get management reports for your sample store.*

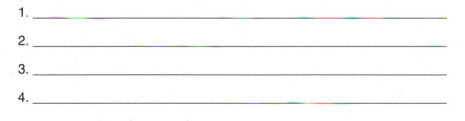

Figure 12.14
Account setup for Yahoo!Store test drive

Carefully follow the instructions on the screen. You must agree to the store merchant service agreement before proceeding with the store. The test drive includes a 5 minute guided tour that shows you how to create a store by adding categories, products, and so forth.

7 There are many useful online tips for merchants who want to build a successful store. Access Yahoo's "10 Secrets of Selling Online" at *http://store.yahoo.com/vw/secrets.html*. Pick four secrets and write a brief description of the advice the author provides for each item.

1. _____

2. _____

3. _____

4. _____

Use a Web Package Software

You can buy Web package software that automates the preparation of the Web store, similar to the way Yahoo!Store does. The software asks you questions about products and services you plan to present in your online store. From the answers you provide, the software builds the database and the HTML files to support your store. Then you need to locate a host server for the Web site. Typically, this alternative also includes registration of your domain name, described in Activity 12.3. IBM's $40 "Startup for E-business" is an example of Web package software.

Webmaster

A **Webmaster** is an individual within an organization who is responsible for developing and maintaining the Web site. The Webmaster's e-mail address is often listed at the bottom of a Web page as the contact for suggestions or complaints about out-of-date material or nonfunctioning links. The Webmaster must know HTML commands and have programming skills. The Webmaster will have access to the Web server that hosts the organization's Web site. Some companies outsource the Webmaster's duties to an outside Web developer.

THINKING ABOUT TECHNOLOGY

Most experts say that a Web site must be continually updated to keep it fresh. Why do you think this is important, especially for E-commerce sites?

Registering and Promoting Your Web Site

ACTIVITY
12.3

Objective:
In this activity, you will learn how to register the domain name and promote your Web site.

At this writing, the InterNIC Web site at *http://www.internic.net/* is responsible for domain name registrations. Most organizations choose domain names that contain a form of the organization's name, to make the site's owner easy to identify from its address. For instance, the U.S. Senate domain name is *senate.gov,* Purdue University's domain name is *purdue.edu,* and the Coca-Cola domain name is *coke.com.* Some companies register more than one name: *coca-cola.com* is also registered to Coca-Cola.

The last three letters in each of these domain names is an abbreviation. The ending *.com* refers to commercial organizations or businesses. The ending *.edu* represents institutions of higher education. And *.gov* refers to United States government organizations. These three-letter abbreviations are **top-level domain names,** designating the type of organization that owns the site. Other common top-level domains include *.net* (network providers) and *.org* (other organizations, including nonprofit organizations).

1. It is easy to search for a particular domain name to see if it has been previously registered. Go to the InterNIC Web site shown in Figure 12.15 and type your last name followed by *.com* in the search box. For example, I asked InterNIC to search on *mclaren.com.* It found a marketing company in Canada that had registered *mclaren.com* in 1995.

   Who has already registered "your" site? _____

   What is the purpose of that Web site? _____

   Try searching for your first and last name together, as in catherine-smith.com. Is your full name available as a domain? _____

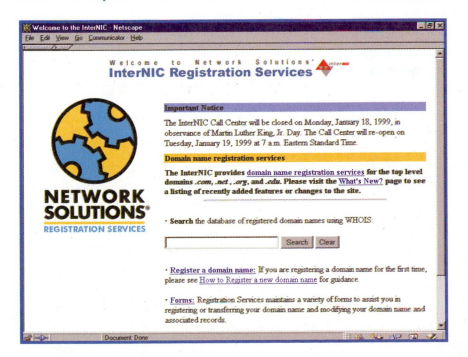

Figure 12.15
Domain name registration site

2 Click the Resources link in the InterNIC Web site.

How much does it cost to register a domain name with InterNIC?

_____

This fee covers the initial registration and updates for a two-year period. You can pay this fee online with InterNIC's secure payment system. Sixty days before the end of the two-year registration period you will be billed for the next two years.

How much is the renewal fee? _____

What happens if you neglect to pay the renewal fee?_____

_____

With most Web site hosting services, it is possible to use your own domain name or the name of the Web server site followed by your name. For example, the imaginary law firm of McLaren and McLaren could register _mclarenlaw.com_ as its domain name. _http://www.xyzhost.com/mclaren_ could refer to the McLaren company's site hosted at _xyzhost.com_.

3 You can use a Web site to promote your new domain name by submitting it to major search engines and online directories. Hundreds of these sites appear when you search for "submit" on Yahoo. As an example, Figure 12.16 shows the Submit Pro site at _http://www.submit-pro.com/_. Go to this site and find the following information:

How much does this service cost?_____

To how many search engines and catalogs does this site submit your domain name? _____

How do you enter the information at this site? _____

_____

Net Ethics   *Domain Name Piracy*

InterNIC registers domain names on a first-come, first-served basis. Do you think it is appropriate for a company to take another company's unregistered name and register it as its own domain name with InterNIC? Should a company whose trademark is properly registered be able to protect that trademark from being used in other domain names?

Figure 12.16
Submit your Web site

THINKING ABOUT TECHNOLOGY

Why do you think that most organizations want to have their own regis-tered domain name? Should a company be able to sell a domain name to another organization?

NET VOCABULARY

Define the following terms:

1. clip art
2. domain name
3. file transfer protocol (FTP)
4. GIF
5. HTML tags
6. hypertext markup language (HTML)
7. InterNIC
8. JPEG
9. publish
10. top-level domain name
11. 24 by 7
12. Web editor
13. Web server
14. Webmaster

NET REVIEW

Give a short answer to the following questions:

1. What language is used to prepare Web pages?

2. Why would you want to use a Web editor instead of manually preparing a Web page?

3. What are the disadvantages of using a Web editor?

4. List the mandatory components of a Web site.

5. How do you transfer files to a Web server?

6. What is a Webmaster and why is this person important to a Web site?

7. How do you register a domain name?

8. Why do you need a domain name?

9. How much does it cost to register a personal domain name for the Internet?

Net Project

CREATE YOUR OWN PERSONAL ONLINE STORE

You want to develop an E-commerce Web site for your online sporting goods store, using Yahoo!Store. Go to Yahoo!Store at *http://store.yahoo.com*. Use the same site you started in Activity 12-2. Make sure you choose the 10-day free store link and don't submit your credit card number for a permanent site! Follow the directions in the Yahoo Web site to build your store.

Pick a unique account name for your store. Use your own name and e-mail address as contact information. Add fitness products for your store from the table below. The part number is shown first, along with its description and retail price. Shipping costs are $34 for the first two items and $8 for the other three items.

EX123-4	Exercise bike	$199.95
EX127-2	Space-saver treadmill	$349.00
EX234-1	Jogging weight (5#)	$2.95
EX234-6	Dumbbell (10#)	$5.95
EX390-0	Deluxe jump rope	$12.59

Write a brief description of your E-commerce site, including its URL. Include a printout of the main catalog showing these fitness items.

NET PROJECT TEAMWORK   Add Images to Your Online Store

Each member of your team should search the Internet for suitable photographs or clip art for each of your products. You can save the picture/image file on your own disk by right-clicking the image and choosing the appropriate command from the menu. Add the images to your online store to make your pages as appealing as possible. Remember that copyright laws apply to many Web sites and only use images that do not violate these laws.

WRITING ABOUT TECHNOLOGY   Managing Your Site

Prepare a brief description of the management reports available for a Yahoo online store. How could the business owner make use of the reports about the E-commerce site?

Developing a Web Site
with Microsoft® FrontPage

Chapter Objectives:

In this chapter, you will learn how to create a Web site using Microsoft Front-Page 98. After reading Chapter 13, you will be able to

1 evaluate examples of good Web sites and identify principles of good Web design.

2 create a personal FrontPage web using the personal web wizard.

3 use the FrontPage Editor to customize a FrontPage web.

Net Terms

download

thumbnail

plug-in

frame

FrontPage

FrontPage web

FrontPage Explorer

theme

FrontPage Editor

tasks list

publish

Design Webs Like a Pro

In the last chapter, you learned about the components of a Web site. This chapter will show you how to actually create a Web site using Microsoft FrontPage, the most popular Web editor. To complete the activities in this chapter, you will need to have the Front-Page software installed on your computer. If this is not possible, you can still learn about Web page development by following the activities in this chapter and looking closely at the illustrations.

The chapter begins with some examples of good Web site design, including several award-winning sites. Good Web sites share several common design principles. Most award-winning sites provide attractive graphics that load quickly, organize information for easy access, and don't require any special plug-ins for your browser. Good sites remain fresh, with new information added regularly to capture viewers' interest.

You've visited many sites in your Web tours throughout this book. You are probably starting to form opinions about what makes an effective, vibrant site that will draw visitors again and again. In this chapter, you'll look at some sites that have been honored for their quality, learn why they work so well, and begin to learn how sites are created.

Figure 13.1 shows the home page from Toyota. This site

even reminds you that it is a good site! The home page is easy to read, fits on one screen, has pleasing use of color and space, and provides the most important information for the user. The search tool makes finding facts easy for users who don't immediately see what they want in the categories listed across the top. It provides links to specific product lines. Links to consumer information, such as the site privacy statement and corporate information, are not hidden off the screen.

Expertly designed corporate sites and small sites designed by individuals not only share design principles but also are created with the same kinds of Web authoring tools. Many companies sell Web authoring software. Some general-purpose packages like FrontPage and Netscape Composer are good for beginners and experts alike. Other packages are developed for special audiences. CourseInfo, by Blackboard, Inc., is a package aimed at teachers who want to make a Web site for a class. It even lets teachers post tests online. IBM's Startup for E-business is a package for developing an E-commerce site.

This chapter will show how Microsoft FrontPage, the most popular Web editor, can be used to create a Web site. If you have FrontPage, you'll be able to experiment with your own site as you follow the activities. If not, follow the steps to see how straightforward creating a site can be.

If you have another Web editor, you should be able to complete similar steps, working with hyperlinks, graphics, background colors, and different fonts. Whether or not you will be able to publish your site depends on your facilities.

Will what you learn in this chapter make you an expert Web designer? No, not quite yet! What it will do is get you started thinking about ways you can incorporate good design ideas into the pages you develop. As you use Web authoring tools to experiment, you'll have fun creating attractive and useful pages. And when you are ready to create your own site, you'll be able to learn your software's more advanced features.

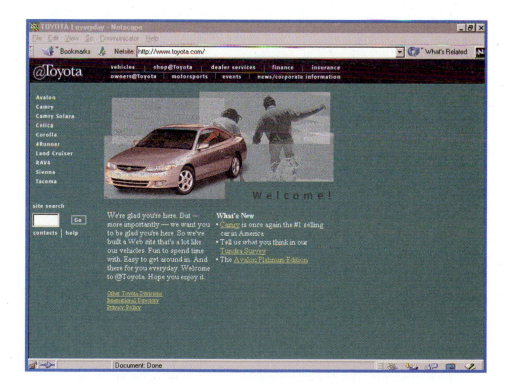

Figure 13.1
Toyota home page

Good Web Design

While it is relatively easy to make a home page, it's much more difficult to make a great Web site. Much depends on the purpose of the site. A home page for an individual can be prepared in a matter of hours, while a Web site for a small business could take weeks. Building a Web site for a large organization could take months or years. In fact, to reduce the time, most large organizations would assign several people to the task.

Good Web sites share some common design principles:

1. Organize your site into sections, with a separate page for each section. An outline is useful for planning this design.

2. Make your starting home page functional and attractive.

3. Display current information, and update frequently to keep the site fresh.

4. Design so that your pages will transfer or **download** quickly from the server to the user's computer for display.
   - Use small images (say, less than 50 KB).
   - Instead of displaying a full-size image, use a smaller version called a **thumbnail** that users can click to call up the larger image if they want.
   - Instead of one large page, break up the site into several smaller pages.

5. Use colors (for background, text, hyperlinks, etc.) that will display and print well. Remember that light text colors on a dark background may "disappear" when printed.

6. Write in standard HTML (older browser versions may not be able to handle your page). Caution: Although FrontPage produces standard HTML, it also contains features not supported by all Web servers and browsers.

7. Avoid elements that require browser plug-ins (or offer an alternate version that doesn't require the plug-ins). A **plug-in** is a specialty program that works with a major software to enhance its capabilities.

8. Avoid frames. A **frame** is a rectangular section of the screen that scrolls separately from other sections. A frame is commonly used for a table of contents. When users click a link in that frame, the related contents appear in the larger frame. Not all browsers can handle frames, and they take up a lot of space on the screen.

9. Although many users have 800x600 screen resolution, develop your site for 640x480 resolution to avoid horizontal scrolling.

10. Include interactivity with users by providing hyperlinks and an e-mail link.

11. Provide an internal search tool for large sites. Some Web servers can build a site index automatically.

Award-winning Web sites offer good design ideas, even for small sites. When you find a site that looks good, add it to your bookmark list, so you can revisit the site and learn from its design.

1 Each year, the NetGuide Awards recognize outstanding Web sites. Figure 13.2 shows the NetGuide winners site. Go to this section of NetGuide to learn more about the awards.

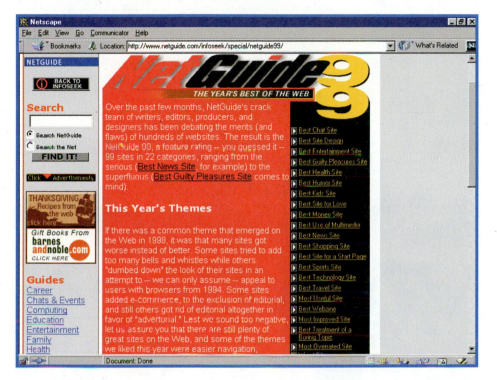

Figure 13.2
NetGuide Year's Best of the Web site

Slide your mouse down the categories on the right side. What happens, and how does this catch your eye? _____

_____

Visit the Worst Site category and list one poor design characteristic for each site there.

_____   _____

_____   _____

2 Dell Computers and Amazon.com have frequently been cited as winning Web sites. Visit the Dell site, shown in Figure 13.3.

How many distinct sections or regions do you see on the Dell opening page?_____

_____

What happens when you move the mouse to a line that begins with a right-pointing triangle (or one that appears in bold)? _____

_____

_____

What is the purpose of the gray banner running across the top of this page (and all Dell pages)? (Hint: Scroll the mouse across this area and observe the status line of your browser.) _____

_____

What is the purpose of the blue background section at the left side of the Web site? _____

_____

This opening page fits on one screen yet contains a great deal of information. Do you think it is too compressed? Why or why not?

_____

Figure 13.3
Dell Computers Web site

3️⃣ Open the PC Magazine site and find its Top 100 Web sites page. For 1998, the magazine expanded the list of categories to 20, with 5 winners in each category. Any site included on this list should be considered an example of good Web design.

List one Top 100 site from each of the following categories and briefly describe one element of the design of the site that you find particularly good.

Computer Companies _____

Finance/Investing _____

News _____

Shopping _____

Travel _____

The Webnet Webratings site at *www.webratings.net* is Australia's largest WWW rating service. Sites are rated from 1 to 5, with 5 being the highest quality. Search its database for the top worldwide sites. The list is updated weekly. You can even submit your own site's URL to this free service.

THINKING ABOUT TECHNOLOGY

Evaluate the design of a Web site that you visit frequently. Describe its good features and any design mistakes. Overall, do you think this site is well designed? Why or why not?

Net Business   *WebLife, Incorporated (www.weblifeinc.com)*

Zack Johnson graduated from engineering school in 1998 and opened his own Internet design and development company. He employs six professionals, mostly local college students, to design, develop, and host Web sites for clients. His market niche falls between the big design houses and the one-person operations. He markets his services by charging a lower hourly rate than most, and including two site revisions in the initial price. He does some Web development by hand using HTML commands as well as using Web development software like FrontPage. For some applications, Zack builds the Web page "on the fly" by plugging in data from a database like Microsoft Access. For an example of his work, see Larry Helman Realtors at www.larryhelman.com. At the time of this writing, Web Life has a special: home page plus up to 10 additional pages including a custom e-mail page and custom navigation bar, up to 10 photographs of products or processes, registration of the customer's domain name, and submission of the site's URL to 400 major search engines for $750.

Why do you think this small firm can charge a smaller hourly rate than larger Web developers? Do you think that $750 for preparing a small business Web site is a fair price? Why or why not? For a small Web development firm that is just getting started, how do you think Zack should promote his company to solicit new business?

For some practical development advice and online workshops, offered in a very upbeat and low-key style, visit WebMonkey (*www.webmonkey.com*), a how-to guide for Web developers. You'll find tips from the pros for beginners as well as experienced developers.

ACTIVITY

13.2

Objective:

In this activity, you will explore the basic features of Web design software, by using FrontPage 98 to create a personal web.

Creating a Personal Web with FrontPage 98

FrontPage is Microsoft's easy-to-use Web site development and management tool. With FrontPage, you can create and maintain a FrontPage web or an individual home page. A FrontPage web is Microsoft's name for the set of HTML and image files that comprise a particular Web site, including the hyperlinks that let users navigate between the pages. We'll use "Web" to refer to the World Wide Web, and "web" to refer to the FrontPage web.

FrontPage consists of two basic tools, Explorer and Editor, and some optional components, such as Image Composer and Personal Web Server. FrontPage Explorer is the tool for creating, viewing, and managing your web of pages. You can use Explorer to import objects into the web and to establish themes for the web. A theme is a design template that is used on all pages of a web. It controls the colors, background image, and basic layout of the page. By choosing a theme in FrontPage, you will create a consistent "look" across all pages in your web. You will learn more about themes later.

FrontPage Editor lets you create and make changes to individual pages in your web. You can start with a new blank page in the Editor or you can edit an existing page with the File|Open command. From Explorer, you can double-click any page in your web to open it in the Editor for changes. The menu bar and toolbar of Editor resemble those of Microsoft Word and other word processors. You can highlight text in Editor and then format that text by clicking a button, just as with a word processor.

NET TIP

Every Computer is Different

Based on previous work on your computer, Explorer may list different existing webs in the top of your Getting Started dialog box.

1 Click the Start button in the taskbar and select Microsoft FrontPage from the programs installed on your computer. You will see a Getting Started dialog box similar to Figure 13.4. The top portion of the dialog box lets you select an existing web and the bottom portion lets you create a new web. Select the "Create a New FrontPage Web" button and click OK.

2 FrontPage will display the New FrontPage Web dialog box shown in Figure 13.5. Notice that FrontPage defaults to the Personal Web Wizard in the top box. Leave that setting as is. Choose a different name for your web in the lower box, step 2. The name of your web will appear whenever someone opens your site on the Internet, so pick something appropriate. Then click OK.

3 Your new web now appears in the Explorer navigation view, as shown in Figure 13.6. The FrontPage wizard built four HTML page files for your personal web, as shown in the top of Explorer. Details and location of the files are shown in the lower portion of your screen. These files contain the outline for a personal web, but you will need to fill in your own information.

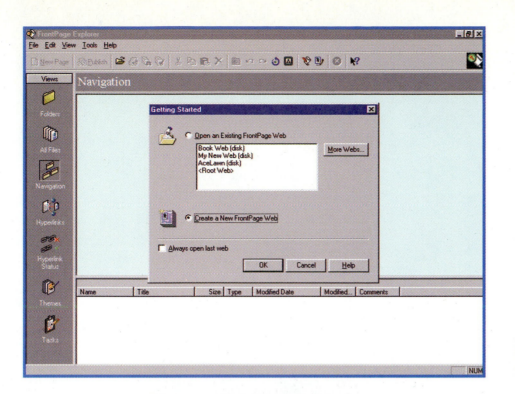

Figure 13.4
FrontPage Getting
Started dialog box

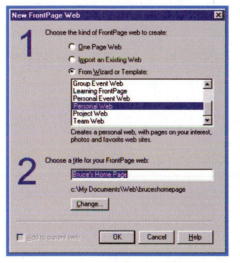

Figure 13.5
New FrontPage Web dialog box

If you're looking for more graphic images to put on your page, visit the Graphics gallery (*www.developer.com/down-loads/d_images.html*) at Developer.com. There you'll find the reusable image library, which contains over 100,000 images that you may download and use free of charge.

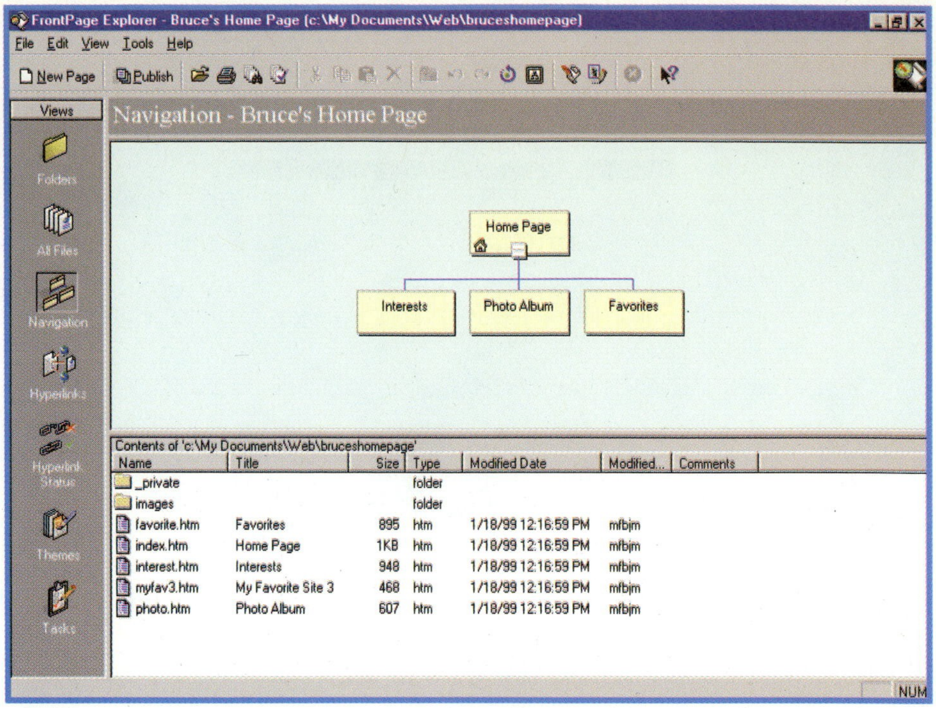

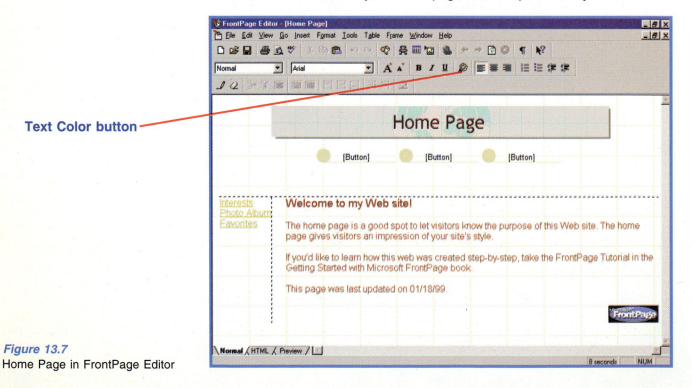

Figure 13.6
FrontPage Explorer in
Navigation view

④ To view the contents of your home page in Editor, double-click it in Explorer. Your home page will open in FrontPage Editor and look like Figure 13.7. The elements on this page came from the Personal Web Wizard. The design formatting is the default theme, Global Marketing. This page is an HTML document, even though you don't see any HTML tags in this view. By clicking the HTML tab at the bottom of your screen, you can see what the document's HTML code looks like. To see what the page will look like when published, click the Preview tab. Print each of the three views of your home page and compare what you see.

Text Color button

Figure 13.7
Home Page in FrontPage Editor

5. Now you will make some changes in your home page. Be sure the Normal tab is highlighted.

   a. In the first line, *Welcome to my Web site*, replace the word "my" with your own name, as in *Welcome to Bruce McLaren's Web site.* You can make your changes the same way you would in your word processor.

   b. Highlight the first line you just changed, and then click the Text Color button in the toolbar, shown in Figure 13.7. (Or use the Format|Fonts menu bar command.) Select Red for the text color and click OK.

   c. Delete the second paragraph in this page. Replace it with a paragraph about yourself.

   d. Delete the third paragraph about the FrontPage tutorial.

   e. Leave the last paragraph – it contains a special date field that is automatically updated whenever you make changes to the page. Your home page should now look like Figure 13.8. Print and save your page.

What else do you think should appear on your opening home page? Remember that there are three other pages in this Web site.

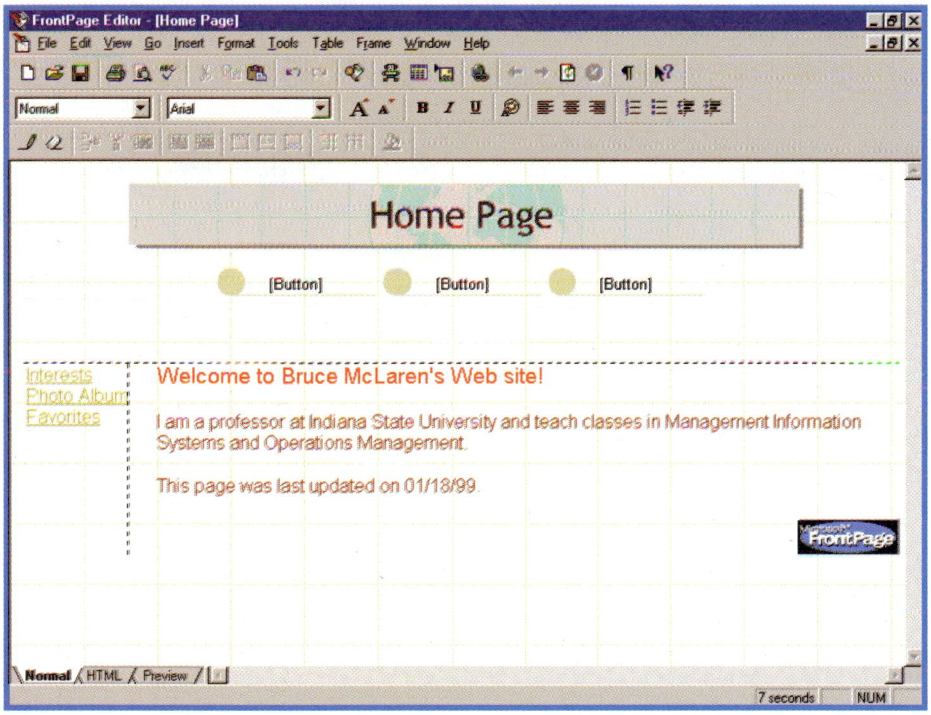

Figure 13.8
Modified Home Page in Editor

THINKING ABOUT TECHNOLOGY

Wizards, such as this one that lets you place your words into a template, have made it much easier for software users to do complicated tasks. As a new user of FrontPage, would you rather understand the background of each of the steps along the way, or do you appreciate being able to leave it up to the wizard?

ACTIVITY

13.3

Objective:

In this activity, you'll learn how to customize your FrontPage web by changing its appearance and its contents.

Customizing Your FrontPage Web

The FrontPage Personal Web Wizard provides a home page and three other pages. As you saw in the previous activity, these pages are named and have an established structure. When you work with these pages, you can not only enter your own words, but also change the background or theme, bring in a picture or clip art, and add links to other pages on the Internet. If the web you created in Activity 13.2 is not open, open it now and look at your home page in Editor.

1. Take a look at the three hyperlinks that the wizard placed on your home page. Place the mouse pointer on the Interests link. What is the URL for this link? (Hint: Look in the status bar at the bottom of the page.) Hold down the Crtl key and click to move to the Interests page.

2. Delete the line that begins "Here is a good place…" Replace the words in each of the bulleted interests with descriptions of your interests. For the first bullet, write a few sentences about your hometown. Write about one of your hobbies in the second bullet. In the third bullet, write about your favorite college or pro sports team. To add another bullet, just press Enter at the end of the previous bullet. Include a related URL for one of your interests. Figure 13.9 shows an example. Experiment with fonts and colors for these sentences.

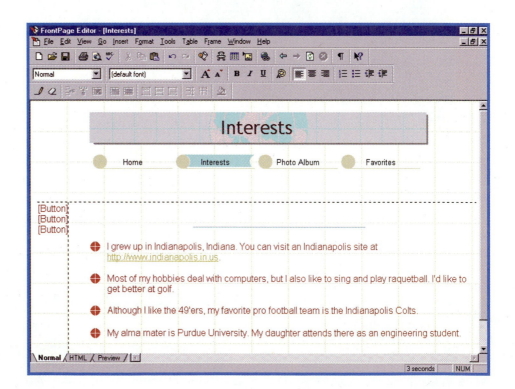

Figure 13.9
Updated Interests page

3 Would you like to give your web a new look? Return to Explorer's Navigation page by clicking the Show FrontPage Explorer icon shown in Figure 13.10. From the Views along the left side, select Themes View. Click the button for Use Selected Theme. Click several theme choices and preview their designs on the right. Figure 13.11 shows a sample of the Blueprint theme.

Figure 13.10
Show FrontPage
Explorer icon

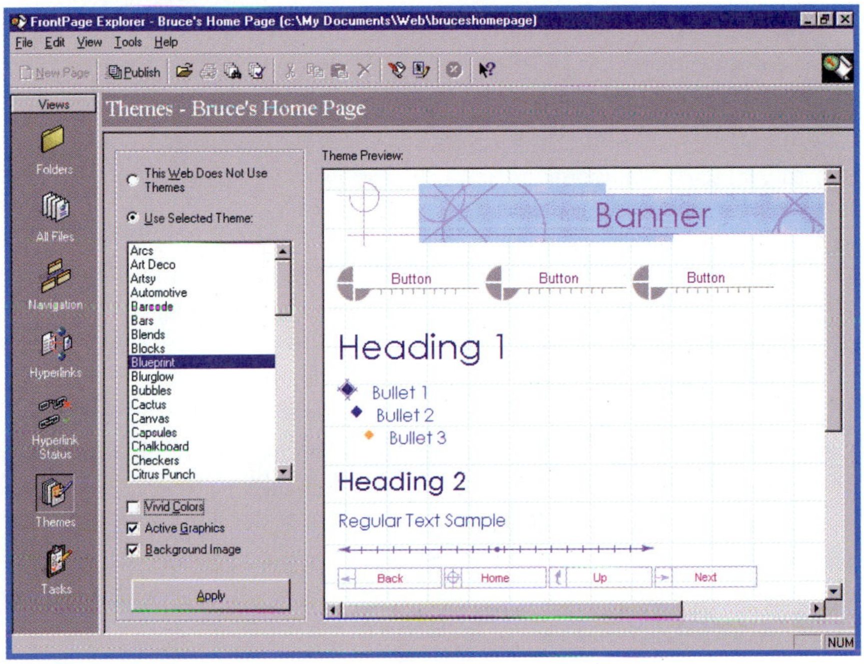

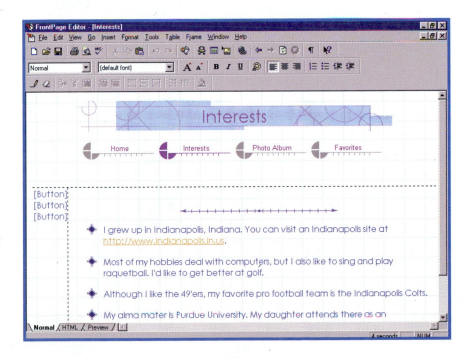

Figure 13.11
FrontPage Explorer
Themes view

When you have found a theme you like, click the Apply button. To check out your web's new look, click the FrontPage Editor icon. Print your Interests page. Figure 13.12 shows the Interests page with the Blueprint theme. Do you think the blue text of the Blueprint theme is a good choice?

Figure 13.12
Interests page with
Blueprint theme

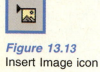

Figure 13.13
Insert Image icon

④ Now let's add an image to your page. Crtl-click the Photo Album button at the top of the Interests page to open the Photo Album page in Editor. As you can see, FrontPage supplies a couple of pictures for this page as part of the template. You can replace these with your own. Click a picture to select it, and press the delete button. Then delete the other picture and both photo captions. Click to set your cursor where you want to insert your own art. For this activity, we'll insert clip art, but you can insert any image you have captured as an electronic file. Click the Insert Image icon shown in Figure 13.13, and select Clip Art. Scroll through the clip art and picture selections that FrontPage supplies. Find one you like and click Insert. Your image will appear at your cursor's location.

Click the art you just inserted to select it. You will see little box-like "handles" appear around it. Move your mouse over a handle until the cursor turns into a double-headed arrow. Then click and drag to resize the art. You can resize it in any direction by dragging the handle on the side you want to change.

Now click the art to select it, and click the Center icon shown in Figure 13.14 to center it horizontally on the page. You can also click-and-drag to move the art around. Figure 13.15 shows the Photo Album page after the Microsoft Strategy Harmony clip art was inserted and the text was changed. When you are finished making your changes, save and print your Photo Album page.

Figure 13.14
Center icon

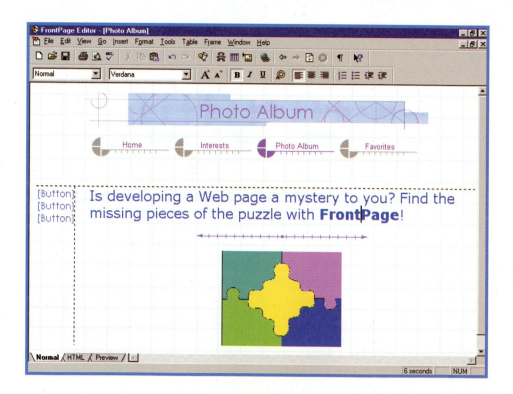

Figure 13.15
Photo Album page with new text and image

5. Now let's add some hyperlinks to other Web pages from your Front-Page web. Crtl-click to go to your Favorites page. Replace the sentences at the top with *My Favorite Links:*. Replace the text next to the bullets with *CNN, The Washington Post,* and *CBS Sportsline.*

Highlight each of the hyperlink phrases, one at a time, and click the Create or Edit Hyperlink icon shown in Figure 13.16 (or use the Insert|Hyperlink command). Enter the URL for that link and click OK. URLs appear below.

CNN   *http://cnn.com*

Washington Post   *http://www.washingtonpost.com*

CBS Sportsline   *http://www.sportsline.com*

Figure 13.17 shows the page and hyperlinks. Notice that the mouse pointer is touching the CNN link, and that the URL associated with that hyperlink appears in the status bar. Print and save your Favorites page.

Figure 13.16
Create or Edit
Hyperlink icon

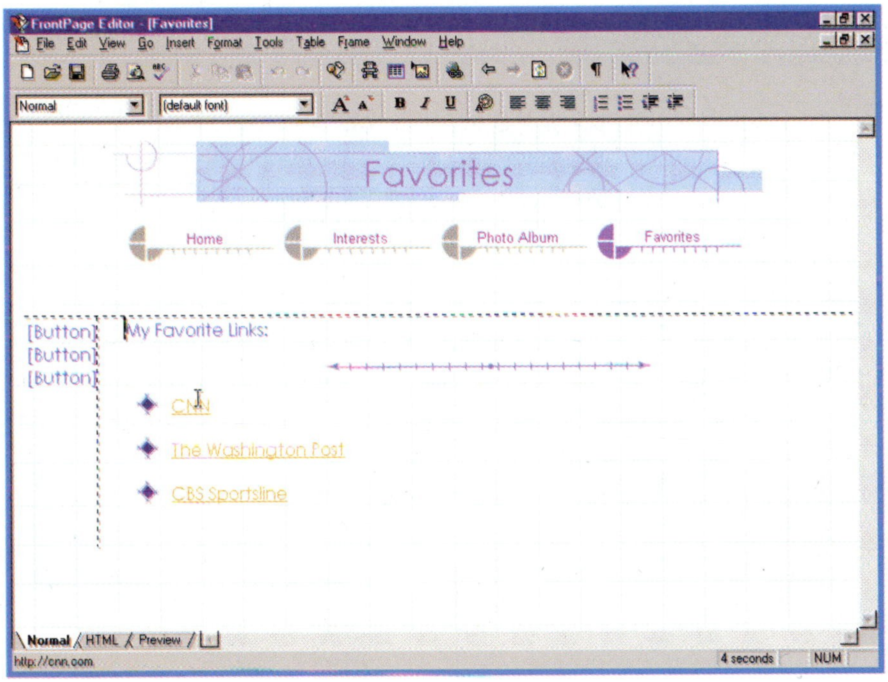

Figure 13.17
Favorites page

6. Click the Show FrontPage Explorer icon in the toolbar to switch back to Explorer. Click the Hyperlinks button in the left panel to display your home page in Hyperlinks view. This view displays all the links in your web. Your screen should look similar to Figure 13.18.

NET TIP

To-Do Tasks

*Explorer has another feature that helps you manage your web. It maintains a "to-do" **tasks list,** where you can list items to finish your web as you think of them. For instance, you can list broken hyperlinks that need to be fixed. You can also add tasks from Editor and associate each task with a particular web page or with the whole web.*

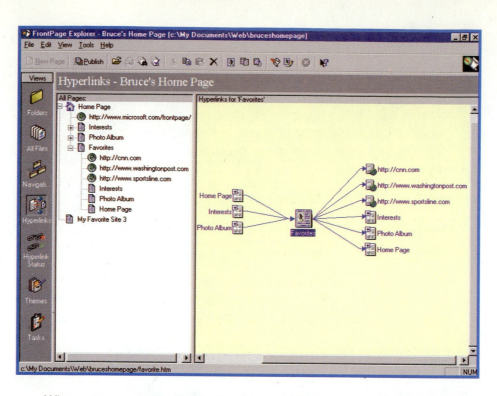

Figure 13.18
Hyperlinks view

Figure 13.19
Verify Hyperlinks icon

When you are connected to the Internet, Explorer can check all of your hyperlinks to see that they still work. If you can connect to the Net, do so now. Then in the Hyperlinks view of your FrontPage web, click the Hyperlink Status button in the left panel. To begin the check, click the Verify Hyperlinks icon shown in Figure 13.19 (or choose Tools|Verify Hyperlinks from the menu) and click Start. You will see green light symbols next to the hyperlinks that still work and red lights next to those that failed. In the hyperlink check shown in Figure 13.20, the green lights indicate that all hyperlinks checked out OK.

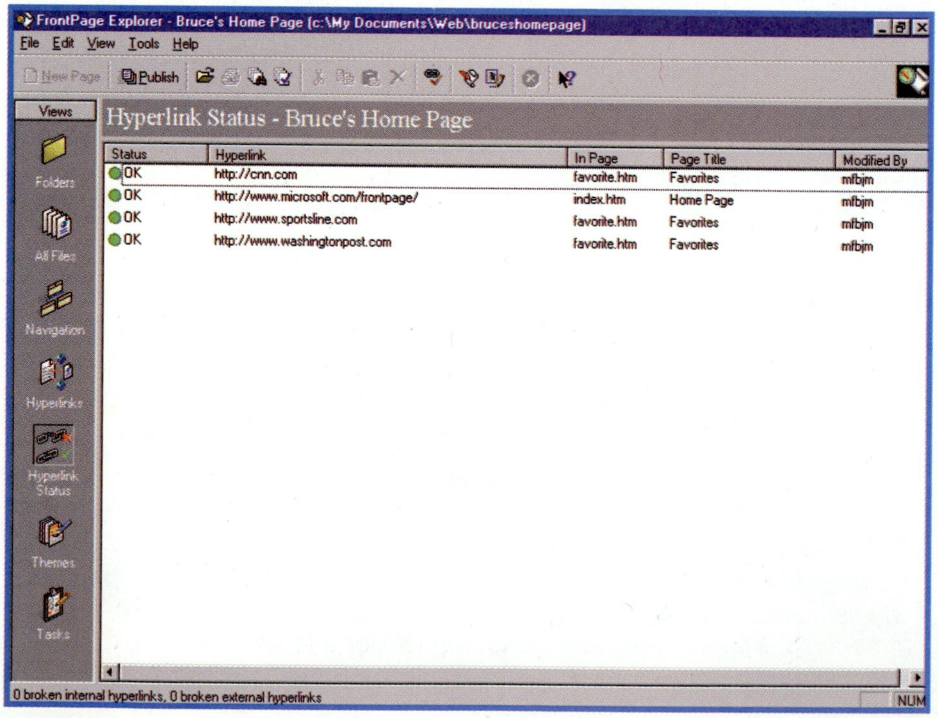

Figure 13.20
Hyperlinks view with
verified links

7 Now you'll change the name of one of the pages in your web. In Explorer, single-click the Favorites page in Navigation view to select it. Press F2 or use the Edit|Rename command. Type *Links* and press Enter. To verify that the name has been changed in all pages, double-click the Home Page in Explorer to open it in Editor. Then click the Preview tab. Notice that FrontPage has changed the name of the Favorites page to Links in the navigation buttons at the top of each page. Figure 13.21 shows the final Home Page, previewed in Netscape.

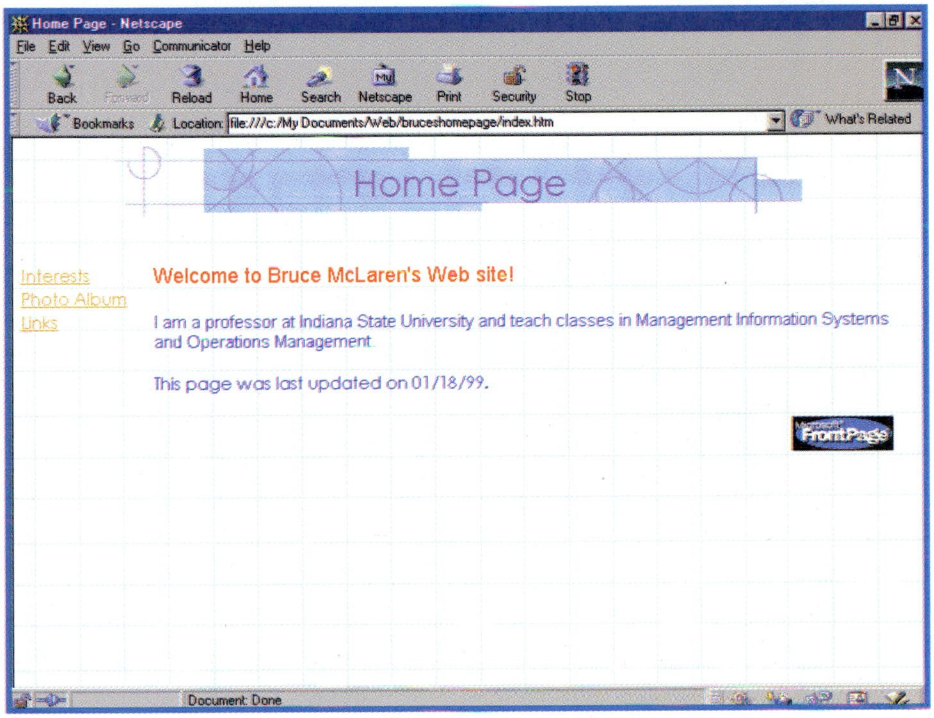

Figure 13.21
Final Home Page in Netscape browser

NET TIP
URL for your Front-Page web

*For now, each page in your web is saved on your hard drive. The URL begins with file:///. When you **publish** your web, its pages are copied to the Web server and its URL will refer to your Web server. Use the Publish button in Explorer to publish your web.*

THINKING ABOUT TECHNOLOGY

Why would it be helpful to use a FrontPage theme when designing a Web site for an organization? How could the common elements in the theme aid in your Web design? Have you noticed common elements in other Web sites?

NET FACT

There's Much More to FrontPage

In this introductory book, you are experiencing just a small sample of the many features FrontPage has to offer. It has many other wizards, or you can create your own pages without the help of a wizard. When you gain experience with FrontPage, you can create a sophisticated site with extensive links, art and animation, and links to a database. You can create a guest book, a form for user registration, and a search page. If you are interested in learning more about FrontPage, check out the FrontPage Web site at *www.microsoft.com/frontpage*. When you are ready to create you own site on the World Wide Web using FrontPage, you can buy an easy-to-follow tutorial to guide you through the program's many features. Just go to South-Western Educational Publishing's Computer Education page at *www.swep.com/computered*, and order *Microsoft FrontPage 2000*, by Ciampa.

CHAPTER Review

NET VOCABULARY

Define the following terms:

1. download
2. frame
3. FrontPage
4. FrontPage Editor

5. FrontPage Explorer
6. FrontPage web
7. plug-in
8. publish

9. tasks list
10. theme
11. thumbnail

NET REVIEW

Give a short answer to the following questions.

1. How can you make a Web page download more quickly?

2. What functions can you perform in FrontPage Explorer?

3. What do wizards do in FrontPage?

4. How can you view the actual HTML codes that FrontPage generates?

5. From Editor, how can you open another page in the same web?

6. How can you create a hyperlink in FrontPage?

7. How can you publish the pages in your FrontPage web?

CREATE A SMALL BUSINESS HOME PAGE

Imagine you are the owner of a lawn maintenance business called Ace Lawn Care in a small college town. You offer year-round maintenance services for lawns as well as snow removal. One reason for preparing your Web page is to offer lawn care services on rental properties for owners or residents who are gone for the summer.

First list the goals for your Web page. What kinds of services will you advertise there? What information do you need to include on your site? You can make up the address, telephone number, fax number, and e-mail address. What pages will you use for your Web site? Write up the design in outline form.

Use FrontPage to create a prototype Web site for Ace Lawn Care. You might find the Corporate Presence Wizard helpful in building your site. That wizard will ask you detailed questions about what components you want it to put into the Web site, such as

- Main pages to include (Home, What's New, Products/Services, Table of Contents, Feedback Form, Search Form)
- Topics for each type of page
- Number of products and services
- What information to get from the feedback form
- What information should appear at the top and bottom of each page
- What theme to use

After answering these questions, the wizard will build the web pages and place sample text into each file, just like the Personal Web Wizard did with your personal web. Then you can go into the Editor and customize the text to fit your business. Print a copy of all the pages of your site.

NET PROJECT TEAMWORK

Perfect Your Site

Together, your team should prepare a site for your company, Ace Lawn Care, as described in the Net Project. Then each team member should go to the Internet and search for Web sites of lawn maintenance companies. Each person should select a different Web site that can contribute good design ideas to your team's site and print out the pages. Together, your team should decide how to improve your site, based on the sample Web pages each of you found. Then make your site the best, most appealing business site you can.

Prepare to present your finished Web site to the class. Discuss its features and why you decided to include them. Explain how your site will help your company attract business.

WRITING ABOUT TECHNOLOGY

FrontPage: What's Your Verdict?

Now that you have had a chance to work with FrontPage, write a paper for the owner of a small business like Ace Lawn Care, explaining why FrontPage would be a good tool for creating an E-commerce Web site. Do you think the average non-technical Internet user could create an attractive Web site using FrontPage.

Browser Basics

This appendix will give you a quick tutorial on how to use the two most popular Web browsers: Netscape Navigator and Microsoft Internet Explorer. You will learn how to get around the Web using links and URLs. You will also learn about how to use the features of your browser to find information within a site, access Help files, print, and bookmark your favorite sites.

THE HYPERTEXT CONCEPT

Hypertext links, or **hyperlinks**, are links from one Web page to another or from one location to another within the same page. Hypertext linking capabilities are the foundation of the World Wide Web. The Web is organized as pages that users can display one at a time. Hypertext links within the pages allow you to jump from one page to another or to other locations in the same page with the click of the mouse.

Hypertext links can appear as simply words on the Web page, usually underlined and in a different color, such as blue or red. Embedded in this link is the address of another Web location. When clicked, the link takes you to the embedded address.

Hypertext links can also appear as icons or images. You can tell that you have encountered a link when you move your mouse over something on the page and your cursor changes to a hand. When you see the hand, you know that you can click in that spot to go to the Web location described by the words or image you see. For example, at bookseller Amazon.com's Web site, pictures of books contain hypertext links. When you click the picture of a book, the embedded link will take you to a page containing detailed information about that particular book. Clicking the underscored author's name will take you to a list of other books by that same author.

Parts of an image can contain links as well. For example, a campus map on a university Web site might

Net Terms

Hypertext links

hyperlinks

browser

Uniform Resource Locator (URL)

HyperText Transport Protocol

cache

bookmark

contain links to more detailed information. The information you get depends on where you click on the map. If you click, say, the computer lab building, the link might take you to a description of how to get there, its hours, and the resources you will find there.

Well-organized hypertext links can help you easily navigate to the information you want. The top of a Web page might have an index with linked section headings. You can click on a section heading to go directly to that page or part of the document. Well-designed Web pages will also provide hyperlinks that help you go back to the index or home page or to another page when you get to the end of the one you are reading.

Hypertext links can also be organized in layers of detail. Home pages often provide broad overview links. Clicking on one of these takes you to a list of more specific options. For example, at *altavista.com*, you can click the Shopping link from among the categories offered on the home page. At the shopping page, you can choose links to different types of products. If you click Sporting Goods, you can then choose from links to different types of sports. This kind of organization of links helps you to progressively narrow your search until you find just what you want

WEB BROWSERS

A Web **browser** is a program that enables you to view Web pages. When you enter an address in the browser or click a hyperlink, the browser displays the linked page on your screen. The two most common browsers are Netscape Navigator and Microsoft Internet Explorer.

Some of the developers of Mosaic, the first major Web browser, formed the Netscape Company, and produced the next big leap in Web browsers: Netscape Navigator. Navigator, now part of the larger package of Web tools called Communicator, became the leading Web browser in a very short time. Communicator is available at no cost on the Netscape home page.

Microsoft's Internet Explorer is the only major competitor to Netscape Navigator. In late fall 1997, Microsoft introduced version 4.0 of Internet Explorer that is comparable to Netscape Communicator 4.5. Internet Explorer is available at no cost from Microsoft's Web site. Figure A.1 shows the Microsoft home page displayed in the Internet Explorer browser.

The competition between Netscape and Internet Explorer is healthy, but may result in incompatibilities with some Web pages. However, the Internet Explorer commands are *very* similar to Netscape Navigator commands. If you are familiar with one browser, you will have little trouble switching to the other.

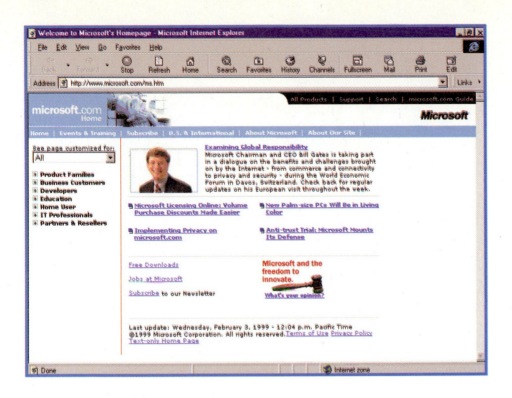

Figure A.1
Microsoft Web site

USING A BROWSER TO EXPLORE THE WEB

This section explains Web browsing using Netscape Navigator for most of the examples. If you have Internet Explorer, the process will be nearly identical.

Starting Your Browser

During the installation process, your browser will install itself in the Start menu and should leave a shortcut icon on your desktop. To start Navigator, click the Start button, click Programs, and then select Netscape Navigator in the Netscape Communicator program group. Or, you can double-click the Netscape Navigator (or Communicator) icon on your desktop. To start Internet Explorer from the Start button, click Programs, and then select Internet Explorer in the Internet Explorer program group. Or, double-click the Internet Explorer icon on your desktop.

Because your browser requires an Internet connection, it will check for a current connection. If it doesn't find one and you are using dial-up networking, your browser will bring up the Connect To dialog box and wait for you to initiate the connection. It is possible to bring up your browser *without* the Internet connection if you want to display a Web page contained in a file on your disk.

When you first connect to the Internet, your browser will display the default home page. If you have just installed Navigator, it will open to the Netscape Netcenter home page at *http://home.netscape.com/*, shown in Figure A.2. Internet Explorer initially opens to the Microsoft home page. Later in this appendix you will learn how you can change to a different starting page if you like.

> **NET TIP**
> **Start Menu Shortcut**
>
> *If you right-drag the Web browser shortcut from your desktop to the Start button, a new shortcut to the browser will appear above Programs when you click the Start button.*

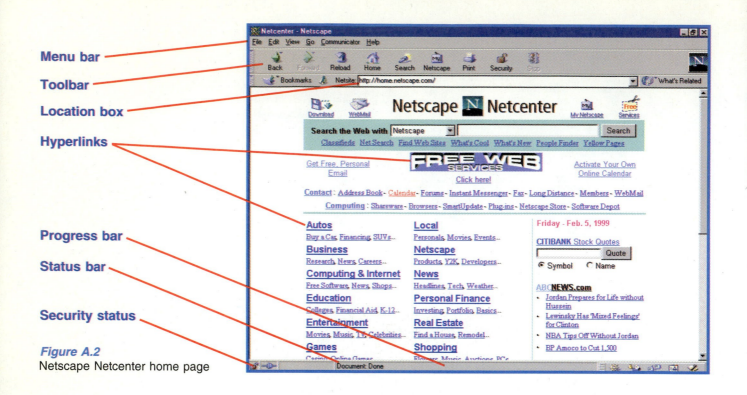

Menu bar

Toolbar

Location box

Hyperlinks

Progress bar

Status bar

Security status

Figure A.2
Netscape Netcenter home page

The Main Browser Window

Figure A.2 shows the standard menus, buttons, and tools in Navigator. Like other Windows applications, Navigator features a standard menu bar, with toolbar buttons just beneath it for frequently used commands. The location box just beneath the toolbar shows the Internet address of the particular document being displayed at the moment. You can go to a new location by entering another address in the location box. The Netscape N symbol in the upper right corner of the window is animated. When Navigator is retrieving a page, you'll see meteors flashing by the N.

The large window in the middle of the screen displays the Web document—in this case, the Netscape Netcenter home page. A Web site's home page is a good starting point for exploring the site. Like a book's table of contents, a site's home page gives an overview of what the site contains. Hyperlinks on the home page help you start "turning the pages" to find the information you want.

At the bottom of the page is the status bar. The browser uses the status bar to give you messages about its progress as it retrieves the page you selected. To the left of the status bar is a progress bar. As the browser is retrieving a page, this bar fills with moving color to indicate that the browser is actively locating and retrieving the page.

The padlock at the lower left indicates whether the page you are viewing is secure or not. An open lock means that transactions you send from this page transmit across the Internet as plain text. A closed lock indicates that transmissions are encoded for privacy. You'll learn about security in Appendix C.

Figure A.2 also shows examples of two types of hyperlinks. The underlined words are hyperlinks. So is the graphic "Free Web Services." When you move the mouse pointer over a hyperlink, the cursor will turn to a hand and the embedded address will appear in the status bar.

Uniform Resource Locator (URL)

The **Uniform Resource Locator (URL)** is the address of a Web page. It defines for your browser the route to take to find the page. The URL for Netscape Netcenter shown in the location box of Figure A.2 is *http://home.netscape.com/*.

Every page on the Web has a URL that tells the browser where to find it on the Internet. A URL has several parts:

- *http://* stands for **HyperText Transport Protocol**, the communication rules used to connect to servers on the Web and transmit pages to a browser. You don't have to type the http:// portion with today's browsers. Since every URL begins this way, the browser will insert it automatically in front of whatever you type in the location box.
- *home.netscape.com* is the domain address for the Web server on the Internet that holds this Netscape site. Many URLs on the Web begin with the initials "www".
- Following the extension (*.com* in this case) is a path to a particular page on the site. For example, if you pass your mouse over different hyperlinks on the Netscape Netcenter page and watch the status bar, you will see letters, numbers, and symbols added to the end of *http://home.netcenter.com*, each locating the specific page for the browser.

Retrieving a Page

You can retrieve a Web page by either clicking a hyperlink or keying the URL into the Location box. The browser knows from the address which server contains the page. It then requests the page from that server and displays it on your screen.

After you click a text hyperlink, you may see it turn to a different color. In Netscape, links usually change from blue to purple. This change in color tells you that you have recently followed that link. By default, this link will stay purple for 30 days before returning to blue.

To key in a URL, use Netscape's File|Open Page command or click the Location box in the toolbar. For Internet Explorer, use the File|Open command or click the Address box in the toolbar. Then type the exact URL into the box and click Open or press the Enter key. You must have the complete URL for the site and type it accurately. If you don't know the URL of a particular site, you can often guess by keying *www.* followed by the organization's name and the appropriate extension (*.edu* for schools, *.com* for businesses, or *.gov* for a government site). Then press Enter. If you guessed right, the browser will go there.

> **NET TIP**
> **Browsers Remember**
>
> *Both Internet Explorer and Netscape Navigator (version 4.0 and later) "remember" previously visited site URLs and will automatically fill in the Address or Location box as you enter a URL. Not only does this feature save time, but it also prevents keying errors.*

Viewing Previous Pages

Your browser has two buttons in the toolbar for viewing pages previously viewed during this session. The Back button (or Go|Back from the menu bar) will take you backward to the page you viewed immediately before the page currently displayed on your screen. The Forward button (or Go|Forward from the menu bar) will reverse that command. It will take you forward to the page you viewed immediately after the one currently displayed on your screen. You can also right-click the browser window and select Back or Forward from that menu.

Remember, both buttons navigate to pages you have viewed already in this session. If you haven't viewed a page after the one currently displayed, the Forward button (or Forward menu selection) will be dim. This means it is inactive.

The Go menu will also display most of the sites you have visited during this browser session. Click Go, and then select the page you want to return to. To get back to your browser's home page, click Home in the Go menu or click the Home button.

When you visit Web pages, your browser keeps data from these pages in a temporary storage area called a **cache**. This temporary storage on your machine allows your browser to redisplay these sites more quickly than would be possible if it requested the pages again from the server. A cache is particularly helpful when you redisplay images. Since images take much longer to load than text, the cache will significantly reduce the loading time for pages containing large image files.

Changing Your Default Home Page

You don't have to use the browser's default home page as your starting point when you connect to the Internet. You can change it to any page you want. To change the default home page in Navigator, use the Edit|Preferences|Navigator command and enter the URL in the Location box. Figure A.3 shows the process for changing the default to the Yahoo home page. If you are currently displaying the page you want for your default home page, simply click the Use Current Page button. The next time you start Navigator or click the Home button, your new selection will take effect.

Interrupting a Web Page

If you entered the wrong URL or the current page is taking longer to load than you want to wait, you can interrupt the transfer of a Web page by clicking the Stop button in the toolbar or by pressing the Esc key. Your browser will display whatever was transferred before you stopped it.

Your browser transfers the text portions of the Web page first and then the graphic images. Some images are large and take a long time to load. Pressing the Stop button will display the received portion of the page and might allow you to select the next link. If you interrupt a graphic image in the middle, it will be partially saved in the cache.

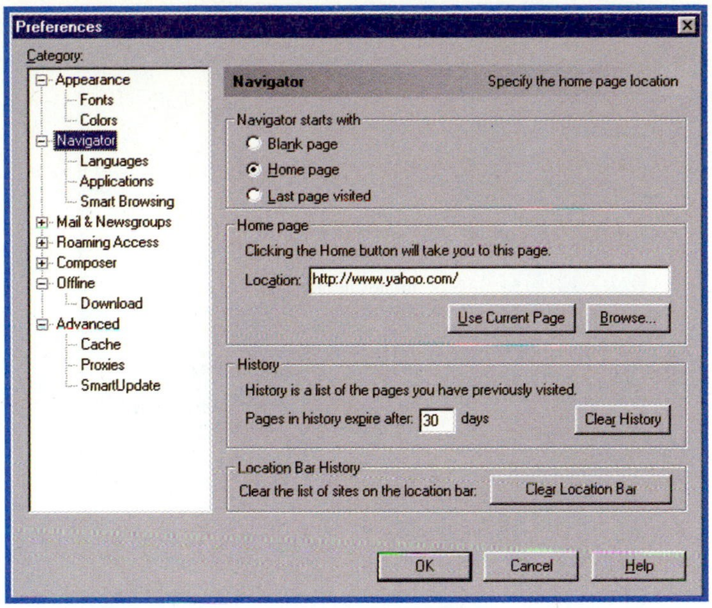

Figure A.3
Netscape Navigator
Preferences dialog box

The next time you visit that site, your browser will retrieve the cached portion and download the remaining unsaved portion of the image from the site.

Reloading a Web Page

If something goes wrong with the display of a page, you can click Netscape's Reload button, or use the View|Reload command or its shortcut, Ctrl+R. Netscape will request that the Web page be retransmitted. With Internet Explorer, click the Refresh button, or use the View|Refresh command.

Getting Help

When you open a menu from the menu bar and highlight a command in the menu by moving your cursor over it, the status bar will give you a one-sentence description of what that command will do. You can learn about various commands by selecting a menu item and then moving the cursor over each command to read the description in the status bar. Netscape also uses tooltips–move the cursor onto a button for a moment, and Netscape will display a phrase that describes what that button will do.

The most common operations are available with the browser's toolbar buttons. If your Navigator screen doesn't show the toolbar buttons, use the View|Show Navigation Toolbar command to turn it on. If you would like to display the button icons along with their names in the toolbar, use Netscape's Edit|Preferences|Appearance command and make that selection.

Many dialog boxes have a Help button for assistance with choices in that box. Choosing the Help button brings up a hyperlinked Help window. From there, you can scroll the contents window on the left, or use the Index button and search for help by keyword. The Find button will search through the actual help display on the right.

Appendix A   Browser Basics   **263**

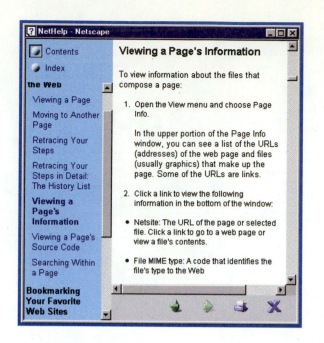

Figure A.4
Netscape NetHelp window

For general help, press the F1 function key or use the Help|Help Contents command in Navigator. Figure A.4 shows the Netscape NetHelp window.

In Internet Explorer, get help by pressing F1 or using the Help|Contents and Index command. A similar hyperlinked Help window appears, in which you can select the desired help topic in the left pane and see the help information in the right pane. Figure A.5 shows the Internet Explorer Help window.

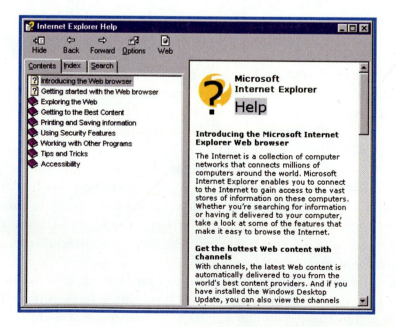

Figure A.5
Internet Explorer Help window

Printing a Web Page

To print a Web page, click the Print button in the toolbar or use the File|Print command. In the Print dialog box, you can choose to print all of the displayed Web page or specify a range to print. You can also select the number of copies and the print resolution. Click OK to begin printing.

Keep in mind that many Web pages are essentially graphic images and may not look as good on a low-resolution printer as they do on your monitor. If you have a color printer such as an inkjet, printed images should look very good.

Using the Find Command for the Current Page

Although most Web pages are relatively short and are subdivided into sections, some are very long, making it difficult to search manually for a particular keyword. You can scroll up and down in the currently displayed page with the vertical scroll bar, just like any other Windows document. Most Web browsers allow the use of the PageUp and PageDn keys, provided that your cursor is set in the browser window, not the Location box.

You can use the Edit|Find (or Ctrl+F) command to locate keywords in the *currently displayed* Web page. You'll be asked to enter the keyword string in the Find What text box and select the search direction, as shown in Figure A.6. Click the Find button, and your browser will search from that point in the desired direction. If a match is found, it will move the pointer to the next point at which the keywords are found and highlight the keyword on the screen. The Find command can help with large or complex Web pages. Note that Find may not discover keywords that reside in forms. The Internet Explorer Find box is similar but adds the Match Whole Word Only option.

NET TIP
Print Button

If you click the Print button in Internet Explorer, the entire document is printed without displaying the Print dialog box. This is similar to the Print button's function in Microsoft Office.

NET TIP
Print Preview

If the Web page you have displayed is very long, use Navigator's File|Print Preview command and scroll through the preview. Then print only those pages that are of interest to you by specifying their page numbers in the Print dialog box. Internet Explorer does not have a Print preview feature.

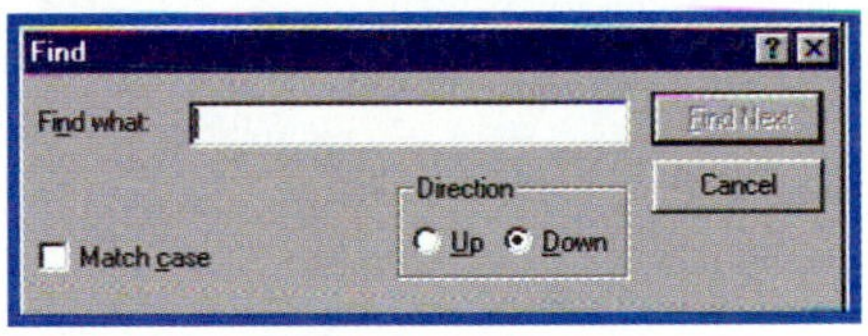

Figure A.6
Netscape Find command dialog box

Using Bookmarks and Favorites

A **bookmark** is a Web address stored for easy retrieval later. You can use the browser's bookmark feature to store the URLs of your favorite Web sites. Then you can return to the sites easily, without having to memorize their URLs. You can simply click the bookmark.

You can organize your bookmarks in folders and edit their names and sequence in the bookmark list. In Navigator, the bookmark feature is called Bookmarks. In Internet Explorer, bookmarks are called Favorites. They are essentially identical.

Adding a Bookmark. To add a location to your bookmark list, first go to that Web page. In Navigator, click the Bookmarks button and select the Add Bookmark command. The location and description of that location will be placed at the bottom of your bookmark list. In Internet Explorer, click Favorites and then Add to Favorites to add the current page to the Favorites list. Internet Explorer maintains the bookmarks in alphabetical order in the Favorites list.

Jumping to a Bookmarked Location. To jump to a page in your bookmark list, click the Bookmarks button in the Navigator toolbar (or the Favorites button in Internet Explorer). Then click the bookmark of the site you want to visit. Your browser will retrieve that page.

Figure A.7 shows some bookmarks in Navigator. Notice that some of the bookmarks are folders. You can create folders to organize your bookmarks, just like you organize your files in Windows Explorer. In Navigator, you can create a folder from the Bookmarks|Edit Bookmarks menu. In Internet Explorer, you can add a new folder from the Favorites|Organize Favorites menu. To display the bookmarks within a folder, click the folder to open it. Folders can contain other folders, too.

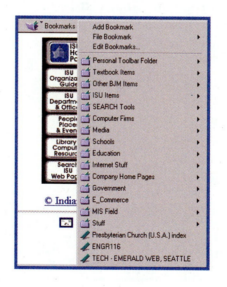

Figure A.7
Netscape Bookmark list

E-Mail Basics

This appendix introduces you to electronic mail—the basic tool for sending messages to other users over the Internet. The major e-mail programs operate similarly. If you have a different program from the one illustrated here, you will still be able to apply the concepts to whatever program you have.

HOW E-MAIL WORKS

Electronic mail, or **e-mail**, is a message transmitted electronically over the Internet or a local area network to one or more receivers. If you are connected to the Internet through an Internet service provider (ISP), messages sent to you will be stored on a computer at your ISP until you request them. If you are part of a local area network (LAN), a business's internal network, messages sent to you will be stored in your mailbox on the network's server computer.

E-mail shares some similarities with regular or "snail" mail. With e-mail, you must have the receiver's address. You write the message and then "mail" it by using the Send command. The message is routed from your computer to the receiver's mailbox. But unlike regular mail, e-mail is usually delivered in minutes or even seconds. When you request mail from your mailbox, your ISP (or network server) transmits the mail to your computer and removes it from its computer. After reading your mail, you can delete it or store it on your computer for future reference.

An e-mail message is a lot like a regular letter or memo. It contains a header with the receiver's address, the sender's address, the subject of the message, and the date and time when the message was sent. After the header comes the body or text of the message itself. You can also choose to add a signature block to the end of the message.

When you receive an e-mail message, you will see additional text in the header area, reflecting the handling of your message by the outgoing and incoming mail systems. Figure B.1 shows a typical e-mail

Key Terms

electronic mail (e-mail)

clipboard

address Book

filter

netiquette

spamming

emoticon

message next to the mailboxes window. As new messages arrive from your ISP or network server, they are stored in your "In" mailbox, or "Inbox," shown at top. We will describe parts of this e-mail window later in this appendix.

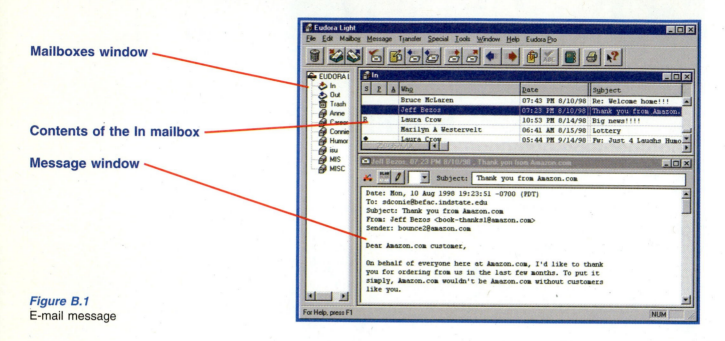

Mailboxes window

Contents of the In mailbox

Message window

Figure B.1
E-mail message

Advantages of E-mail

E-mail is very fast—your mail is usually delivered immediately if the receiver's mailbox is in the same local area network. It will be delivered in a few minutes when it is sent over the Internet. E-mail is entirely electronic and doesn't require paper copies unless you want a printed version. Because the message is electronic, you can use other computer tools, such as a spell checker, in creating your message. Most ISPs include electronic mail services as part of their Internet connection fees. Some may charge a nominal fee for low-volume usage.

E-mail is convenient. When you are working on the computer and want to communicate with someone else, it is easy to send an e-mail message. It is particularly convenient for brief messages that don't require the face-to-face or voice-to-voice interaction that some discussions might require. You can arrange meetings, keep up with your friends, or send pictures to family across the country by e-mail.

With Windows or Macintosh, it is easy to copy material from other documents and insert it into an e-mail message. The reverse is also true: You can copy material from an incoming e-mail message into other messages or documents.

Disadvantages of E-mail

E-mail works only if both parties agree to use it to communicate. If either party does not (or cannot) check the mailbox, communication does not take place. Although most e-mail systems are compatible, some advanced e-mail programs add formatting codes that may confuse the receiver's e-mail program.

E-mail is not as personal as meeting with people face-to-face or talking to them by phone. Using e-mail, you can't read the meaning transmitted by body language or voice. You also don't get the immediate response that you get from talking with someone directly. Even though e-mail transmits quickly, the receiver must read it before communication is complete.

E-mail is *not* the same as U. S. mail with respect to privacy. Although the law forbids reading other people's postal mail, electronic mail is not protected. In fact, an employee's e-mail is considered the property of the organization. Company officials can—and do—read employees' e-mail.

E-mail Address

Your e-mail address is based on your user name and the domain name of your ISP or organization. For example, my e-mail address is *mfbjm@befac.indstate.edu*. The letters *mfbjm* are my user name, *befac* is the name of the network server that contains my mailbox, *indstate* is the designation for Indiana State University, and *edu* represents an educational institution. *indstate.edu* is the domain name that uniquely identifies the server computer at Indiana State.

If you connect to the Internet through an ISP, the domain name in your e-mail address will be that of your ISP. For example, an address with the ISP America Online would take this form: *username@aol.com*.

If you don't know your receiver's e-mail address, there are several ways to find it. Many people now advertise their e-mail address in phone directories and on business cards. If you have an e-mail message sent by that person, that message will contain the person's e-mail address. Many ISPs and organizations let you search their electronic directories for addresses of people who belong to the same ISP or organization as you do. You can also look up an e-mail address on the Internet. Popular search sites like Yahoo and Altavista have a "people finder" feature for finding addresses.

USING E-MAIL

Before you can send or receive messages, you must have an Internet connection and an e-mail account. If your company or school has an e-mail system, your account will be established automatically when you become part of the organization. If you connect through an ISP, your e-mail account will be set up when you establish your Internet account with the ISP.

Eudora Light

Eudora Light is the shareware version of the popular Eudora e-mail software. You can download a free copy of this software from Qualcomm Corporation. To download the setup file, go to the Eudora Web page at *http://www.eudora.com/* and follow the links to the download page. The remainder of this appendix will demonstrate how to perform essential e-mail tasks using Eudora Light for illustrations. Other e-mail programs will operate similarly.

Creating a New Message

Here is the general procedure for sending a message:

1. Start the e-mail software from an icon on your desktop or from the Start button.
2. Specify that you want to create a new message by clicking the New Mail Message icon or clicking File|New Mail Message in some e-mail programs.
3. Supply the receiver's e-mail address and create an appropriate subject header for your message.
4. Key your message into the message window. Be sure to proofread your message before sending it.
5. Click the Send button to transmit it to its destination.

Parts of the New Message Window. The Eudora message header consists of six parts, as shown in Figure B.2. You can send messages or copies to any number of receivers. Simply include all addresses in the appropriate address box. Most e-mail programs will remember your address and will automatically enter it for you in the "From" box.

In the Subject box, key in a brief description of the topic of your message. Your receivers will see this subject in their mailbox listing, so choose a subject wording that tells them at a glance what your message is about.

You may write a message directly to someone but want others to receive a copy. If you want everyone to know who received copies, enter the addresses of the people to be copied in the Cc (for "carbon copy") box. If you don't want others to know who got copies, use the Bcc (for "blind carbon copy") box.

You can attach electronic files of any kind to an e-mail message. When you attach a file, the file name will appear in the Attachment box of Eudora. In other e-mail programs, the file name and an icon appear in the message box. You will learn more about attaching files later in this appendix.

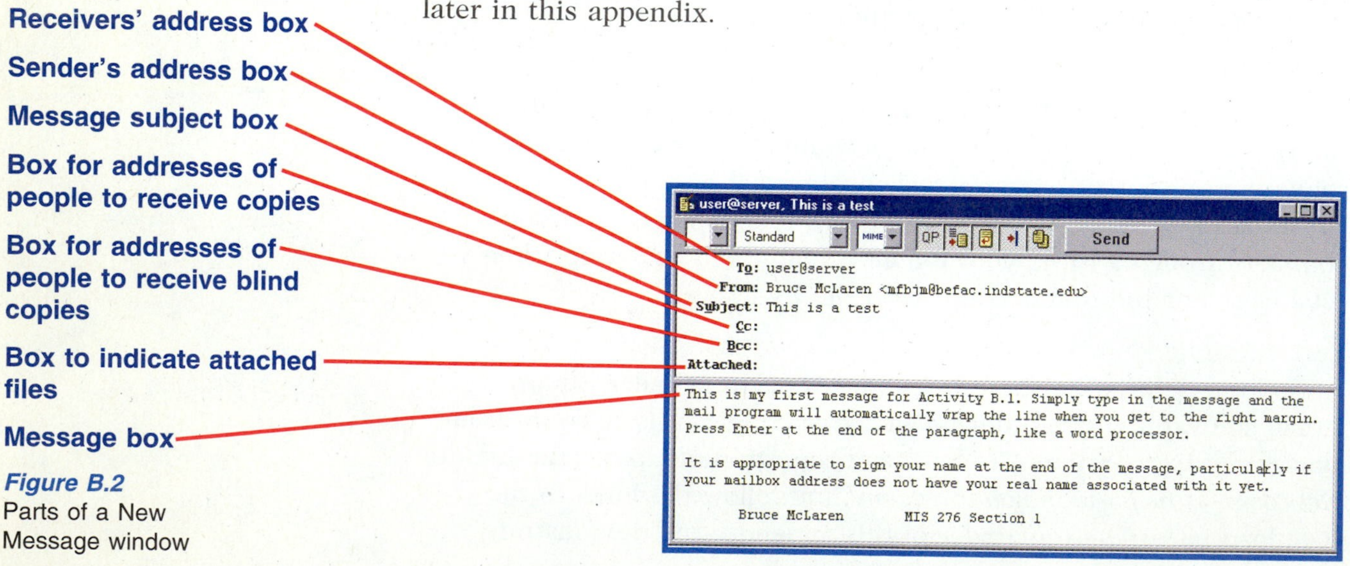

Receivers' address box

Sender's address box

Message subject box

Box for addresses of people to receive copies

Box for addresses of people to receive blind copies

Box to indicate attached files

Message box

Figure B.2
Parts of a New Message window

Creating the Message. Most e-mail systems contain a limited-feature word processor for creating and editing your messages. Simply begin keying on the first line of the message box and continue keying until you reach the end of the paragraph. The editor will wrap your message at the end of the line, so press the Enter key only at the end of a paragraph. Use the arrow keys or the mouse to move the cursor to different places in the message. The e-mail program's word processor will have commands for such things as deleting a word, deleting a line, and so forth. Eudora uses many of the same text editing shortcut commands as MS Word. Delete and Backspace have the usual effects. Ctrl+Delete deletes the word to the right of the cursor location. Ctrl+Backspace deletes the word to the left of the cursor location. Ctrl+Home moves to the top of the message. Ctrl+End moves to the end of the message.

Some e-mail programs will automatically reformat lines for you as you insert or delete text, while others require that you issue the reformat command yourself. If you are using a Windows-based e-mail program, most of the usual Windows commands will work. For example, you can use the Windows **clipboard** to copy or cut text from one message and paste it elsewhere in the same message or into a different message. You can even bring text into an e-mail message from another Windows document via the clipboard.

Sending the Message. Once you have finished your message, proofread it before sending it on its way. If your mail system has a spell checker, use it now. When you are ready to send the message, click the Send button illustrated in Figure B.3. Most mail programs automatically keep a copy of all outgoing messages. Eudora stores these copies in the Out mailbox. Other e-mail programs store the copies in a mailbox called something like "Sent Items." Your mailbox can rapidly fill with these copies. You should periodically empty your Out or Sent Items mailbox of unneeded messages (printing any you wish to save).

Figure B.3
Eudora's Send button

Reading a Message

Depending on how your e-mail program is configured, it may prompt you when you have unread mail in your mailbox, or you may not know if you have new mail until you request it. To request your mail, click the Check Mail button in the toolbar (Eudora's is shown in Figure B.4). Other programs may label this button something like "Send and Receive." You can also check for mail using a menu command. In Eudora, that command is File|Check Mail.

Some mail systems (including Eudora) require you to enter a password before you can retrieve messages. You can configure most e-mail programs to "remember" your password so that you don't have to enter it each time. Be cautious with this setting, however. In an environment where other people have access to your computer, unscrupulous users can gain access to your mail account and send objectionable messages under your name.

Figure B.4
Eudora's Check Mail button

Select the message you want to read in your incoming mailbox and double-click to open it. The message will be displayed in the message window, as shown in Figure B.1 on page 268. After reading the message, you have several options: delete it, save it in a mailbox, forward or redirect it to another user's mailbox, or prepare a reply to the original sender. Most e-mail programs will let you leave the read mail in the In mailbox. This is helpful if you want the message to appear as a reminder to answer it or do something else with it later.

NET TIP

Reply to Whom?

One caution is in order for replying to a message originally sent to a group of people. Do you want your reply to go to just the original sender or to the entire group? Most e-mail programs let you choose All or Sender. You could be embarrassed if you accidentally send to all receivers a reply you intended for the original sender only.

Replying to a Message

Often, you will want to reply to the message you just read. To do so, highlight the message and use the Message|Reply command or click the Reply button in the toolbar. (Eudora's Reply button is pictured in Figure B.5.) The e-mail program will open a new message window and place the address of the original sender in the To box and your e-mail address in the From box. You can use the same subject, modify it, or replace it with your own subject. Then move to the New Message window and create your reply.

Most e-mail programs will include a copy of the original message with your reply. To distinguish the original from the reply, the program may put a > or other character before each line of the original message. You can key your responses next to relevant portions of the original message, or key your entire reply in one place. You can also delete parts of the original message that aren't relevant to your reply.

Figure B.5
Eudora's Reply button

Printing a Message

To print a message with Eudora and other e-mail programs, select the message and click the Print button, similar to the one pictured in Figure B.6. If you instead use the File|Print command, a dialog box will appear that will let you choose which pages to print (default is all pages) and some other printer options.

Figure B.6
Eudora's Print button

Eudora will print a special header and footer in bold for each page of the message. The sender's name, date, time, and subject appear in the header, while the receiver's address and page number appear in the footer. Like Eudora, other e-mail programs let you choose options such as the font, page margins, and print quality. Use the Tools|Options|Fonts command to select the screen and printer fonts for your messages.

Figure B.7
Eudora's Forward button

Forwarding a Message

To forward a message to another user, highlight that message in the mailbox and choose the Message|Forward command or click Forward button in the toolbar, pictured in Figure B.7. Eudora will open a message window with the contents of the original message, each line preceded by a >. Enter the address of the person to whom you are sending the message. You can make changes or comments as needed to the body of the message. Click the Send button or press Ctrl+E to forward the message.

Figure B.8
Eudora's Delete
Message button

Deleting a Message

To delete a message in Eudora, select the message and click the trash can icon (pictured in Figure B.8), or use the Message|Delete command or Ctrl+D. Other programs may use a large X or some other icon for deleting a message.

When you delete a message, it will be copied to the Trash mailbox folder (or Deleted Items folder in other programs). To get rid of your deleted messages completely, you must empty the trash. To do this in Eudora, use the Empty Trash command from the Special menu. In other programs, you will find a similar command, such as Empty Deleted Items in the Tools menu of Microsoft Internet Mail. Like the Windows Recycling Bin and the Macintosh Trash Can, this two-step process allows you to retrieve a "deleted" message from the trash before it is gone completely. Most users appreciate the value of this extra step.

USING E-MAIL FEATURES

Many e-mail programs offer features such as group mailings, attaching document files to the message, and multiple mailboxes. Some also allow you to request notification when a message you sent has been delivered and read by the receiver.

Address Book

You can use your e-mail program's **address book** to store names and e-mail addresses of the people with whom you communicate. Some address books can also store other information about your correspondents, such as street addresses, phone numbers, and even notes about them that you want to record on their address cards. To create an address card, open the address book by clicking its icon. Click New in Eudora. (Other programs call this button New Card or New Contact.) A dialog box will appear, similar to the one pictured in Figure B.9. Fill in the person's name, e-mail address, and other contact information, and then save the card.

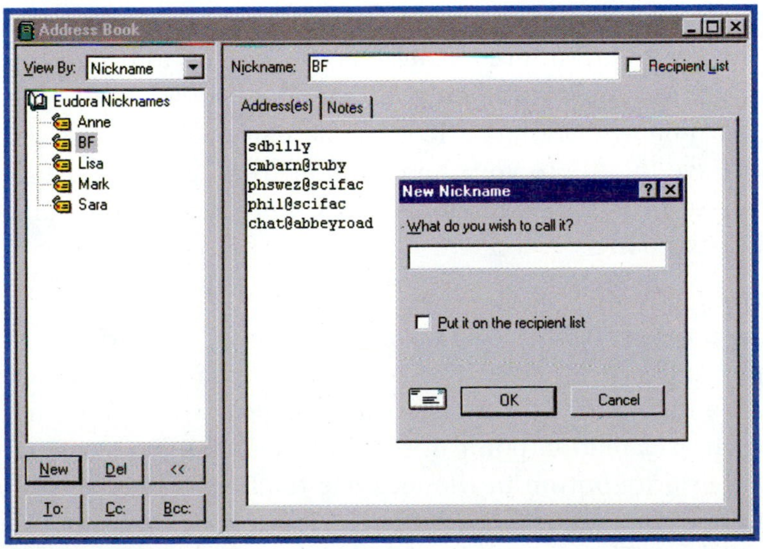

Figure B.9
Eudora's Address Book
dialog box

NET FACT

Emoticons

The whimsical images known as **emoticons** are a set of keyboard characters that, when viewed sideways, indicate the writer's emotion. Because they can be created with any keyboard, they are popular for expressing feelings in e-mail messages. It is much more difficult to communicate subtle meanings with an e-mail message than with a phone call or face-to-face meeting. This is a good reason to use emoticons. But when you want to project professionalism, use emoticons sparingly.

Here are some typical emoticons:

:-)	smile
:-D	wide smile or grin
;-)	wink or light sarcasm
:-1	indifference
:-(	frown or anger
:-0	shock or surprise
:-/	perplexed

Figure B.10
Eudora's Attach File button

Once stored, you can retrieve someone's e-mail address from the address book whenever you want to address a message to that person. To use the address book for addressing a new message, create a new message and type in the name that you used in the address book. Your e-mail program will fill in the full e-mail address when your message is sent. Or in some programs, you can click To in your new message header to bring up the address book. Then click the person's name from the list in your address book, and the e-mail address will be inserted into the To box.

You can also create a group mailing list and store it under one group name in your address book. To create a group list, open the address book by clicking its icon on the toolbar or using the Tools|Address Book command. In the Address Book dialog box, click the New button (or New Group in other programs). Then list the e-mail addresses of all the users you want in the group, separated by commas. In some programs, you can add user addresses to the group by selecting them from the address book. Give your group a name. Then close the address book. When you want to send a message to everyone in the group, just enter the group name in the message's To box or select the group name from the address book.

Attach Document File

Most e-mail programs allow you to transmit other files as attachments to your e-mail message. You may want to send someone a report you wrote in Word, a graphic image stored as an electronic file, or even a program file. Whatever you have stored on disk you can transmit to someone else as an e-mail attachment.

To attach a file, create a new e-mail message as usual. Then click the Attach File button in Eudora, shown in Figure B.10. In other programs, this button might be called something like Insert File. You can also use the Message|Attach File command in Eudora, or a similar one in other programs. A dialog box will appear, asking you the name of the file you want to attach. Select the name and enter it. The file name will appear in your message.

When you send the message, the attached document will be carried along. At the destination, the receiver will be told that the message has an attachment. When you receive an attachment, you can open it by double-clicking its icon or file name in the message. You can also save the file to your hard disk or to a floppy by using the File|Save Attachment command. Then specify where you want to save the attachment.

Priority Level

Some e-mail programs allow you to assign a "high" priority to an important message, so that it will stand out from other unread messages. The high-priority message usually appears in a different color or with an exclamation point in the receiver's mailbox. In Eudora, click the Priority button in the message toolbar to select a priority level. Eudora maintains five priority levels, from lowest through normal to highest. The priority level will show with your message's listing in the receiver's mailbox. Take care not to abuse the high or highest priority—remember the boy who cried "Wolf!"

Cancel Message

Few systems let you cancel a message that has already been sent. This feature, although rare, can be particularly useful when you have sent a message in error, or when you sent a hasty response that you later regret. The Cancel feature is not available with Eudora.

Mailbox System

Most systems let you set up a mailbox or folder system, in which you can store messages according to their content. It is a convenient way to organize messages. Standard Eudora mailboxes include:

- In mailbox, where incoming messages are placed
- Out mailbox, where copies of messages you sent are stored
- Trash mailbox, for messages you no longer want to keep

When you have many messages stored, it's hard to find a particular message. To get organized, you can create a filing system of mailbox folders, similar to the folder system on your hard drive. Designing a useful structure early on will save you grief later as your messages multiply. Suppose you are working on projects and have exchanged e-mail messages with several colleagues. You might want to file their replies in a mailbox associated with each project. That way, in the future you can more easily refer to messages about that project.

Creating a Mailbox. To create a mailbox in Eudora, use the Mailbox|New command and enter the mailbox name. If you want the mailbox to be stored as a separate Windows folder, click that box. Click OK to create the mailbox. The current mailbox names are displayed in the mailbox window at the left side of the Eudora window.

Transferring a Message to a Mailbox. You can transfer a message to a mailbox in Eudora by selecting that message, and then using the Transfer command from the menu bar. Slide the cursor down to the desired mailbox, and then click its name. Eudora will move your message from its current mailbox to the selected mailbox.

Message Signatures

Most mail systems let you create a personal e-mail signature that is automatically added to the end of outgoing messages, saving you time. Rather than resembling your written signature for checks or correspondence, the mail signature contains your name and address and any other information you would like to accompany your messages to all receivers. Many people include their telephone number and Web site address.

To create or edit a signature in Eudora, use the Tools|Signature command. Enter the information you would like in your signature, similar to Figure B.11, and then close the Signature dialog box. Eudora will add this signature text to the end of all outgoing messages unless you turn off the signature by using the Signature button in the New Message window.

> **NET TIP**
> **Drag-and-Drop**
>
> *You can also drag a message from one mailbox to another mailbox with the left mouse button.*

Figure B.11
Author's e-mail signature

E-Mail Netiquette

To make good use of e-mail, observe a few commonsense "rules of the road" in your messages. These suggestions are part of etiquette on the Internet, or **netiquette**.

- Identify yourself in the message. Fill in your personal name in the mail configuration, so that your name appears with your e-mail address in the From message header box.
- Avoid inflammatory or intimidating statements. Consider your response carefully before snapping off something you'll be sorry about later.
- Use ordinary capitalization. ALL CAPS is equivalent to "shouting" in e-mail.
- Read your mail promptly. Most senders expect their messages to be read as soon as they are received.
- Use emoticons when appropriate. (Emoticons are described elsewhere in this appendix.)
- Keep message length to a minimum, particularly when sending to a group or attaching a file. Most people don't want to wade through lengthy dissertations to get to the meaning in your message.
- Do repeat portions of your sender's message when replying. That way, the receiver will have a context for your reply.
- Minimize the number of people to whom you send copies of messages. Most users are busy and don't want to spend time reading messages that are not relevant to them. Sending copies of one message to many people is called **spamming**.

Spam

An infamous spamming incident occurred in 1994 when an Arizona law firm sent thousands of messages offering their immigration services to discussion and news groups. Some people estimate that up to 20% of the e-mail at AOL is junk e-mail.

Message Filters

Some mail systems provide **filters** that let you specify criteria for allowing some messages to pass through to your In mailbox while rejecting others, or for directing incoming messages to different mailboxes. A filter can help you keep unwanted e-mail from cluttering your In mailbox. You can specify e-mail addresses or subjects to be filtered. You can use filters to direct incoming e-mail into particular mailboxes by subject or sender. That way, you can read new mail according to its subject or by priority. If someone is using e-mail to bother you, you can filter mail from these individuals into the Trash mailbox.

Eudora Light supports use of e-mail filters through the Tools|Filters command. You can specify the content of any of the header blocks (To, From, Subject, and so forth) and give the filter condition (contains, doesn't contain, starts with, ends with, and so forth). The action section lets you specify what to do when a message matches that condition: open, copy to, or transfer to another mailbox.

Spelling Check

Many e-mail systems employ a spelling checker, similar to one in a word processing software. When you are dashing off a quick e-mail message, it's easy to make errors. If your e-mail package has a spell checker, use it! Most require that you manually invoke the spell check rather than check automatically. If you don't have a spell checker, then proofread carefully before you send the message.

Web Security

In this appendix, you will learn how e-merchants secure information sent over the Internet and how electronic payment systems work.

PROVIDING PRIVACY FOR E-COMMERCE VISITORS

You have seen many examples of electronic commerce in this book, from Amazon.com to ZDNet.com. Virtually every e-commerce site has an online catalog, a shopping cart to keep track of your purchases, and a method for gathering information about payment, usually with a credit card. To protect sensitive customer information, your browser encrypts the data before it is sent back to the e-commerce Web site. *Encrypted* data is scrambled or coded to prevent unauthorized individuals from understanding it if they intercept it as it travels across the Internet to its destination.

Secure Sockets Layer

Secure sockets layer (SSL) is the most common method for encrypting data on the Web. Browsers that support SSL are able to communicate with a Web server that encrypts data. Both Netscape Navigator (v. 2.0 and later) and Internet Explorer support SSL. The symbol for a secure session is a closed lock in the status bar. Figure C.1 shows the Netscape Navigator browser with a secure connection, as indicated by the closed lock in the status bar. Notice that the URL in the Location box begins with **https://** for **HyperText Transport Protocol Secure.** The https:// designation in the URL directs the transmission to a secure Web server. Normal unencrypted sessions begin with http://.

Not all of a merchant's Web site needs to be encrypted. Public areas for displaying product information don't involve sensitive information. Most e-commerce Web sites only encrypt the checkout area. Encrypting the Web page slows down the process of sending information between the Web server and your browser. Like Lands' End in Figure C.1, merchants often offer three options for placing

Net Terms

secure sockets layer (SSL)

HyperText Transport Protocol Secure (https)

encryption key

digital certificate

spoofing

Pretty Good Privacy (PGP)

firewall

digital cash

smart cards

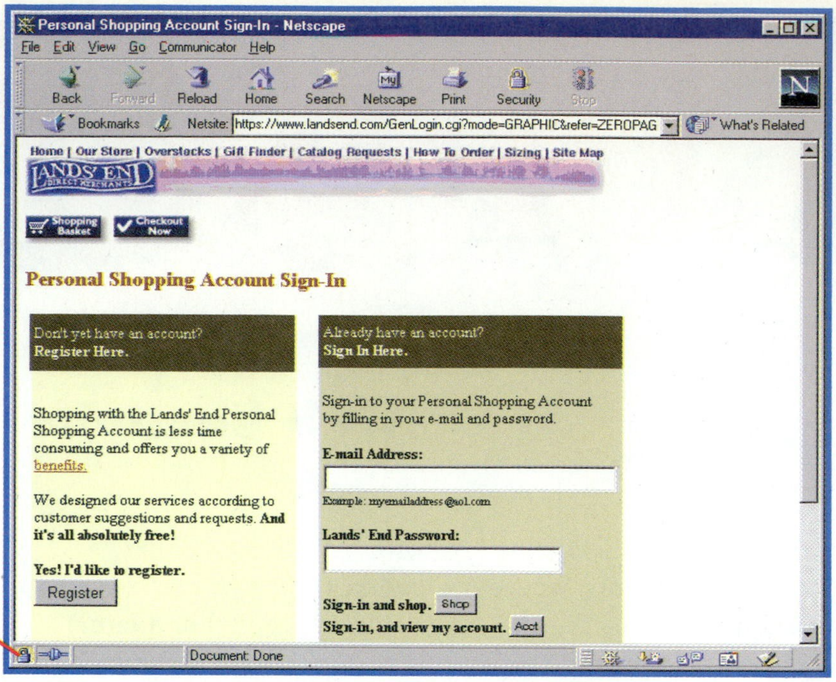

Secure transaction icon

Figure C.1
Secure browser session

an order: order online using the secure session, phone in the order with a toll-free number, or fax the order.

Although details about encryption methods are beyond the scope of this book, the procedure is a fairly straightforward. The **encryption key** is a series of digits that are added to the original text using a formula. At the other end, the message must be decoded by applying another key.

The Caesar cipher is a simple version of encryption. Suppose you replaced each letter of the original text with a letter 11 places later in the alphabet. When you got to Z, you would start over again at A. For example, NETSCAPE would appear as YPEDNLAP, as shown in Table C.1. If you want to do one yourself, prepare a sheet of paper with the letters A-Z and their place position from 1 to 26. When you add the key (11 in this case), be sure to start over again at A if you go past 26.

NET TIP

Passwords

When choosing a password, don't use names of friends or relatives. Your password ought to be at least 5 or 6 characters long with a mixture of upper- and lower-case letters and digits. For example, use something like frY8bee. You should change your password every few months.

Table C.1
Caesar Cipher Example

Text	Place Position	Place Position +11	Cipher Text
N	14	25	Y
E	5	16	P
T	20	31 -> 5	E
S	19	30 -> 4	D
C	3	14	N
A	1	12	L
P	16	27 -> 1	A
E	5	16	P

The longer the key, the more secure the encrypted information. Hackers try to break the code by repeatedly trying all possible combinations for the key. The international version of Netscape Communicator uses a 40-bit key and the U.S. version has a 128-bit key. Some online banking Web sites require the 128-bit version, but most secure sites will work properly with the 40-bit version. It is estimated that a high-speed computer could "crack" a 40-bit key in several hours but would take centuries to break a 128-bit key, even working around the clock.

Public Key Encryption

Most encryption systems on the Web use two keys – a public key and a private key. The browser uses the public key to encrypt information at the customer's computer. The private key is held only at the Web server. The private key can unlock the message, and having two keys means that the Web server does not have to transmit its key to customers' browsers, avoiding the possibility of an unauthorized person gaining access to the private key during transmission.

Digital Certificates

A **digital certificate** is a digital ID that verifies the identity of the owner of the Web site. When you initiate a secure connection with a Web site, your browser requests a copy of the digital certificate from the Web server. That certificate contains the public key to encrypt further transmissions to that site. It also assures you that you are dealing with the real owner of the Web site.

Digital certificates are issued by commercial organizations like VeriSign that research the business and verify that the Web address does indeed belong to the authorized owner. This is one way to prevent **spoofing**, in which a third party "steals" the Web site and sets up a storefront to steal information about the site's customers.

Pretty Good Privacy (PGP)

Pretty Good Privacy (PGP) is a low-cost encryption software developed by Pretty Good Privacy, Inc. In fact, it is free for non-commercial use. Using some of the same encryption technology as commercial techniques, PGP is available in many forms. While it is used primarily for encrypting e-mail messages between individuals, it can also be used to encrypt FTP and Web traffic. PGP uses the public key method of encryption. For more information, see the FAQ list at *http://www.pgp.net/pgpnet/pgp-faq/*.

Authentication

Another way of securing information is to provide for an authenticated session. *Authentication* is a process for establishing the user's identity, usually requiring a username and password. When a Web site uses authentication, the login screen, such as that shown in Figure C.2, asks for an account ID (username) and password. Only users whose account ID and password match the data on file at the Web server will be granted permission to access the next Web page. It is possible to both authenticate *and* encrypt the same Web page.

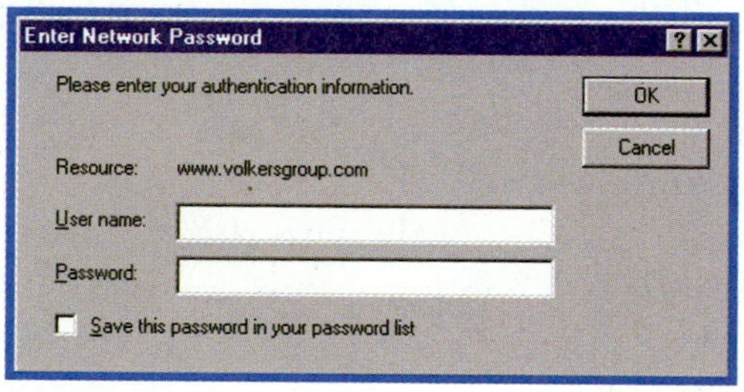

Figure C.2
Authentication login screen

> **NET TIP**
> **Passwords**
>
> *When choosing a password, don't use names of friends or relatives. Your password ought to be at least 5 or 6 characters long with a mixture of upper- and lower-case letters and digits. For example, use something like frY8bee. You should change your password every few months.*

Of course, no authentication security measure is truly foolproof. If you leave your account ID and password out in the open, someone could copy the information and use it to access the server. Make sure your password is hard for someone else to guess. Make sure you log out from the session when you leave the computer, even if only for a few minutes.

Lands' End offers another layer of security in addition to SSL. You can create a personal shopping account at Lands' End and create a password. When you arrive at the site, you'll be asked to sign in and verify your identity through the password. Of course, this can backfire if customers have trouble remembering all their passwords at different Web sites!

Cookies

You've read about cookies earlier in this book. A *cookie* is a small text file stored on your computer that contains some identifying information. The Web server must have permission before it can direct your browser to save information in the cookie file. For example, when you buy something at Amazon.com, a cookie file is created and stored on your hard drive. When you revisit Amazon.com, the Web server directs your browser to open the cookie file and send its contents to the server. The server can look up information about your previous purchases and display information in the Web site that matches your reading interests. Notice in Figure C.3 that Amazon.com identified me by name – evidently picking up this information from a cookie file.

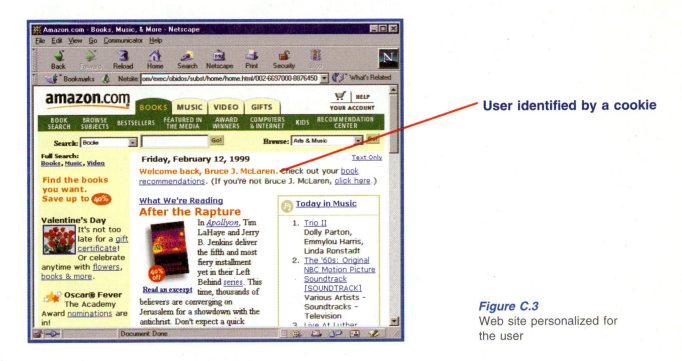

User identified by a cookie

Figure C.3
Web site personalized for the user

Figure C.3
Web site personalized for the user

Customers who do not want cookies stored on their computer can turn off this feature with a browser command. In Netscape, choose the Edit|Preferences command and select the Advanced screen. There you can disable cookies altogether, accept certain cookies, or ask to be warned each time a cookie is accessed. In Internet Explorer, the same choices are available by using the View|Internet Options command and selecting the Advanced tab. In general, you will benefit from cookies, because you don't have as much to type to identify yourself. Rarely is any sensitive information stored in the cookie file.

Firewalls

Customers expect e-merchants to protect information about them from outside users. This can be accomplished with physical security at the data center as well as implementing a firewall.

A **firewall** is hardware and/or software that isolates an organization's computers from the outside world. A firewall prevents outside users from accessing information inside the firewall. It also may selectively prevent individuals in the organization from accessing information outside the firewall. Visualize the firewall as a checkpoint that all information must pass through.

Another role of a firewall is to restrict internal users from accessing certain sites on the Internet. In other words, as your browser requests a certain URL, the firewall software must decide whether you are eligible to access that site. Some organizations restrict certain users from accessing anything outside the firewall. Other employees might have partial access.

Yet another role of the firewall software is to log the sites that users visit. For example, your employer would know if you regularly visit espn.com while on the job.

PAYING FOR MERCHANDISE ONLINE

From your e-commerce experience earlier in the book, you have learned that most users pay for goods ordered online with a credit card. With proper encryption, there is little reason to think that credit card information is any less secure than when you call a toll-free number and give your credit information over the phone. In fact, if you order merchandise with a portable telephone, someone could intercept the telephone call from the street in front of your house!

Credit Card Processing

To be able to accept credit card payments, a merchant opens a credit card agreement with a financial institution, probably a bank. The merchant pays a small fee for this service. The same is true for online credit card sales. Some ISPs offer credit card processing bundled along with other merchant services when you host your site with that ISP.

Most e-commerce sites process credit cards immediately, verifying the customer's credit worthiness online and making a decision about the credit sale at the same time. Of course, if you are using an ISP to host your site, the ISP will probably already have links to the credit card verifying sites and the necessary links for your site. In fact, you will probably use a standard Web site to verify and process payment. If you are hosting your own e-commerce Web site, then you must create the credit card validation pages yourself. Some packages, like IBM's Startup for e-business, offer instant credit card processing.

Visa and Master Card have been working on SET – Secure Electronic Transaction standard for credit card payments. This standard will improve the ability for e-merchants to make sales online. In this system, your credit card number is sent over the Internet in pieces, making it more difficult for thieves to steal your information.

Digital Cash

Some customers do not want to give their credit card information online. Customers can instead use **digital cash**, an online account that customers deposit funds into and then use to pay for purchases. Think of this like the electronic debit card – you provide authentication information, and the merchant receives payment from your digital cash account. It is somewhat safer than the credit card because only you can give the authentication information and the account information remains offline, at the digital cash company, not the merchant. The downside is that you can only shop at merchants who are compatible with your digital cash institution.

CyberCash is one of the digital cash providers. Figure C.4 shows the CyberCash home page. If you go to this site, notice the number of affiliations with other financial institutions – more banks are cooperating with online payment methods. As e-commerce grows, emphasis on making payments more efficient and more secure will also grow. In fact, CyberCash offers an array of Internet payment services to e-commerce merchants, including online credit card processing.

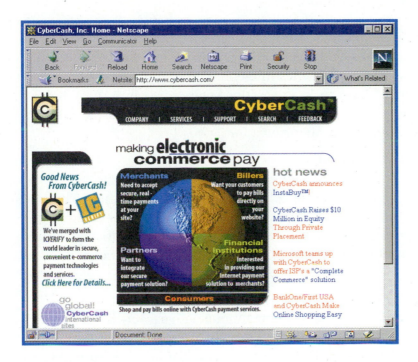

Figure C.4
CyberCash home page

In most cases there is no cost to the consumer for using these digital cash solutions. Rather, the merchant pays a fee, similar to the credit card arrangement. CyberCash offers a service called Cyber-Coin for micropayment purchases – typically in the range of $0.25 to $10. These small sales are not economical for regular credit card processing, and this service expands the possibility of spontaneous sales (lottery tickets, pay per view, information) over the Internet. CyberCash has worked to make it easy to transfer funds from your own bank to a CyberCash account. Some digital money providers refer to the account as an electronic wallet.

Some electronic payment methods keep your credit card information off the Internet altogether. When you make a purchase, you authorize the payment provider to make a direct charge against your credit card on behalf of the merchant. Your credit card information never appears on the Internet, safeguarding the information. This is similar to having a personal payment account with a merchant, established offline via telephone. When you are ready to pay, you give the personal account information but not the credit card information. Of course, you must still safeguard the personal account information through secure sessions, but should the information get out, it is only "good" for purchases made at that merchant.

Smart Cards

Smart cards are credit cards with a built-in microprocessor and memory used for identification or financial transactions. These cards might contain a cash balance, or could have a non-reproducible serial number or PIN. When customers are ready to make a purchase, they insert the card into a reader attached to their computer. Thus, only the person in possession of the card can conduct a transaction.

The downside is that customers must have a card reader attached to their computer. For now, that is not practical. But in the future, smart cards could become commonplace, particularly if there are serious security breaches in e-commerce. In late 1998, Microsoft announced interest in integrating smart cards into the Windows architecture. See the eCash Web site at *www.ecash.com* for more information about Microsoft's initiatives.

The Old Fashioned Way

Of course, it is still possible to shop electronically yet pay with check, money order, or other offline payment method. This adds a few days to the purchase cycle and introduces new security risks through the mail. But for consumers who aren't satisfied with any amount of online security, they can still shop online and pay using one of these other methods.

The Final Guarantee

Several e-merchants have announced guarantees against any customer losses due to fraudulent use of credit card information. OfficeMax and Lands' End both have elaborate security and privacy discussions in their Web sites. In fact, Lands' End states that since going online in 1995, there have been no confirmed cases of fraud reported by customers as a result of credit card purchases there. Both firms say that they will pick up all liability owed by the customer in such cases, including the first $50.

Glossary

acronym A group of letters, usually the first letters of the words of a phrase, that form an abbreviation for the phrase. Sometimes acronyms can be pronounced as words and become a recognized term. "FBI" and "scuba" are both acronyms.

address book E-mail program feature that stores names and e-mail addresses that can be retrieved easily for addressing e-mail messages.

alt-text lines Short text phrases that appear in an image's location while the image is loading.

animated GIF ad Web advertisement containing a graphic image that moves.

assessment tool A questionnaire or other means for gathering information. When tallied, your answers to the questions will indicate your interests or other characteristics about you.

auction service Online site that allows anyone to offer an item for sale to the highest bidder.

authentication The process of establishing the user's identity, usually requiring a username and password.

automatic withdrawal Regular, pre-authorized payments taken from a bank account. Customers often use these for loan payments or savings plans.

banner ad A large, splashy advertisement that appears on a Web page and often has a hyperlink to the advertiser's own Web site.

bookmark Web address stored for easy retrieval later.

browser Program, such as Netscape Navigator or Microsoft Internet Explorer, that enables users to view Web pages.

business-to-business sales Sales made by one business to another.

cache Temporary storage area in a computer that helps a browser display previously visited Web pages more quickly than it could by requesting the page from the server again.

career A profession for which you receive training and may hold several jobs during your lifetime. A career is usually a long-term pursuit.

clearinghouse An agency that gathers, stores, and exchanges information. Online job clearinghouses are large databases that store information about jobs and job seekers, and match jobs with people.

clip art A collection of electronic drawings, pictures, and icons, created for use in Web pages and other documents.

clipboard Feature that allows information to be cut or copied from one document and pasted into another document or into another location in the same document.

consumer The ultimate owner or user of a product.

cookie A file of information about you that some Web sites create and store on your hard drive when you visit the site.

cooperative ads Pairs of ads placed in complementary sites. Viewers at one site would likely be interested in products at the other site.

CPM Cost per thousand impressions, the basis used for determining advertising rates.

data port An RJ-11 analog telephone jack that lets a user connect a computer's modem through a telephone when a direct wall connection is unavailable.

database A large collection of information arranged in linked tables for easy search and retrieval.

demographics Characteristics of human populations, such as age, gender, income, and ethnic background.

digital cash Online accounts that customers deposit funds into and then use to pay for purchases.

digital certificate A digital ID that verifies the identity of the owner of the Web site.

direct deposit Paperless transfer of funds from an employer or other agency to the account of an employee or beneficiary.

discount broker An investment agent who buys and sells securities at the client's request, but does not provide extensive advice or other services.

domain name The last part of a URL that includes the organization's unique name followed by a top-level domain name designating the type of organization, such as *.com* for "commercial" or *.edu* for "educational."

download   Transfer of electronic files from one computer to another.

dynamic ads   Ads that appear when certain keywords are entered in a search engine.

e-commerce (electronic commerce)   Any electronic business transaction or exchange of information to conduct business.

electronic mail (e-mail)   A message transmitted electronically over the Internet or local area network to one or more receivers.

electronic shopping cart   A small program at a retail Web site that keeps track of your selections as you shop.

e-mail ads   Personalized e-mail advertising messages sent to a particular customer, usually with a link to the advertiser's Web site.

embedded hyperlink   A link between one object and another that, when clicked, opens your browser and loads the linked document or Web site. Hyperlinks can be embedded within an e-mail message as well as in any other kind of text or graphics.

emoticon   Icon created with keyboard characters that, when viewed sideways, indicates the writer's emotion.

encryption   Coding data for security.

encryption key   A series of digits added to the original text using a formula, for secure transmission over the Web.

entrepreneur   Someone who starts and operates a new business.

extranet   An intranet that uses the Internet to transmit private information beyond the company's own premises, but keeps its pages private by requiring user authentication.

FAQ (frequently asked questions)   A list of answers to common questions that customers ask.

file transfer protocol (FTP)   Method for transferring files over the Internet from one computer to another.

filter   In e-mail, criteria you specify for allowing some messages to pass through to your In mailbox while rejecting others, or for directing messages to different mailboxes.

firewall   Hardware and/or software that isolates an organization's computers from the outside world.

frame   A rectangular section of a Web page that scrolls separately from the main section.

FrontPage   Web site development and management software from Microsoft Corporation.

FrontPage Editor   The FrontPage tool used to create and make changes to individual web pages.

FrontPage Explorer   The FrontPage tool for creating, viewing, and managing your web of pages.

FrontPage web   The collection of HTML and image files that comprise a particular Web site, including the hyperlinks that let users navigate between the pages.

GIF (graphics interchange format)   The universal standard format for storing images for display in Web browsers. It is used for most lettering, small pictures, and animations.

hit counter   An electronic counting device that keeps track of the number of visits to a Web page during a particular time period and provides limited identity information about viewers.

HTML tags   Computer codes that tell your Web browser how to display information on your screen. HTML tags are surrounded by < > symbols. For example, <B> means to turn on bold and </B> means to turn off bold. HTML tags are used to indicate such features as bold, character size, font color, hyperlinks, and images.

HTML-enhanced e-mail   E-mail programs capable of displaying messages with embedded HTML commands that link to Web pages.

Hypertext links (hyperlinks)   Links from one Web page to another or from one location to another within the same page.

hypertext markup language (HTML)   Language used to create Web pages by adding formatting tags to text.

HyperText Transport Protocol (HTTP)   The communication rules used to connect to servers on the Web and transmit pages to a browser.

HyperText Transport Protocol Secure (HTTPS)   Method for accessing a secure Web server.

image map   A picture that is separated into sections, each of which contains a link that will take users to different Web locations.

interest (loan)   A fee for the use of borrowed funds.

interest rate (loan) The percentage of a loan amount charged to the borrower.

Internet A network of public networks, generally available everywhere.

InterNIC The organization that registers domain names.

intranet A private information network for company employees that is available only within the company's premises.

job A specific position you hold with a specific employer.

JPEG (Joint Photographic Experts Group) Standard graphics format for compressing still images, such as large photographs and art for use in Web browsers. JPEG files do not render lettering well.

lemon Car with so many problems that the manufacturer repurchased it.

mailing list service Automated e-mail system on the Internet to which users may subscribe to receive regular news on a specified topic.

market share One company's portion of a product's total sales.

meta-site The prefix "meta," from the Greek for "between, with, or after," has come to mean "going a level above or beyond." So a meta-site would be a super site with many links, larger and more extensive than a customary Web site.

mirror site A twin Web site placed in another country or continent to reduce the download time by eliminating the need to connect to the distant master site.

mortgage A loan for the purchase of real estate.

MP3 A compression format that has revolutionized the way high-quality digital music can be delivered over the Internet.

multinational corporation A business based in one country but with branches, plants, or business partners in other countries.

netiquette Etiquette on the Internet.

online mall Internet site that offers links to a large number of stores in one convenient place.

packets Blocks of data used to transmit Web pages and messages through the Internet.

PDF (portable document format) A file format generated by the Adobe Acrobat program that makes it possible to download and read files on different computers, using the free Acrobat Reader program.

pixel (PIX [picture] ELement) One or more dots that operate as the smallest element on a video display screen.

plug-in A specialty program that works with a major software to enhance its capabilities.

Pop-up ads Ads that appear in a separate browser window on top of the base Web page, which remains open in the background.

portal sites Web sites, such as search engines, that offer users a good starting point for entering the Web.

portfolio A collection of stocks, bonds, and other investments.

powered by Run by a search engine or database that provides the background resources for a site.

Pretty Good Privacy (PGP) A low-cost encryption software developed by Pretty Good Privacy, Inc.

publish To transfer an HTML file from your computer to a Web server.

pull technology Internet information retrieval system in which users actively seek information by visiting sites.

push technology Internet information retrieval system in which users specify the information they want, and the system finds and downloads it automatically to the users' computer.

reach The number of potential customers who view an ad.

recall A manufacturer's request to return a product because of severe risks to health or safety.

resume A list of personal information, educational background, and professional experience.

retailing Selling goods and services to the ultimate consumer.

richness (in advertising) Degree to which ad content can be designed for a specific market segment.

rotation ad Banner ad that rotates between advertisers. Each time the page comes up, the advertiser changes.

secure sockets layer (SSL) Most common method for encrypting data on the Web.

security Protection from unauthorized access to data.

smart cards Credit cards with a built-in microprocessor and memory used for identification or financial transactions.

socially responsible investing A policy of promoting environmentally and socially responsible operating practices by investing in corporations with good records in these areas.

SOHO Acronym for "small office/home office."

spamming Sending copies of an e-mail message to many people.

spoofing "Stealing" a Web site to set up a storefront to steal information about the site's customers.

static ad Advertisement that always appears in a given location on the Web page, regardless of the keywords used to get to the page.

tasks list In FrontPage, a helpful utility in Explorer to keep track of "to-do" items associated with a project.

term (loan) The duration of a loan.

theme In FrontPage, a collection of design elements, such as colors, fonts, bullets, background images, and navigation bars, that are applied to all pages in a web, giving the site a consistent "look."

thumbnail A smaller version of the full image used to reduce download time. The viewer can click the thumbnail image to display the full image in the browser.

ticker symbol Company abbreviation made up of several letters, used for reference in stock quotes.

top-level domain name Three-letter abbreviation at the end of a domain name, designating the type of organization that owns the site.

24 by 7 24 hours a day, 7 days a week.

uniform resource locator (URL) The address of a Web page, that defines for the browser the route to take to find the page.

Web editor An easy-to-use program for creating Web pages. The Web editor resembles a word processor and automatically inserts the proper HTML tags into the file when you have selected a certain format or feature.

Web server Computer that holds the pages and images that form a Web site and accepts requests from Web browsers to download them. The Web server is the host for the Web site. The Web server must be connected to the Internet all of the time, so that users can view the Web site.

web spider Robotic search tool that is constantly examining sites around the Web and adding them to a search engine's catalog or index.

Webmaster Web developer who is responsible for creating and maintaining the HTML files that comprise a Web site. The Webmaster knows HTML and usually has programming skills.

wholesale Sale of mechandise by one business to another for resale.

zine Net-speak for "magazine."

INDEX

A

ad rates, 179
alt-text line, 180-181
Amazon.com, 12, 162
animated GIG ads, 180
apartment hunting, 52
assessment tools, 43
asynchronous business activities, 199
auctions online, 113-116
auction service, 113
authentication software, 208
auto insurance options, 70
automatic withdrawals, 57

B

banking online, 59-61
banner ad, 158
banner advertising, 179-185
Better Business Bureau, 152
BidFind, 114
Bigfoot home page, 89
Binary Compass, 143
BizRate, 143
bookmarks and favorites, 265-266
browser,
basics, 257
hyperlinks, 260
location box, 260
main window, 260
menu bar, 260
progress bar, 260
security status, 260
starting your, 259
status bar, 260
toolbar, 260
business plan, components of, 34
business purchases, 96
business-to-business, 2
creating a site, 112

C

car loan applications online, 61
car purchases online, 106-108
career
planning, 42-44
resume writing tips, 45
searching for, 40-41
clearinghouses, 46
clip art, 218
CNET, 82
CNN Financial home page, 58
CollegeNet search, 54
company information on the web, 9-11
comparison shopping, 143, 148
consumer, 18
Consumer Information Center, 138
consumer issues, 137-138
Consumer Reports online, 148
cooperative ads, 181
cookies, 98, 160
copyrighted images, 219
copyrighted materials, 19
corporations on the net, 33
cost of living calculator, 51
country code domain names, 195
Coupon Directory site, 150
CPM, 182
credit card security, 161
currency converter, 202
customer support icon, 144
cyberspeak, 88

d

data port, 81
database, 77
database server, 224
delivering products online, 164
demographics, 172
Department of Labor Women's Bureau
homepage, 92
digital advertising, 172-173
direct deposit, 57
discount brokers, 62
doctors on the internet, 5

domain names, 195, 215, 233
domain name piracy, 235
download, 240
downloading an image, 128-130
dynamic ads, 181

E

e-commerce (*electronic commerce*),
5, 18, 39
e-mail ads, 171
E-TRADE, 63
eToys, 120
educational institutions, 53-54
electronic catalogs, 23
electronic shopping cart, 119
embedded hyperlink, 158
entrepreneur, 28
ethics training, 91
Excite home page, 7
extranet, 208

F

FAQ (*frequently asked questions*), 167
favorites and bookmarks, 265-266
Federal Trade Commission, 142
Federal Web locator, 90
FedEx tracking page, 166
financial watchdogs, 142
financing a home, 66-68
floral services links, 125
flowers, shopping for, 102-103,
125-127
food, shopping for, 103-104
Forrester Research, 69
frame, 240
FrontPage
center icon, 250
create or edit hyperlink icon, 251
creating a personal web, 244-247
customizing a home page, 248-253

developing a web site with, 238
Explorer icon, 249
favorites page, 251
getting started dialog box, 245
  hyperlinks, 248
insert image icon, 250
text color button, 246
themes view, 249
URL for, 253
verify hyperlink icon, 252
web design, 240-242

General Mill home page, 4
GIF (graphic interchange format),
  180, 219
global e-commerce, 193
global language statistics, 207
government links, 90-92

hailed sites, 36
help online, 22
hit counter, 158
HTML (*hypertext markup language*),
  216
HTML files, 216
HTML tags, 216
humor services, 85
hyperlinks, 257
hypertext links, 257

image files, 218
image map links, 200
images, downloading, 128
information providers, 88
information services, 75
Institute for Business and Professional
  Ethics, 5
insurance online, 69-70
interest, 66
interest rate, 66

international access, 206
international banking, 61
international business information,
  204-207
international shopping icon, 144
internal search box, 223
Internet
  as personal information source, 39
  connection, 221
  lawyer, 138
  marketing, 156-157
  retailing on, 18, 20-22
  search tool, 223
Internet Explorer, 258
Internet Explorer commands, 267
InterNIC, 215
interview information, 44
intranet, 208
investing online, 62-65
IRS home page, 71

job clearinghouses, 46
job links search engine, 41
job search, 48-50
JPEG(*Joint Photographic Experts
  Group*), 219

lemon, 146
locating a country, 195

mailing list service, 1
making purchases online, 119-121
maps online, 52, 83, 164, 200
marketing on the internet, 156-157
meta-sites, 41
Metrics link, 15
Microsoft's automatic subscription,
  178
Microsoft's Internet explorer, 258
mirror subscription, 196
Monster Board search form, 49
mortgage, 66
Mortgage Mart, 66

Mosaic, 217, 258
MP3, 164
multinational corporations, 198-199
music purchases online, 123-124

National Fraud Information Center,
  146
National Hurricane Center, 87
National Parks Service, 90
National Weather Service sites, 85-86
Neilsen Company, 15
net privacy, 185
Netscape
  business source site, 19
  Communicator commands, 267
  Navigator, 258
  Netcenter home page, 260
  Net Search home page services, 76
  Travel channel, 78
news and weather online, 84-87
nonprofits on the web, 37
non-sales benefits, 4

online
  car loan applications, 61
  car purchases, 106-108
  catalogs, 23
  consumer activity, 11
  Consumer Reports, 148
  investing, 62-65
job listings, 7
malls, 99-100
maps, 52, 83, 164, 200
subscriptions, 131
Online Banking Association, 59

packets, 196
PBS Internet timeline, 3
PDF (*portable document format*), 167
personal finance online, 57-58
pixels, 179
planning for career, 42-44
plug-in, 240
pop-up ads, 184
portable files (*see PDF*)

portal sites, 181
portfolio, 62
post-sale phase, 157, 167-169
"powered by", 79
pre-sale phase, 156-160
print button, 265
print preview, 265
privacy and security, 139
promoting a site, 186
publish, 226
pull technology, 64
push technology, 64

quality assurance engineer (*QAE*), 79
Quicken's Home and Mortgage site, 67

reach, 172
real estate search, 24-25
registration information, 128
REI Horizon Maps, 164
relocation information, 51-52
resume, 40, 45-47
resume scanning, 47
resume writing tips, 45
retail purchases, 96
retailing, 18
richness, 172
rotation ad, 182

safety bulletins, 150
sales tax, 152
saving images from the web, 180
scanning resumes, 47
search engines, 84
search tool, 223
searchable site icon, 144
seasonal sites, 125
secure ordering icon, 144
secure transactions, 161
security and privacy, 139
security indicator icon, 122
security measures, 120
shopping cart icon, 144

site-use considerations, 54
Small Business Administration
    homepage, 31
small business's use of internet, 30-31
Smart Money portfolio, 64
Snap.com, 82
SOHO(small office/home office), 112
SRI (*socially responsible investing*),
    65
stock photo sites, 130
subscriptions online, 131
sweepstakes and giveaways, 159

taking orders, 157, 161-163
tax tips, 71-72
Tenagra Corporation, 13
term of a mortgage, 66
The Wall Street Journal homepage,
    132
thumbnail, 240
ticker symbol, 62
ticket sales, 105
™ symbol, 19
top-level domain names, 233
trade organizations, 26
travel planning, 77
Travelocity, 79
TRUSTe trustmark, 140-141

unsubscribing, 175
URL, 215, 261
U.S. Consumer Gateway, 150

Villanova Center for Information Law
    and Policy, 91

weather and news online, 84-87
web browser, 258-267
web developer, 186, 214

web editor, 220
web master, 232
web package software, 231
web page
    getting help, 263
    interrupting a, 262
    printing, 265
    reloading, 263
    retrieving a, 261
    viewing previous, 262
web site
    building an effective, 214
    components of, 216-219
    methods for developing a, 226-230
    registering a, 233
web spider, 186
wholesale, 109

Yahoo, 27, 76
    shopping, 97
    store requirements, 227
    Travel link, 78

ZDNet anchor desk, 8
Zine, 110
zip code information, 89